D1561960

The Best Guide to Korean Conversation!

KOREAN
PHRASE BOOK
FOR TRAVELERS

All-Romanized

By B.J. Jones

HOLLYM

Elizabeth NJ · Seoul

Korean Phrase Book for Travelers

Copyright © 1987
by Hollym Corporation; Publishers

All rights reserved.

First English edition published in 1987
Seventeenth printing, 2003
by Hollym International Corp.
18 Donald Place, Elizabeth, NJ 07208, U.S.A.
Phone: (908) 353-1655   Fax: (908) 353-0255
http://www.hollym.com

Published simultaneously in Korea
by Hollym Corporation; Publishers
13-13 Gwancheol-dong, Jongno-gu,
Seoul 110-111, Korea
Phone: (02) 735-7551~4   Fax: (02) 730-5149, 8192
http://www.hollym.co.kr e-mail: info@hollym.co.kr

ISBN: 0-930878-20-5
Library of Congress Catalog Card Number: 87-82975

Printed in Korea

Preface

This phrase book is primarily written for helping the reader feel more at ease in basic Korean conversations. In this respect, the book is different characteristically from the ones which are designed to teach a complete list of grammars and vocabularies necessary for Korean conversations.

Basic words and phrases in the book will get you quickly and easily anywhere you need and enable you to cope with practical problems such as medical, theft, loss of the valuables, replacement or repair of watches, cameras and others.

The reader will benefit from other aspects of the book including the section of pronunciation, a brief review of grammar and reference: the pronunciation guide accompanies the words and phrases, the topic of which can quickly be found by reference to the contents list; the grammatical presentation gives you an idea of the Korean language structure and usage of the phrases; the reference section provides you with the signs, the names of the months, days of the week, times and holidays.

Romanization of Korean alphabet in this book is based on the Ministry-of-Education system generally accepted in Korea, a modified form of McCune-Reischauer system.

This phrase book will certainly help you to be readily understood on everyday occasions during your vacation or travel in Korea.

B. J. Jones

Contents

Introduction to Korean

Of their most distinctive traits Koreans list their language first. The Korean language is a member of the Ural-Altaic Family, closer to Hungarian, Finnish or Turkish than to other Oriental languages. They also have their own efficient phonetic alphabet(한글 *Han-gŭl*) invented by King Sejong in the 15th century, and also they make use of Chinese ideographs for everyday life along with the alphabet.

The Koreans are rich in the intricacies and sophistication of a 5000-year-old culture. You will find that in many ways it is complex and subtle, in other ways simple and direct. It reflects how the Korean people think and reason, and deeply held values, many quite different from western ones. As you use the phrases in this book, you may begin to perceive how the Koreans look at life, and your interactions well become easier and more natural.

Pronunciation Guide

VOWELS

Korean vowels are more like those of Spanish than English. The English sounds given here are, of course, approximate ones.

Romanization Used in This Book	*English Spelling*	*Example*
a	as in f**a**ther	kabang (가방)
ŏ	as in h**u**t	ŏmŏni (어머니)
o	as in h**o**me	ot (옷)
u	as in d**o**	tubu (두부)
ŭ	as in tak**e**n	ŭnhaeng (은행)
i	as in **i**nk	iri (이리)
ae	as in h**a**t	kaekch'a (객차)
e	as in m**e**t	cheil (제일)
oe	as in K**ö**ln	oeguk (외국)
ya	as in **ya**rd	yagu (야구)
yŏ	as in **yea**rn	yŏja (여자)
yo	as in **yo**ke	yogŭm (요금)
yu	as in **you**	yudo (유도)
yae	as in **ya**m	yaegi (애기)
ye	as in **ye**s	yeyak (예약)
ŭi	as in tak**e**n+**we**	ŭisa (의사)
wa	as in **wa**n	wan-gujŏm (완구점)
wo	as in **wo**n	wol (월)
wae	as in **wa**g	wae (왜)
we	as in **we**t	wenmank'ŭm (웬만큼)
wi	as in **wie**ld	wie (위)

CONSONANTS

With a few exceptions, Korean consonants are similar to those of English. Note the differences:

Romanization Used in This Book		English Spelling	Example
k	⎫	as in **g**as	kagu (가구)
t	⎬ beginning	as in **d**og	tong (둥)
p	⎪ of word	as in **b**ag	paduk (바둑)
ch	⎭	as in **J**ane	Cheju (제주)
k'		as in **k**ite	k'al (칼)
t'		as in **t**ime	yŏnt'an (연탄)
p'		as in **p**ine	Kimp'o (김포)
ch'		as in **ch**ild	ch'ang (창)
kk		as in **sk**i	kkaman (까만)
tt		as in **st**ick	ttang (땅)
pp		as in **sp**eak	ppang (빵)
tch		as in pi**zz**a	tchaksu (짝수)

The Fundamentals

BASIC EXPRESSIONS

Basic Words

near	가까이에	kakkaie
outside	밖에	pakke
inside	안에	ane
down	아래로	araero
up	위로	wiro
in	안에	ane
from	__부터	__put'ŏ (after voiceless) __but'ŏ (after voiced)
after	후에	hue
before	전에	chŏne
on	위에	wie
at	__에	__e
to	__(으)로	__(ŭ)ro
during	동안	tong-an
or	또는/그렇지 않으면/혹은	ttonŭn/kŭrŏch'i anŭmyŏn/ho-gŭn

and (between sentences)	그리고	kŭrigo
and (between nouns)	__와 __과	__wa (after vowels) __kwa (after consonants)
also	__도/또한	__do/ttohan
but	그러나/_지만	kŭrŏna/_jiman
here	여기	yŏgi
there	거기	kŏgi
over there	저기	chŏgi
this/that/that over there (pron.)	이것/그것/저것	igŏt/kŭgŏt/chŏgŏt
this/that/that over there	이/그/저	i/kŭ/chŏ

Pronouns

I	나/저	na/chŏ (to superiors)
you (sing.)	당신	tangshin
he/she	그/그녀	kŭ/kŭnyŏ
we	우리	uri
you (pl.)	당신들	tangshindŭl
they	그들	kŭdŭl

※ To form the possessives, simply add the particle *ŭi* to the above pronouns:

my	나의/저의	naŭi/chŏŭi

Adjectives

It's hot and humid.	무덥습니다.	Mudŏpsŭmnida.
It's hot.	덥습니다.	Tŏpsŭmnida.
It's cold.	춥습니다.	Ch'upsŭmnida.
hot/cold	뜨겁습니다. /차갑습니다.	Ttŭgŏpsŭmnida. /Ch'agapsŭmnida.
same	같습니다.	Kassŭmnida.
warm/cool	따뜻합니다. /시원합니다.	Ttattŭt'amnida. /Shiwonhamnida.
big/small	큽니다. /작습니다.	K'ŭmnida. /Chaksŭmnida.
long/short	깁니다. /짧습니다.	Kimnida. /Tchalssŭmnida.
strong/weak	강합니다. /약합니다.	Kanghamnida. /Yak'amnida.
pretty, beautiful/ ugly	멋있읍니다. /보기 흉합니다.	Mŏdissŭmnida. /Pogi hyunghamnida.
delicious/awful tasting	맛있읍니다. /맛이 없읍니다.	Madissŭmnida. /Mashi ŏpsŭmnida.
good, fine/bad	좋습니다. /좋지 않습니다.	Chossŭmnida. /Choch'i ansŭmnida.
fast, quick/slow	빠릅니다. /느립니다.	Pparŭmnida. /Nŭrimnida.
high/low	높습니다. /낮습니다.	Nopsŭmnida. /Nassŭmnida.

expensive/cheap	비쌉니다. /쌉니다. Pissamnida. /Ssamnida.
far/near	멉니다. /가깝습니다. Mŏmnida. /Kakkapsŭmnida.
wide/narrow	넓습니다. /좁습니다. Nŏlsŭmnida. /Chopsŭmnida.
heavy/light	무겁습니다. /가볍습니다. Mu- gŏpsŭmnida. /Kabyŏpsŭmnida.
new/old	새 것입니다. /낡았읍니다. Sae kŏshimnida. /Nalgassŭmnida.
young/old	어립니다. /늙었읍니다. Ŏrimnida. /Nŭlgŏssŭmnida.
dark/light	어둡습니다. /밝습니다. Ŏdupsŭmnida. /Paksŭmnida.
quiet/noisy	조용합니다. /시끄럽습니다. Choyonghamnida. /Shikkŭrŏp- sŭmnida.
a lot, many/a lit- tle, few	많습니다. /적습니다. Manssŭmnida. /Chŏksŭmnida.
intelligent/stupid	똑똑합니다. /바보입니다. Ttokttok'amnida. /Paboimnida.
right/wrong	맞습니다. /틀립니다. Massŭmnida. /T'ŭllimnida.
easy/difficult	쉽습니다. /어렵습니다. Swipsŭmnida. /Ŏryŏpsŭmnida.
early/late	이릅니다. /늦었읍니다. Irŭmnida. /Nŭjŏssŭmnida.

Greetings

How do you do?	처음 뵙겠읍니다(아무쪼록 잘 부탁 하겠읍니다). **Ch'ŏŭm poepkes- sŭmnida. (Amutchorok chal put'ak'agessŭmnida.)**
How do you do? (reply)	처음 뵙겠읍니다(저야말로 잘 부탁 하겠읍니다). **Ch'ŏŭm poepkes- sŭmnida. (Chŏyamallo chal put'ak'agessŭmnida.)**
Pleased to meet you.	만나 뵈어 반갑습니다. **Manna poeŏ pan-gapsŭmnida.**
Good morning. Good afternoon. Good evening.	안녕하십니까? **Annyŏnghashimnikka?** 안녕하세요? **Annyŏnghaseyo?**
Good night.	안녕히 주무세요. / 안녕. **Annyŏnghi chumuseyo. / An- nyŏng**(between friends).
How are you?	안녕하세요? **Annyŏnghaseyo?**
Fine, thank you.	네, 덕분에요. **Ne, tŏkpuneyo.**
Goodbye.	① 안녕히 가세요. **Annyŏnghi kaseyo**(seeing someone off). ② 안녕히 계세요. **Annyŏnghi kyeseyo**(leaving someone who remains).
See you again. See you later.	또 뵙겠읍니다. **Tto poepkessŭmnida.**

Everyday Words and Phrases

Hello (for telephone calls, for getting someone's attention).	여보세요. Yŏboseyo.
Excuse me.	미안합니다. /실례합니다. Mianhamnida/Shillyehamnida.
Please.	부탁합니다. Put'ak'amnida.
I'm sorry.	미안합니다. /죄송합니다. Mian- hamnida. /Choesonghamnida.
You're welcome.	천만에요. Ch'ŏnmaneyo.
Thank you.	감사합니다. Kamsahamnida.
Yes.	예. /네. Ye/Ne.
No	아니오. Anio.
Mr./Mrs./Miss/ Ms.	씨 ssi
Of course.	물론이지요. Mullonijiyo.
Maybe.	아마. /어쩌면. Ama. /Ŏtchŏmyŏn.
Pardon me, but ___.	실례합니다만 ___. Shillyehamnidaman ___.
It's all right. It doesn't matter.	괜찮습니다. ahso Kwaench'anssŭmnida.
Let's go.	갑시다. Kapshida.
Shall we go?	우리 갈까요? Uri kalkkayo?

With pleasure.	네, 그러죠. Ne, kŭrŏjyo.
I don't mind.	네, 그러세요. Ne, kŭrŏseyo.
Oh, I see,	아, 알겠읍니다. A, algessŭmnida.
Is that so?	그러세요? Kŭrŏseyo?
Really?	정말입니까? Chŏngmarimnikka?
I think so.	저도 그렇게 생각합니다. Chŏdo kŭrŏk'e saenggak'amnida.
I don't think so.	전 그렇게 생각하지 않습니다. Chŏn kŭrŏk'e saenggak'aji an- ssŭmnida.
Let's go/eat.	갑/먹읍시다. Kap/Mŏgŭpshida.
No, thank you.	아니오, 괜찮습니다. Anio, kwaench'anssŭmnida.
I don't want it.	그건 필요하지 않습니다. Kŭgŏn p'iryohaji anssŭmnida.
It's interesting/ fun.	그거 재밌는데요. Kŭgŏ chaeminnŭndeyo.
It's over./I'm fin- ished.	이제 끝났읍니다. Ije kkŭnnassŭmnida.
Just a moment, please.	잠깐만 기다리세요. Chamkkanman kidariseyo.
Yes, it is.	네, 그렇습니다. Ne, kŭrŏssŭmnida.

The Fundamentals

No, it isn't.	아니오, 그렇지 않습니다. Anio, kŭrŏch'i anssŭmnida.
Not yet.	아직. Ajik (in negation).
Soon.	곧. Kot.
Right away.	빨리. Ppalli.
Now.	자금. Chigŭm.
Later.	나중에. Najung-e.

Language Problems

I don't understand Korean.	한국어는 못합니다. Han-gugŏnŭn mot'amnida.
Could you repeat it, please?	다시 한 번 말씀해 주시겠어요? Tashi han pŏn malssŭmhae chushigessŏyo?
Please speak slowly.	천천히 말씀해 주세요. Ch'ŏn-ch'ŏnhi malssŭmhae chuseyo.
Write it down on the paper, please.	종이에 써 보세요. Chong-ie ssŏ poseyo.
Is there anyone who understands English?	영어 알아듣는 사람 있으세요? Yŏng-ŏ aradŭnnŭn saram issŭseyo?
Do you speak English?	영어 하십니까? Yŏng-ŏ hashimnikka?
What's this called in Korean?	이것을 한국어로 뭐라고 하지요? Igŏsŭl Han-gugŏro mworago hajiyo?

What do you call this?	이것을 뭐라고 합니까? Igŏsŭl mworago hamnikka?
Excuse me, could you help me, please?	죄송합니다만 좀 도와 주시겠읍니까? Choesonghamnidaman chom towa chushigessŭmnikka?
Please point to the phrase in this book.	그 말을 이 책에서 좀 지적해 주세요. Kŭ marŭl i ch'aegesŏ chom chijŏk'ae chuseyo.
I speak a little Korean.	한국어를 약간 합니다. Han-gugŏrŭl yakkan hamnida.
I know very little Korean.	한국어를 거의 모릅니다. Han-gugŏrŭl kŏŭi morŭmnida.
Do you understand?	알겠읍니까? Algessŭmnikka?
Yes, I understand.	예, 알겠읍니다. Ye, algessŭmnida.
No, I don't understand.	아니오, 모르겠읍니다. Anio, morŭgessŭmnida.
Do you understand English?	영어 알아들으세요? Yŏng-ŏ aradŭrŭseyo?

Questions

When?	언제?	Ŏnje?
Where?	어디서?	Ŏdisŏ?
Why?	왜?	Wae?
Who?	누가?	Nuga?

Which?	어느 것을?	Ŏnŭ kŏsŭl? (Obj.)
	어느 것이?	Ŏnŭ kŏshi? (Subj.)
What?	무엇을?	Muŏsŭl? (Obj.)
	무엇이?	Muŏshi? (Subj.)
How?	어떻게?	Ŏttok'e?
How much?	얼마나 많이?	Ŏlmana mani?
How much (money)?	얼맙니까?	Ŏlmamnikka?

What's the matter? 무슨 일입니까?
Musŭn irimnikka?

What's this? 이건 뭡니까?
Igŏn mwomnikka?

Where's the ___? __이[가] 어디에 있읍니까?
__ī[ga] ŏdie issŭmnikka?

bathroom	화장실이	Hwajangshiri
dining room	식당이	Shiktang-i
entrance	입구가	Ipkuga
exit	출구가	Ch'ulguga
telephone	전화가	Chŏnhwaga
police box	파출소가	P'ach'ulsoga
drugstore	약국이	Yakkugi
counter	카운터가	K'aunt'ŏga

Physical Conditions

I'm tired.	피곤한데요.	P'igonhandeyo.
I'm sleepy.	졸린데요.	Chollindeyo.
I'm sick.	몸이 안 좋은데요.	
	Momi an choŭndeyo.	

I'm fine.	건강합니다. Kŏn-ganghamnida.
I'm all right.	전 괜찮습니다. Chŏn kwaench'ansŭmnida.
I'm thirsty.	목이 마르군요. Mogi marŭgunnyo.
I'm hungry.	배가 고픈데요. Paega kop'ŭndeyo.
I'm full.	배불러요. Paebullŏyo.

Needs

I want ___.	___ 싶습니다. ___ shipsŭmnida.
I want to go to ___.	___에 가고 싶습니다. ___e kago shipsŭmnida.
I want to see ___.	___을[를] 보고 싶습니다. ___ (r)ŭl pogo shipsŭmnida.
I want to buy ___.	___을[를] 사고 싶습니다. ___ (r)ŭl sago shipsŭmnida.
I want to eat ___.	___을[를] 먹고 싶습니다. ___ (r)ŭl mŏkko shipsŭmnida.
I want to drink ___.	___을[를] 마시고 싶습니다. ___ (r)ŭl mashigo shipsŭmnida.
Could you tell me where the ___ is?	___이[가] 어디에 있는지 가르쳐 주시겠읍니까? ___i[ga] ŏdie innŭnji karŭch'yŏ chushigessŭmnikka?

Could you give me ____?	____ 좀 주시겠어요? ____ chom chushigessŏyo?
I need ____.	____이[가] 필요합니다. ____i[ga] p'iryohamnida.

LOSS OR THEFT

I'm in Korea on business.	업무차 한국에 왔읍니다. Ŏmmŭ-ch'a Han-guge wassŭmnida.
as a tourist	관광차 Kwan-gwangch'a
I'm staying at ____.	____에 머물고 있읍니다. ____e mŏmulgo issŭmnida.
My telephone number is ____.	제 전화 번호는 ____입니다. Che chŏnhwa pŏnhonŭn ____ imnida.
I've lost my way.	길을 잃었읍니다. Kirŭl irŏssŭmnida.
Can you direct me to ____?	____이[가] 어디에 있읍니까? ____i[ga] ŏdie issŭmnikka?
Excuse me.	실례하겠읍니다. Shillyehagessŭmnida.
Would you call the police for me please?	경찰 좀 불러 주시겠어요? Kyŏngch'al chom pullŏ chu-shigessŏyo?
What's the telephone number for the police?	경찰 전화 번호가 어떻게 됩니까? Kyŏngch'al chŏnhwa pŏnhoga ŏttŏk'e toemnikka?

I seem to have lost my wallet.	지갑을 잃어버린 것 같아요.	Chigabŭl irŏbŏrin kŏt kat'ayo.
passport	여권을	Yŏkwonŭl
plane tickets	비행기 표를	Pihaenggi p'yorŭl
camera	카메라를	K'amerarŭl
What shall I do?	어떻게 하죠?	Ŏttŏk'e hajyo?
I want to report a theft.	도난 신고를 하려고 합니다.	Tonan shin-gorŭl haryŏgo hamnida.
an accident	사고	Sago
I think my money has been stolen.	돈을 잃어버린 것 같아요.	Tonŭl irŏbŏrin kŏt kat'ayo.
Someone just grabbed my camera.	누가 제 카메라를 채 갔읍니다.	Nuga che k'amerarŭl ch'ae kassŭmnida.
purse	핸드백을	haendŭbaegŭl
Can you help me?	좀 도와 주시겠읍니까?	Chom towa chushigessŭmnikka?
My name is ___.	제 이름은 ___입니다.	Che irŭmŭn ___imnida.
I'm an American citizen.	전 미국에서 왔읍니다.	Chŏn Migugesŏ wassŭmnida.
a British	영국에서	Yŏnggugesŏ
a French	프랑스에서	P'ŭrangsŭesŏ

The expressions in this section are the ones you'll use again and again—the fundamental building blocks of conversation, the way to express your wants or needs, and some simple forms you can use to construct all sorts of questions. It's a good idea to practice these phrases until you know them by heart.

Korea and Its People

WEATHER AND SEASONS

It's a nice day, isn't it?	날씨 좋죠? Nalssi choch'yo?
It's terrible weather, isn't it?	무슨 날씨가 이렇죠? Musŭn nalssiga irŏch'yo?
It's <u>hot</u> today, isn't <u>it</u>?	오늘 덥죠? Onŭl <u>tŏpchyo</u>?

cool	서늘하죠	sŏnŭrhajyo
cold	춥죠	ch'upchyo
warm	따뜻하죠	ttattŭt'ajyo

It's <u>fine</u>.	날씨 좋습니다. <u>Nalssi chossŭmnida.</u>
cloudy	구름이 끼었군요 Kurŭmi kkiŏtkunnyo
raining	비가 오는군요 Piga onŭn-gunnyo
snowing	눈이 오는군요 Nuni onŭn-gunnyo
Will it stop <u>raining</u>/<u>snowing</u> <u>soon?</u>	비가/눈이 곧 그칠까요? <u>Piga</u>/<u>Nuni</u> kot kŭch'ilkkayo?
I hope it will <u>clear up</u>.	개면 좋겠읍니다. Kaemyŏn chok'essŭmnida.

When does the rainy season begin?	장마철은 언제 시작됩니까? Changmach'ŏrŭn ŏnje shijak- toemnikka?
When does the rainy season end?	장마철은 언제 끝납니까? Changmach'ŏrŭn ŏnje kkŭn- namnikka?
When do the cherry blossoms bloom?	벗꽃은 언제 핍니까? Pŏtkkoch'ŭn ŏnje p'imnikka?
When do the autumn leaves begin?	단풍은 언제 볼 수 있읍니까? Tanp'ung-ŭn ŏnje pol su is- sŭmnikka?
What's tomorrow's weather forecast?	내일 일기 예보는 어떻습니까? Naeil ilgi yebonŭn ŏttŏssŭm- nikka?
Do you think a typhoon is coming?	태풍이 불겠읍니까? T'aep'ung-i pulgessŭmnikka?

Frequently-Used Words

warm	따뜻하다	ttattŭt'ada
hot	덥다	tŏpta
hot and humid	무덥다	mudŏpta
cool	시원하다	shiwonhada
cold	춥다	ch'upta
dry	건조하다	kŏnjohada
humid	습하다	sŭp'ada

climate	기후	kihu
weather	날씨	nalssi
clear (sky)	맑은 (하늘)	malgŭn (hanŭl)
cloudy	흐리다	hŭrida
wind	바람	param
rain	비	pi
rainy season	장마철	changmach'ŏl
snow	눈	nun
typhoon	태풍	t'aep'ung
season	계절	kyejŏl
four seasons	4 계절	sa kyejŏl
spring	봄	pom
March/April/May	3월/4월/5월	samwol/sawol/owol
summer	여름	yŏrŭm
June/July/August	6월/7월/8월	yuwol/ch'irwol/p'arwol
fall	가을	kaŭl
September/October/November	9월/10월/11월	kuwol/shiwol/shibirwol
winter	겨울	kyŏul
December/January/February	12월/1월/2월	shibiwol/irwol/iwol

ABOUT THE LAND

capital	수도	sudo
city	도시	toshi
big city	대도시	taedoshi
countryside	시골	shigol
village	마을	maŭl
hot springs	온천	onch'ŏn
ocean	-양, 바다	-yang, pada
coast	해안	haean
bay	만	man
island	-도, 섬	-to/-do (after voiced), sŏm
mountain range	산맥	sanmaek
mountain	산	san
hill	언덕	ŏndŏk
river	강	kang
lake	호수	hosu
waterfall	폭포	p'okp'o
map	지도	chido
national park	국립 공원	kungnip kongwon

Korea	한국	Han-guk
population	인구	in-gu
land area	면적	myŏnjŏk

The Korean Peninsula extends due south of Manchuria, curving gently east and then west like jade commas dangling from the golden crowns of its ancient kings. Its nine provinces are:

경기도	Kyŏnggi-do
강원도	Kangwon-do
충청북도	Ch'ungch'ŏngbuk-do
충청남도	Ch'ungch'ŏngnam-do
전라북도	Chŏllabuk-do
전라남도	Chŏllanam-do
경상북도	Kyŏngsangbuk-do
경상남도	Kyŏngsangnam-do
제주도	Cheju-do

WITH PEOPLE

Personal Information

Do you have any children?	자녀분은 있으십니까? Chanyŏbunŭn issŭshimnikka?
How old are you?	연세가 나이가 } 어떻게 되십니까? Yŏnsega (to senior) } ŏttŏk'e toeshimni- Naiga } kka?

I'm over 20.　　　20세가 넘었읍니다.
　　　　　　　　　Iship sega nŏmŏssŭmnida.

I'm <u>20</u> years old.　20세입니다.
　　　　　　　　　<u>I</u>ship seimnida.

21	21	Iship il
22	22	Iship i
23	23	Iship sam
24	24	Iship sa
25	25	Iship o
26	26	Ishim nyuk
27	27	Iship ch'il
28	28	Iship p'al
29	29	Iship ku
30	30	Samship
35	35	Samship o
40	40	Saship
45	45	Saship o
50	50	Oship
55	55	Oship o
60	60	Yukship
65	65	Yukship o
70	70	Ch'ilship
75	75	Ch'ilship o
80	80	P'alship

Are you married?　　결혼하셨읍니까?
　　　　　　　　　Kyŏrhonhasyŏssŭmnikka?

I'm married.　　　결혼했읍니다.
　　　　　　　　　Kyŏrhonhaessŭmnida.

I'm single.　　　　독신입니다.
　　　　　　　　　Tokshinimnida.

What do you do?	어떤 일을 하십니까? Ŏttŏn irŭl hashimnikka?
I'm an architect.	건축 일을 하고 있읍니다. K<u>ŏnch'uk irŭl</u> hago issŭm-nida.

a publisher	출판업을	Ch'ulp'anŏbŭl
a driver	운전을	Unjŏnŭl
a merchant	장사를	Changsarŭl
a musician	음악을	Ŭmagŭl

I'm a student.	학생입니다. <u>Haksaeng</u>-imnida.

a teacher	교사	Kyosa
a professor	교수	Kyosu
a housewife	주부	Chubu
an office worker	회사원	Hoesawon
a secretary	비서	Pisŏ
an engineer	엔지니어	Enjiniŏ
in the military	군인	Kunin
a doctor	의사	Ŭisa
a dentist	치과 의사	Ch'ikwa ŭisa
a nurse	간호원	Kanhowon
a lawyer	변호사	Pyŏnhosa

I'm a company president/an industrialist.	사업을 하나 하고 있읍니다. Saŏbŭl hana hago issŭmnida.
I'm a company executive.	회사에서 임원을 맡고 있읍니다. Hoesa-esŏ imwonŭl matko issŭmnida.
I'm a painter.	그림을 그리고 있읍니다. Kŭrimŭl kŭrigo issŭmnida.

I'm a writer.	글을 쓰고 있읍니다. Kŭrŭl ssŭgo issŭmnida.
I'm a politician.	정치 일을 하고 있읍니다. Chŏngch'i irŭl hago issŭmni-da.
Where are you from?	고향이 어디세요? Kohyang-i ŏdiseyo?
I'm from <u>America</u>.	미국입니다. <u>Migugimnida.</u>

England	영국	Yŏnggug
Germany	독일	Togir
France	프랑스	P'ŭrangsŭ
Canada	캐나다	K'aenada
Australia	호주/오스트레일리아	Hoju/ Osŭt'ŭreillia
New Zealand	뉴질랜드	Nyujillaendŭ

Which country are you from?	어디서 오셨읍니까? Ŏdisŏ osyŏssŭmnikka?
I'm from the United States.	미국에서 왔읍니다. Migugesŏ wassŭmnida.
Where were you born?	어디서 태어나셨읍니까? Ŏdisŏ t'aeŏnasyŏssŭmnikka?
I was born in Rome.	로마에서 태어났읍니다. Roma-esŏ t'aeŏnassŭmnida.
Where do you live?	어디서 사십니까? Ŏdisŏ sashimnikka?
I live in Paris.	전 파리에서 살고 있읍니다. Chŏn P'ariesŏ salgo issŭmnida.

Introduction

How do you do?	처음 뵙겠읍니다. (아무쪼록 잘 부탁하겠읍니다.) Ch'ŏŭm poepkessŭmnida. (Amutchorok chal put'ak'agessŭmnida.)
How do you do? (reply)	처음 뵙겠읍니다. (저야말로 잘 부탁하겠읍니다.) Ch'ŏŭm poepkessŭmnida. (Chŏyamallo chal put'ak'agessŭmnida.)
I'm honored to meet you.	만나 뵈어 영광입니다. Manna poeŏ yŏnggwang-imnida.
I'm glad to meet you.	만나 뵈어 반갑습니다. Manna poeŏ pan-gapsŭmnida.
I'm Joe Smith.	죠 스미스라고 합니다. Joe Smith-rago hamnida.
My name is Jean Brown.	제 이름은 진 브라운입니다. Che irŭmŭn Jean Brown-imnida.
Mr./Ms. *A*, may I introduce Mr./Ms. *B*?	*A*씨, *B*씨를 소개하겠읍니다. *A*ssi, *B*ssirŭl sogaehagessŭmnida.
I would like you to meet Mr./Ms. *C*.	*C*씨를 소개하겠읍니다. *C*ssirŭl sogaehagessŭmnida.
Have you met Mr./Ms. *D*?	*D*씨를 만난 적이 있읍니까? *D*ssirŭl manan chŏgi issŭmnikka?
Mr./Ms. *F*, this is Mr./Ms. *G*.	*F*씨, 이분이 *G*씨입니다. *F*ssi, ibuni *G*ssiimnida.

Korea and Its People

| Pardon me, may I introduce myself? | 인사 드리겠읍니다.
Insa tǔrigessǔmnida. |

This is my <u>friend</u>.

제 친구입니다.
Che ch'in-guimnida.

husband	남편	namp'yŏn
wife	아내	anae
nephew	조카	chok'a
aunt	숙모님	sungmonim
uncle	삼촌	samch'on
son	아들	adŭr
daughter	딸	ttar

This is my father.

제 아버지이십니다.
Che abŏjiishimnida.

This is my mother.

제 어머니이십니다.
Che ŏmŏniishimnida.

Who is that?

저 사람[분]은 누굽니까?
Chŏ saram[pun]ǔn nugumnikka?

Do you know who that is?

저 사람[분]이 누군지 아세요?
Chŏ saram[pun]i nugunji aseyo?

I would like to meet him/her (literally, that person).

저 사람[분]을 한 번 만나 보고싶습니다. Chŏ saram[pun]ǔl han pŏn manna pogo shipsǔmnida.

Would you introduce me to him/her (that person)?

저 사람[분]을 소개해 주시겠읍니까? Chŏ saram[pun]ǔl sogaehae chushigessǔmnikka?

In general, the Koreans prefer "proper" introductions. Some people will be glad to strike up a conversation with a stranger under casual circumstances. You can introduce yourself if you like. But formal introductions are preferable. Whenever possible, have a mutual friend, acquaintance, or colleague introduce you to someone he or she already knows.

Korea and Its People

Names

What's your name?	성함이 어떻게 되십니까? Sŏnghami ŏttŏk'e toeshimnikka?
My name is (full name).	(이름)입니다. / (이름)(이)라고 합니다. (full name)imnida. / (full name)(i)rago hamnida.

Koreans use first names or full names followed by the respectful -ssi. In the case of children, the first names are followed by -a or -ya(after vowels). It's safer for foreigners to use first names or full names plus ssi when addressing Koreans, unless specially asked to do otherwise. Note that when referring to oneself, the ssi is dropped. Also keep in mind that Koreans use the family name first.

Cards

Here's my card.	제 명함입니다. Che myŏnghamimnida.

Thank you very much.	감사합니다. Kamsahamnida.
Here's mine.	제 명함입니다. Che myŏnghamimnida.
May I have your card?	명함 있으십니까? Myŏngham issŭshimnikka?

Koreans routinely exchange business cards during introductions. Korea has been called a vertical society; people deal with each other according to their relative positions on that vertical ladder. Knowing a person's profession or business affiliation, including position within a company, is important. It helps in choosing the right level of language, the right gestures, and other more subtle interactions. It's also convenient to have the card to refer to later. You'll be given a lot of cards in Korea, and you will find it useful to have your own to offer in exchange. You can get cards printed with English on one side and Korean on the other once you arrive. You might prefer just to take your own cards with you, of course.

Greetings and Leavetakings

Welcome.	어서 오십시오. Osŏ oshipshio.
How are you?	안녕하십니까? Annyŏnghashimnikka?

Fine, thanks. And you?	네, 덕분에요. (이름)씨는 어떠세요? Ne, tŏkpuneyo. (name)-ssinŭn ŏttŏseyo?
Good morning. Good afternoon. Good evening.	안녕하세요? Annyŏnghaseyo? 안녕하십니까? Annyŏnghashimnikka?
It's been a long time.	오랜만입니다. Oraenmanimnida.
Thank you for last time.	요전번에는 정말 고마웠읍니다. Yojŏnpŏnenŭn chŏngmal komawassŭmnida.
I must go.	가봐야 되겠읍니다. Kabwaya toegessŭmnida.
I'm afraid I will have to go soon.	곧 가봐야 되겠읍니다. Kot kabwaya toegessŭmnida.
Sorry for taking your time.	시간을 뺏어서 죄송합니다. Shiganŭl ppaesŏsŏ choesonghamnida.
Good night.	안녕히 주무세요. Annyŏnghi chumuseyo.
Goodbye.	안녕히 가세요. Annyŏnghi kaseyo (Seeing someone off).
Well, goodbye.	안녕히 계세요. Annyŏnghi kyeseyo (Leaving someone who remains).

Korea and Its People

See you again.	또 뵙겠읍니다. Tto poepkessŭmnida.
See you tomorrow.	내일 뵙겠읍니다. Naeil poepkessŭmnida.
See you soon.	그럼 근간에 또 뵙겠읍니다. Kŭrŏm kŭn-gane tto poepke- ssŭmnida.
See you later.	나중에 뵙겠읍니다. Najung-e poepkessŭmnida.
So long.	안녕히 가[계]십시오. Annyŏnghi ka[kye]shipshio.
Take care.	조심하십시오. Choshimhashipshio.
Thank you for the delicious food.	맛있게 잘 먹었읍니다. Maditke chal mŏgŏssŭmnida.

Korean culture is not only very old, it's also remarkably intact. Because the Korean people were free from outside contacts for so long, their own traditions became stronger. Even today, with the influence of the West so visible, the Koreans adhere to their unique customs and values. Some Korean cultural requirements may differ from your own. No one expects foreign visitors to act like Koreans. But a few insights into new and different customs can help you speak Korean more easily.

PRESENTS

Receiving

May I open it?	뜯어 봐도 되겠읍니까? Ttŭdŏ pwado toegessŭmnikka?
Thank you very much.	정말 감사합니다. Chŏngmal kamsahamnida.
Thank you very much for such a wonderful gift.	이렇게 좋은 선물을 주시다니 정말 감사합니다.　Irŏk'e choŭn sŏnmurŭl chushidani chŏngmal kamsahamnida.
It's very kind of you.	정말 친절하시군요.　Chŏngmal ch'injŏrhashigunnyo.
That's very thoughtful of you.	정말 사려 깊으시군요.　Chŏng-mal saryŏ kip'ŭshigunnyo.
Thank you very much for your kindness.	친절히 해 주셔서 감사합니다. Ch'injŏrhi hae chusyŏsŏ kam-sahamnida.
I'm very much obliged for your generosity.	송구스럽습니다. Songgusŭrŏpsŭmnida.
I'm most grateful. How nice of you! How generous of you!	정말 감사합니다. Chŏngmal kamsahamnida.

Giving

I hope you like it.	마음에 드시면 좋겠읍니다. Maŭme tŭshimyŏn chok'essŭmnida.
This is a small present for you.	제 작은 선물입니다. Che chagŭn sŏnmurimnida.
It's not anything special, but...	특별한 건 아닙니다만,... T'ŭkpyŏrhan kŏn animnidaman,...
Here's something for you.	이거 받아 주십시오. Igŏ pada chushipshio.
It's from Virginia.	버지니아산입니다. Pŏjiniasanimnida.
It's just a token.	이거 약소합니다. Igŏ yaksohamnida.

On Arrival

CUSTOMS

These are my personal effects.
제 소지품입니다.
Che sojip'umimnida.

It's not new.
신품이 아닙니다.
Shinp'umi animnida.

These are gifts.
이것은 선물입니다.
Igŏsŭn sŏnmurimnida.

May I close the bag now?
이제 가방을 닫아도 되겠읍니까?
Ije kabang-ŭl tadado toegessŭmnikka?

Do I have to pay duty?
관세를 물어야 합니까?
Kwanserŭl murŏya hamnikka?

How much do I pay?
얼마를 내야 합니까?
Ŏlmarŭl naeya hamnikka?

Where do I pay?
어디서 내야 합니까?
Ŏdisŏ naeya hamnikka?

Can I pay with dollars?
달러로 내도 됩니까?
Tallŏro naedo toemnikka?

This is my luggage.
이것이 제 수화물입니다.
Igŏshi che suhwamurimnida.

This is all I have.
전부입니다.
Chŏnbuimnida.

I have nothing to declare.
신고할 것이 없읍니다.
Shin-gohal kŏshi ŏpsŭmnida.

I have <u>two cartons of cigarettes</u>.	담배 두 보루가 있읍니다. <u>Tambae tu poruga</u> issŭmnida.
three bottles of whiskey	위스키 세 병이 Wisŭk'i se pyŏng-i
four bottles of gin	진 네 병이 Chin ne pyŏng-i
three bottles of wine	포도주 세 병이 P'odoju se pyŏng-i
Where's customs?	세관이 어디에 있읍니까? Segwani ŏdie issŭmnikka?
Here's my passport.	제 여권입니다. Che yŏkwonimnida.
Here's my customs declaration form.	제 세관 서류입니다. Che segwan sŏryuimnida.

You must present your bags for customs inspection, and they may be opened. An oral declaration of your personal effects will be sufficient except for some circumstances, in which case, you'll have to fill out a written declaration: arrival by ship, or articles in excess of the duty free allowance.

QUARANTINE

Do you need to see my vaccination certificate?	예방 접종 증명서가 필요합니까? Yebang chŏpchong chŭngmyŏngsŏga p'iryohamnikka?

PASSPORT CONTROL

I'm on <u>vacation</u>.
휴가차 왔읍니다.
<u>Hyugach'a</u> wassŭmnida.

  a sightseeing
  tour
  a business trip

관광 여행차 Kwan-gwang
               yŏhaengch'a
사업차 Saŏpch'a

I'll be staying here
<u>a few days.</u>
며칠 동안 여기에 머물 예정입니다.
<u>Myŏch'il</u> tong-an yŏgie mŏmul
yejŏng-imnida.

  a week
  two weeks
  a month

1 주일 Il chuil
2 주일 I chuil
한 달 Han tal

I'm traveling <u>a-lone.</u>
혼자 여행하고 있읍니다. <u>Honja</u>
yŏhaenghago issŭmnida.

  with my hus-
  band
  with my wife

남편과 Namp'yŏn-gwa

아내와 Anaewa

My name is ___.
제 이름은 ___입니다.
Che irŭmŭn ___imnida.

I'm <u>American</u>.
미국에서 왔읍니다.
<u>Migugesŏ</u> wassŭmnida.

  British
  Canadian
  Dutch

영국에서 Yŏnggugesŏ
캐나다에서 K'aenada-esŏ
화란에서 Hwaranesŏ

I'm staying at ___.
___에서 머물고 있읍니다.
___esŏ mŏmulgo issŭmnida.

Here's my pass-port.	제 여권입니다. Che yŏkwonimnida.
Embarkation/ Disembarkation Card	출입국 기록입니다 ch'uripkuk kirogimnida

LUGGAGE CLAIM

That's mine.	그것이 제 겁니다. Kŭgŏshi che kŏmnida.
I can't find my luggage.	제 수화물이 안 보이는데요. Che suhwamuri an poinŭndeyo.
Where's my luggage?	제 수화물은 어디에 있습니까? Che suhwamurŭn ŏdie issŭmnikka?
My luggage is lost.	제 수화물이 없어졌읍니다. Che suhwamuri ŏpsŏjyŏssŭmnida.
Where is the baggage claim?	수화물은 어디서 찾습니까? Suhwamurŭn ŏdisŏ ch'assŭmnikka?
baggage/luggage	수화물 suhwamul
Get that black suitcase for me please.	저 까만 가방 좀 주시겠읍니까? Chŏ kkaman kabang chom chushigessŭmnikka?

	white	흰 hŭin
	red	빨간 ppalgan
	brown	갈색 kalsaek
	big	큰 k'ŭn
	small	작은 chagŭn

PORTERAGE

To the <u>taxi stand</u>, please.
택시 승차장으로 가져가 주세요.
T'aekshi sŭngch'ajang-ŭro ka-jyŏga chuseyo.

  bus stop
버스 정류장으로 Pŏsŭ chŏng-nyujang-ŭro

  hotel bus
호텔 버스로 Hot'el pŏsŭro

  limousine bus
소형 버스로 Sohyŏng pŏsŭro

  shuttle bus
셔틀 버스로 Syŏt'ŭl pŏsŭro

  that building
저 건물로 Chŏ kŏnmullo

  that car
저 차로 Chŏ ch'aro

I want the limousine bus to <u>Sheraton Walker Hill.</u>
<u>워커힐</u> 가는 버스를 타려고 합니다.
<u>Wok'ŏhil</u> kanŭn pŏsŭrŭl t'aryŏgo hamnida.

  Kangnam Express Bus Terminal
강남 터미널   Kangnam t'ominŏl

Here is fine.
여깁니다. / 됐읍니다.
Yŏgimnida. / Twaessŭmnida.

Put them down here please.
여기 놓으세요.   Yŏgi nouseyo.

How much do I owe you?
얼맙니까?   Ŏlmamnikka?

Could you get me a porter?
짐꾼 좀 불러 주시겠읍니까?
Chimkkun chom pullŏ chushigessŭmnikka?

Could you help me?
좀 도와 주시겠읍니까?   Chom towa chushigessŭmnikka?

My luggage is here.	수화물은 여기 있읍니다. Suhwamurŭn yŏgi issŭmnida.
there	거기 kŏgi
over there	저기 chŏgi

I have two pieces of luggage altogether.	수화물은 전부 두 개입니다. Suhwamurŭn chŏnbu tu kaeimnida.
three pieces	3 개 se kae
four pieces	4 개 ne kae
five pieces	5 개 tasŏt kae
six pieces	6 개 yŏsŏt kae

| This one is fragile. | 이건 깨지기 쉽습니다.
Igŏn kkaejigi swipsŭmnida. |

| Please be careful. | 조심하세요. Choshimhaseyo. |

| I'll carry this one myself. | 이건 내가 들겠읍니다.
Igŏn naega tŭlgessŭmnida. |

QUESTIONS ABOUT LOCATION

| Where's the Korea National Tourism Corp. (KNTC) Tourist Information Center? | 한국 관광 공사 관광 안내소가 어디에 있읍니까? Han-guk Kwan-gwang Kongsa Kwan-gwang Annaesoga ŏdie issŭmnikka? |

| Where's the information counter? | 안내소가 어디에 있읍니까?
Annaesoga ŏdie issŭmnikka? |

| Where's the hotel reservation counter? | 호텔 예약 카운터가 어디에 있읍니까? Hot'el yeyak k'aunt'ŏga ŏdie issŭmnikka? |

TRANSPORTATION

Buses

I want to go to ____ in Seoul.	서울 ____에 가려고 합니다. Seoul ____e karyŏgo hamnida.
What's the best way to go?	어떻게 가는 것이 가장 좋습니까? Ŏttŏk'e kanŭn kŏshi kajang chossŭmnikka?
How long does it take?	얼마나 걸립니까? Ŏlmana kŏllimnikka?
When does the next one leave?	다음 차는 언제 떠납니까? Taŭm ch'anŭn ŏnje ttŏnamnikka?
Where do I get it?	어디서 탈 수 있읍니까? Ŏdisŏ t'al su issŭmnikka?
I want to go to the airport bus counter.	공항 버스 카운터에 가려고 합니다. Konghang pŏsŭ k'aunt'ŏe karyŏgo hamnida.
Is there a bus to the ____ Hotel?	____ 호텔 가는 버스가 있읍니까? ____ Hot'el kanŭn pŏsŭga issŭmnikka?

Taxis

Take me to the ____ Hotel, please.	____ 호텔로 가 주세요. ____ Hot'ello ka chuseyo.
Take me to this address please.	이 주소로 가 주세요. I chusoro ka chuseyo.

On arrival

Where can I get a taxi?	택시를 어디에서 탈 수 있읍니까? T'aekshirŭl ŏdiesŏ t'al su i-ssŭmnikka?
How long does it take to Seoul?	서울까지는 얼마나 걸립니까? Seoulkkajinŭn ŏlmana kŏllimnikka?
How much will it cost?	요금은 얼마나 나옵니까? Yogŭmŭn ŏlmana naomnikka?

Hotel Taxis

Is the rate <u>by the hour</u>?	요금은 시간제입니까? Yogŭmŭn <u>shiganje</u>imnikka?
by the day	일일제 irilche
I'd like to get one.	1대 부탁합니다. Han tae put'ak'amnida.
Where can I get a hotel taxi?	호텔 택시를 어디서 탈 수 있읍니까? Hot'el t'aekshirŭl ŏdisŏ t'al su issŭmnikka?
How much will it cost to ___ in Seoul?	서울 ___까지 요금이 얼마나 나옵니까? Seoul ___kkaji yogŭmi ŏlmana naomnikka?

At the Hotel

REACHING THE HOTEL

Where is the bus stop?	버스 정류장이 어딥니까? Pŏsŭ chŏngnyujang-i ŏdimni-kka?
How much is the fare?	요금은 얼맙니까? Yogŭmŭn ŏlmamnikka?
What buses go into town?	어떤 버스가 시내로 갑니까? Ŏttŏn pŏsŭga shinaero kam-nikka?
I'd like to go to the ___ Hotel.	___ 호텔로 가려고 합니다. ___ Hot'ello karyŏgo ham-nida.
Where can I get a taxi?	택시를 어디서 탑니까? T'aekshirŭl ŏdisŏ t'amnikka?

CHECKING IN

I'd like a room <u>with twin beds.</u>	이 인용 침대 방 하나 부탁합니다. <u>I innyong</u> ch'imdae pang hana put'ak'amnida.	
with a shower	샤워실이 있는	Syawoshiri innŭn
with a good view	전망이 좋은	Chŏnmang-i chohŭn
facing the mountain	산이 보이는	Sani poinŭn

facing the ocean	바다가 보이는	Padaga poinŭn
facing the street	도로가 보이는	Toroga poinŭn
facing the courtyard	정원이 보이는	Chŏngwoni poinŭn

I need a baby crib in the room, please.
유아용 침대 좀 부탁합니다.
Yuayong ch'imdae chom put'ak'amnida.

My name is ___.
내 이름은 ___입니다.
Nae irŭmŭn ___imnida.

I have a reservation.
예약을 했읍니다.
Yeyagŭl haessŭmnida.

I don't have a reservation, but can I get a room?
예약은 안했는데 방 있읍니까?
Yeyagŭn anhaennŭnde pang issŭmnikka?

I'd like a single room.
일 인용 방 하나 부탁합니다.
I rinnyong pang hana put'ak'amnida.

two single rooms	일 인용 방 둘	I rinnyong pang tul
a double room	이 인용 방 하나	I innyong pang hana
a single room and a double room	일 인용 방 하나하고 이 인용 방하나	I rinnyong pang hana hago innyong pang hana
a suite	스위트 하나	Sŭwit'ŭ hana

Do you have anything cheaper?
좀 싼 방 있읍니까?
Chom ssan pang issŭmnikka?

I'll be staying just tonight.
오늘 밤만 머물겁니다.
Onŭl pamman mŏmulkŏmnida.

a few days	며칠	Myŏch'il
a week	일 주일	Il chuil
at least a week	적어도 일 주일은	Chŏgŏdo il chuirŭn

I'm not sure yet how long I am staying.
얼마나 머물지는 모르겠읍니다.
Ŏlmana mŏmulchinŭn morŭgessŭmnida.

What floor is it on?
몇 층에 있읍니까?
Myŏt ch'ŭng-e issŭmnikka?

Can I get the room right now?
방에 지금 들어갈 수 있읍니까?
Pang-e chigŭm tŭrŏgal su issŭmnikka?

What's the rate?
숙박료는 얼맘니까?
Sukpangnyonŭn ŏlmamnikka?

Does the rate include the service charge?
숙박료에 봉사료가 포함됩니까?
Sukpangnyo-e pongsaryoga p'ohamdoemnikka?

Does the rate include breakfast?
숙박료에 아침 식사가 포함됩니까?
Sukpangnyo-e ach'imshiksaga p'ohamdoemnikka?

Is there a discount for children?
애들에 대한 할인이 있읍니까?
Aedŭre taehan harini issŭmnikka?

Is there a charge for the baby?
어린애도 요금을 받습니까?
Ŏrinaedo yogŭmŭl passŭmnikka?

Hotel Information

Is there a <u>gym</u>?
체육관이 있읍니까?
Ch'eyukkwani issŭmnikka?

health club	헬스 클럽이	helsŭ k'ŭllŏbi
sauna	사우나가	saunaga
swimming pool	수영장이	suyŏngjang-i
tennis court	테니스 코트가	t'enisŭ k'ot'ŭga

What time does it open?

몇 시에 엽니까?
Myŏt shie yŏmnikka?

Is there a charge?

입장료가 있읍니까?
Ipchangnyoga issŭmnikka?

Can I rent a typewriter?

타자기를 빌 수 있읍니까?
T'ajagirŭl pil su issŭmnikka?

Where's the <u>elevator</u>?

<u>엘리베이터가</u> 어디에 있읍니까?
<u>Ellibeit'ŏga</u> ŏdie issŭmnikka?

telephone	전화가	Chŏnhwaga
bathroom	욕실이	Yokshiri
ladies' room	여자 화장실이	Yŏja hwajangshiri
men's room	남자 화장실이	Namja hwajangshiri

Where do I control the <u>air conditioner</u>?

<u>에어컨은</u> 어디서 조절합니까?
<u>Eŏk'ŏnŭn</u> ŏdisŏ chojŏrhamnikka?

heater

히터는　Hit'ŏnŭn

Where can I plug in my <u>electric razor</u>?

면도기 플러그는 어디다 꽂습니까?
<u>Myŏndogi p'ŭllŏgŭnŭn</u> ŏdida kkossŭmnikka?

hair dryer

헤어 드라이어　Heŏ tŭraiŏ

Do you have an <u>adapter plug</u>?

<u>어댑터 플러그</u> 있읍니까?
<u>Ŏdaept'ŏ p'ŭllŏgŭ</u> issŭmnikka?

electrical transformer	변압기	Pyŏnapki

How does the shower work?
샤워기는 어떻게 사용합니까?
Syawoginŭn ŏttŏk'e sayonghamnikka?

I need a bellhop.
보이 좀 불러 주세요.
Poi chom pullŏ chuseyo.

Please send <u>breakfast</u> to my room.
이 방에 <u>아침</u> 좀 보내 주세요.
I pang-e <u>ach'im</u> chom ponae chuseyo.

some towels	타월	t'awol
some soap	비누	pinu
some hangers	옷걸이	otkŏri
a pillow	베개	pegae
a blanket	모포	mop'o
some ice	얼음	ŏrŭm
some ice water	냉수	naengsu
an ashtray	재떨이	chaettŏri
some toilet paper	화장지	hwajangji
a luggage rack	수화물대	suhwamuldae

Is room service available?
룸 서비스가 있읍니까?
Rum sŏbisŭga issŭmnikka?

Is a masseur/masseuse available?
안마사가 있읍니까?
Anmasaga issŭmnikka?

Is a babysitter available?
애 보는 사람이 있읍니까?
Ae ponŭn sarami issŭmnikka?

Is there a <u>restaurant</u> in the <u>hotel</u>?
호텔 안에 <u>식당</u>이 있읍니까?
Hot'el ane <u>shiktang</u>-i issŭmnikka?

bar	바가	paga
coffee shop	커피 숍이	k'ŏp'i syobi
barbershop	이발소가	ibalsoga
beauty parlor	미장원이	mijangwoni
pharmacy	약국이	yakkugi
newsstand	신문 판매대가	shinmun p'anmaedaega
shopping arcade	쇼핑 아케이드가	syop'ing ak'eidŭga

| Where is it? | 거기가 어딥니까? | Kŏgiga ŏdimnikka? |
| Is an English-language interpreter available? | 영어 통역이 있읍니까? | Yŏng-ŏ t'ong-yŏgi issŭmnikka? |

Changing the Room

Do you have a <u>better</u> room?	<u>더 좋은</u> 방 있읍니까?	<u>Tŏ choŭn</u> pang issŭmnikka?
larger	큰	k'ŭn
smaller	작은	chagŭn
quieter	조용한	choyonghan
I'd like a room <u>with more light</u>.	<u>햇빛이 더 잘 드는</u> 방 좀 부탁합니다.	<u>Haetpich'i tŏ chal tŭnŭn</u> pang chom put'ak'amnida.
on a higher floor	더 높은 층	Tŏ nop'ŭn ch'ŭng
on a lower floor	더 낮은 층	Tŏ najŭn ch'ŭng
Do you have a room with a better view?	전망이 더 좋은 방 있읍니까?	Chŏnmang-i tŏ choŭn pang issŭmnikka?

Could I get a
different room?

다른 방으로 바꿀 수 있읍니까?
Tarŭn pang-ŭro pakkul su
issŭmnikka?

It's <u>too big</u>.

<u>너무 큰</u>데요.
<u>Nŏmu k'ŭn</u>deyo.

too small	너무 작은	Nŏmu chagŭn
too dark	너무 어두운	Nŏmu ŏduun
too noisy	너무 시끄러운	Nŏmu shikkŭrŏun

In the Room

Who is it?

누구십니까?
Nugushimnikka?

Just a minute.

잠깐만 기다리세요.
Chamkkanman kidariseyo.

Come in.

들어오세요. Tŭrŏoseyo.

Put it on the <u>table</u>
please.

<u>테이블</u> 위에 놓으세요.
<u>T'eibŭl</u> wie noŭseyo.

   bed

침대   Ch'imdae

I'd like <u>room serv-
ice</u> please.

<u>룸 서비스</u> 좀 부탁합니다.
<u>Rum sŏbisŭ</u> chom put'ak'am-
nida.

a masseur/a masseuse	안마사	Anmasa
a babysitter	애 보는 사람	Ae ponŭn saram

I'd like a 6 o'clock
wakeup call,
please.

6시에 좀 깨워 주시겠읍니까?
Yŏsŏssie chom kkaewo chu-
shigessŭmnikka?

Problems

The bathtub won't drain properly.	욕조 물이 잘 안 빠집니다. Yokcho muri chal an ppajimnida.
I need a new lightbulb.	새 전구가 있어야겠읍니다. Sae chŏn-guga issŏyagessŭmnida.
The window will not open.	창문이 안 열립니다. Ch'angmuni an yŏllimnida.
Venetian blind won't open.	차양이 안 걷힙니다. Ch'ayang-i an kŏch'imnida.
The window won't close.	창문이 안 닫힙니다. Ch'angmuni an tach'imnida.
Venetian blind will not close.	차양이 안 내려집니다. Ch'ayang-i an naeryŏjimnida.
Can I get it fixed?	내가 고칠 수 있읍니까? Naega koch'il su issŭmnikka?
I've locked myself out.	문이 안으로 잠겼읍니다. Muni anŭro chamgyŏssŭmnida.
I've lost my key.	열쇠를 잃어버렸읍니다. Yŏlsoerŭl irŏbŏryŏssŭmnida.
These shoes aren't mine.	이 구두는 내 것이 아닙니다. I kudunŭn negŏshi animnida.
This laundry isn't mine.	이 세탁물은 내 것이 아닙니다. I set'angmurŭn naegŏshi animnida.
There's no electricity.	전기가 안 들어옵니다. Chŏn-giga an tŭrŏomnida.

The <u>TV</u> doesn't work.	TV가 안 나옵니다. <u>T'ibŭiga</u> an naomnida.
radio	라디오가 Radioga
The electric fan doesn't work.	선풍기가 안 돌아갑니다. Sŏnp'unggiga an toragamnida.
The lamp doesn't work.	불이 안 들어옵니다. Puri an tŭrŏomnida.
The air conditioning doesn't work.	에어컨 작동이 안됩니다. Eŏk'ŏn chaktong-i andoemnida.
There's no heat.	난방이 안됩니다. Nanbang-i andoemnida.
There's no <u>running water</u>.	<u>물</u>이 안 나옵니다. <u>Muri</u> an naomnida.
hot water	더운 물이 Tŏun muri
The toilet won't flush.	화장실 물이 안 나옵니다. Hwajangshil muri an naomnida.
The toilet is stopped up.	화장실이 막혔읍니다. Hwajangshiri mak'yŏssŭmnida.
The sink is stopped up.	싱크대가 막혔읍니다. Shingk'ŭdaega mak'yŏssŭmnida.

SERVICES

With the Telephone Operator

I'd like an outside line.	외부에 전화 좀 하고 싶습니다. Oebue chŏnhwa chom hago shipsŭmnida.

Hello. I'd like to make a long-distance call.

여보세요. 장거리 전화를 하고 싶습니다. Yŏboseyo. Changgŏri chŏnhwarŭl hago shipsŭmnida.

The number is <u>Pusan 44-4567</u>.

번호는 부산 44-4567입니다. Pŏnhonŭn Pusan sasa-e sa-o-ryuk-ch'irimnida.

Taegu 754-8901

대구 754-8901 Taegu ch'iro-sa-e p'al-gu-gong-ir

Hello, operator! I was cut off.

여보세요. 전화가 끊어졌읍니다. Yŏboseyo. Chŏnhwaga kkŭnŏjyŏssŭmnida.

Could you try it again?

다시 한 번 해보시겠어요? Tashi han pŏn haeboshigessŏyo?

With the Desk Clerk

The key for Room 200 please.

200호실 열쇠 좀 주세요. Ibaek'-oshil yŏlsoe chom chuseyo.

Are there any <u>messages</u> for me?

제게 무슨 메시지 있었읍니까? Chege musŭn meshiji issŏssŭmnikka?

letters

편지 P'yŏnji

Could you keep this in your safe?

이것 좀 금고에 넣어 주세요. Igŏt chom kŭmgo-e nŏŏ chuseyo.

I'd like to take my things out of your safe.

제 물건 좀 금고에서 꺼내 주세요. Che mulgŏn chom kŭmgo-esŏ kkŏnae chuseyo.

ORDERING

I'd like ___.	___(으)로 주세요.
	___ (ŭ)ro chuseyo.

Do you have ___?	___ 됩니까?
	___ toemnikka?

May I have some more ___?	___ 좀 더 주세요.
	___ chom tŏ chuseyo.

There isn't any ___.	여기 ___이[가] 없읍니다.
	Yŏgi ___i[ga] ŏpsŭmnida.

Could you bring me ___?	___ 좀 갖다 주세요.
	___ chom katta chuseyo.

Beverages

coffee	커피	k'ŏp'i
tea	홍차	hongch'a
milk	밀크[우유]	milk'ŭ [uyu]
hot milk	데운 우유	teun uyu
hot chocolate	코코아	k'ok'oa

Meat

bacon	베이컨	peik'ŏn
ham	햄	haem
sausages	소시지	soshiji

Bread

| toast | 토스트 | t'osŭt'ŭ |

At the Hotel

rolls	롤 빵	rol ppang
croissant	크롸쌍	K'ŭrwassang
English muffins	머핀	mŏp'in
Danish pastry	과자 빵	kwaja ppang
doughnuts	도나스	tonasŭ

Cereal

| cornflakes | 콘플레이크 | k'onp'ŭlleik'ŭ |
| oatmeal | 오트밀 | ot'ŭmil |

Eggs

scrambled eggs	스크램블한 계란	sŭk'ŭraem-bŭrhan kyeran
fried eggs	계란 프라이	kyeran p'urai
soft boiled eggs	반숙	pansuk
omelet	오믈렛	omŭllet

Other Hot Dishes

pancakes	팬케이크	p'aenk'eik'ŭ
waffles	와플	wap'ŭl
French toast	프렌치 토스트	P'ŭrench'i t'osŭt'ŭ

Accompaniments

jam	잼	chaem
marmalade	마멀레이드	mamŏlleidŭ
honey	꿀	kkul
syrup	시럽	shirŏp

Combinations

ham and eggs	햄 에그	haem egŭ
bacon and eggs	베이컨 에그	peik'ŏn egŭ
sausage and eggs	소시지 에그	soshiji egŭ
ham omelet	햄 오믈렛	haem omŭllet
cheese omelet	치즈 오믈렛	ch'ijŭ omŭllet

Special Requests

decaffeinated coffee	카페인 없는 커피	k'ap'ein ŏmnŭn k'ŏp'i
skim milk	탈지 우유	t'alchi uyu
lowfat milk	저지방 우유	chŏjibang uyu
decaffeinated tea	카페인 없는 홍차	k'ap'ein ŏmnŭn hongch'a
sugar substitute	다이어트 감미료	taiŏt'ŭ kammiryo
I'd like it cooked without <u>salt</u> please.	<u>소금을</u> 넣지 말고 해주세요.	<u>Sogŭmŭl</u> nŏch'i malgo haejuseyo.
butter or oil	버터나 기름을	pŏt'ŏna kirŭmŭl

Juice

orange juice	오렌지 주스	orenji chusŭ
grapefruit juice	그레이프프루트 주스	kŭreip'ŭp'ŭrut'ŭ chusŭ
tomato juice	토마토 주스	t'omat'o chusŭ
pineapple juice	파인애플 주스	p'ainaep'ŭl chusŭ

Fruit

watermelon	수박	subak
apple	사과	sagwa
orange	오렌지	orenji
melon	멜런	mellŏn
Korean pear	배	pae
strawberries	딸기	ttalgi
p'ainaep'ŭl	파인애플	p'ainaep'ŭl

CHECKING OUT

I don't have much time. Could you hurry please?	시간이 없으니 서둘러 주세요.	Shigani ŏpsŭni sŏdullŏ chuseyo.
Does this include the tax and service charge?	세금과 봉사료가 포함된 것입니까?	Segŭmgwa pongsaryoga p'ohamdoen kŏshimnikka?
There seems to be an error in the bill.	계산서가 잘못 된 것 같은데요.	Kyesansŏga chalmot toen kŏt kat'ŭndeyo.
Could you check it again?	다시 한 번 확인해 주세요.	Tashi han pŏn hwaginhae chuseyo.
Could you get me a taxi?	택시 좀 불러 주시겠어요?	T'aekshi chom pullŏ chushigessŏyo?
Can I check my baggage till <u>noon</u>?	짐을 정오까지 좀 맡아 주세요.	Chimŭl chŏng-okkaji chom mat'a chuseyo.

evening	저녁	chŏnyŏ(k)

I'm checking out <u>this morning</u>.

<u>오늘 아침에</u> 나갈 겁니다.
<u>Onŭl ach'ime</u> nagal kŏmnida.

around noon	정오쯤에	Chŏng-otchŭme
early tomorrow	내일 일찍	Naeil iltchik
tomorrow morn-ing	내일 아침에	Naeil ach'ime

Please have my bill ready.

계산서 좀 준비해 놓으세요.
Kyesansŏ chom chunbihae noŭseyo.

Would you send someone to carry my luggage down?

짐 들 사람 좀 불러 주세요.
Chim tŭl saram chom pullŏ chuseyo.

May I have my bill, please. My room is 600.

계산서 좀 부탁합니다. 600 호실입니다. Kyesansŏ chom put'ak'amnida. Yukpaek'oshirimnida.

At the Hotel

ACCOMMODATIONS

When you stay in Korea, you have a choice between Western-style and Korean-style accommodations. The terms "Western-style" and "Korean-style" categorize both the facilities and the service that each type of lodging offers. In each of the two broad categories, you'll find a wide range of possibilities, from costly and luxurious to inexpensive and simple. You might stay at a Western-style hotel when you first arrive, and then a Korean-style inn, or

yŏgwan for a few nights as you travel around.
Sometimes it's possible to have a bit of both
worlds: Some Western-style hotels have a few
Korean-style rooms or suites, and some Korean-style hotels may have a few guest rooms
with beds.

Hotels

First-class hotels in Korea may equal fine hotels anywhere for facilities, quality of service,
and the rate as well. There are options, however. Korea has a great many Western-style
hotels of various types and standards. Current-
ly room rates range from US $ 50 to $ 80
(45, 000—72, 000won) depending on the types
of rooms.

Yŏgwan: Korean Inns

Staying at a **yŏgwan** is a good way to experience everyday Korean customs firsthand.
These inns offer traditional and authentic
Korean flavor, from the architecture and fur-
nishings to the pace and style of life. You'll
have everything you need to be comfortable.
If you do decide to stay at a **yŏgwan**, there
is a range in quality and price (as with
Western-style hotels) from luxurious to simple.
Some inns have private bathrooms, and some
are used to dealing with Western guests.

Youth Hostelling

Is there a bath time?	목욕 시간이 정해져 있읍니까? Mogyok shigani chŏnghaejyŏ issŭmnikka?
Can I use my sleeping bag?	슬리핑 백을 사용할 수 있읍니까? Sŭllip'ing paegŭl sayonghal su issŭmnikka?
Can I rent sleeping sheets?	담요를 빌 수 있읍니까? Tamnyorŭl pil su issŭmnikka?
Is there a curfew?	폐문 시간이 있읍니까? P'yemun shigani issŭmnikka?
When is wakeup time?	언제 기상합니까? Ŏnje kisanghamnikka?
When is "lights-out"?	소등은 언제 합니까? Sodŭng-ŭn ŏnje hamnikka?
Is there a youth hostel nearby?	이 근처에 유스 호스텔이 있읍니까? I kŭnch'ŏe yusŭ hosŭt'eri issŭmnikka?
Can I stay here? I'm a member.	회원인데요. 여기서 머물 수 있읍니까? Hoewonindeyo. Yŏgisŏ mŏmul su issŭmnikka?
Here's my membership card.	제 회원증입니다. Che hoewonchŭng-imnida.
When is meal time?	식사 시간은 언젭니까? Shiksa shiganŭn ŏnjemnikka?

Where's the dining room?	식당은 어딥니까? Shiktang-ŭn ŏdimnikka?
Can I cook for myself?	직접 요리해 먹을 수 있읍니까? Chikchŏp yorihae mŏgŭl su issŭmnikka?

There are also 11 youth hostels in Korea. They offer rather low-priced accommodation for students, foreign athletes, and other economic minded travelers. The charge for one night ranges $4~5 (3,500~4,400won) for a single occupancy. The Korea Youth Hostel Association (Tel. Seoul 226-2896, 275-4203) will help you with all the necessary informations including listings of facilities.

Moving around Town

BUSES

When does the next bus to Kangnam come?

강남 가는 다음 버스가 언제 옵니까? Kangnam kanŭn taŭm pŏsŭga ŏnje omnikka?

How long does it take from here to Kangnam?

여기서 강남까지 얼마나 걸립니까? Yŏgisŏ Kangnamkkaji ŏlmana kŏllimnikka?

How many stops are there from here to Namsan Tower?

여기서 남산 타워까지 몇 정거장이나 됩니까? Yŏgisŏ Namsan T'awokkaji myŏt chŏnggŏjang-ina toemnikka?

How much will it be to Chamshil?

잠실까지 요금이 얼맙니까? Chamshilkkaji yogŭmi ŏlmamnikka?

Do I have to pay the exact change?

잔돈으로 내야 합니까? Chandonŭro naeya hamnikka?

Can I get change?

거스름돈을 받을 수 있읍니까? Kŏsŭrŭmtonŭl padŭl su issŭmnikka?

Where do I put the fare?

요금을 어디다 넣어야 합니까? Yogŭmŭl ŏdida nŏŏya hamnikka?

Could you tell me when to get off?

내릴 곳에서 좀 알려 주시겠읍니까? Naeril kosesŏ chom alnyŏ chushigessŭmnikka?

Where can I get a bus to Myŏngdong?	명동 가는 버스를 어디서 탑니까? Myŏngdong kanŭn pŏsŭrŭl ŏdisŏ t'amnikka?
Where's the nearest bus stop for Chamshil?	잠실에서 가장 가까운 버스 정류장이 어딥니까? Chamshiresŏ kajang kakkaun pŏsŭ chŏngnyujang-i ŏdimnikka?
Can I get a bus to Tongdaemun around here?	이 근처에 동대문 가는 버스가 있읍니까? I kŭnch'ŏe Tongdaemun kanŭn pŏsŭga issŭmnikka?
Which bus do I take to go to Seoul Station?	서울역으로 가려면 어느 버스를 타야 합니까? Seoulnyŏgŭro karyŏmyŏn ŏnŭ pŏsŭrŭl t'aya hamnikka?
Where does this bus go?	이 버스는 어디로 갑니까? I pŏsŭnŭn ŏdiro kamnikka?
Does this bus go to City Hall?	이 버스 시청 갑니까? I pŏsŭ Shich'ŏng kammikka?
Does this bus stop at the Taehan Theater?	이 버스 대한 극장 섭니까? I pŏsŭ Taehan Kŭkchang sŏmnikka?
Where do I get off to go to the British Consulate?	영국 영사관에 가려면 어디서 내려야 합니까? Yŏnguk Yŏngsagwane karyŏmyŏn ŏdisŏ naeryŏya hamnikka?
Do I need to change buses to go to the National Theater?	국립 극장에 가려며 버스를 갈아타야 합니까? Kungnip Kŭkchang-e karyŏmyŏn pŏsŭrŭl karat'aya hamnikka?

| How often does the bus for Seoul Station come? | 서울역 가는 버스가 얼마나 자주 옵니까? Seoulnyŏk kanŭn pŏsŭga ŏlmana chaju omnikka? |

SUBWAYS

What's the next station?	다음 정거장이 어딥니까? Taŭm chŏnggŏjang-i ŏdimnikka?
How many more stops to Chungmu-ro?	충무로까지 몇 정거장이나 더 가야 됩니까? Ch'ungmurokkaji myŏt chŏnggŏjang-ina tŏ kaya toemnikka?
Shinsŏl-dong	신설동 Shinsŏltong
Where is the east exit?	동쪽 출구가 어디에 있습니까? Tongtchok ch'ulguga ŏdie issŭmnikka?
west	서쪽 Sŏtchok
Where is the exit to the Taewoo Building?	대우 빌딩 쪽 출구가 어디에 있습니까? Taewoo Building tchok ch'ulguga ŏdie issŭmnikka?
Sajik Park	사직 공원 Sajik Kongwon
Where is the lost and found office?	분실물 취급소가 어디에 있습니까? Punshilmul ch'wigŭpsoga ŏdie issŭmnikka?
I've left my attache case on the train.	차에 가방을 놓고 내렸습니다. Ch'a-e kabang-ŭl nok'o nae-ryŏssŭmnida.
package	물건을 mulgŏnŭl

Moving around Town

How many stations are there from here to Ch'ŏngnyangni?

여기서 청량리까지 몇 정거장이나 됩니까? Yŏgisŏ Ch'ŏngnyang-nikkaji myŏt chŏnggŏjang-ina toemnikka?

Chonggak

종각 Chonggak

Do I have to change?

갈아타야 됩니까? Karat'aya toemnikka?

At which station do I have to change?

어디서 갈아타야 됩니까? Ŏdisŏ karat'aya toemnikka?

Which line do I change to?

몇 호선으로 갈아타야 됩니까? Myŏt hosŏnŭro karat'aya toemnikka?

Which track does the train leave from?

열차가 어느 트랙에서 출발합니까? Yŏlch'aga ŏnŭ t'ŭraegesŏ chulbarhamnikka?

Where is the platform for the train to Tongdaemun?

동대문으로 가려면 어느 홈에서 타야 됩니까? Tongdaemunŭro karyŏmyŏn ŏnŭ homesŏ t'aya toemnikka?

to Hannamdong

한남동으로 Hannamdong-ŭro

Is this the right platform for the train to Sadang?

사당으로 가려면 이 홈에서 타야 됩니까? Sadangŭro karyŏmyŏn i homesŏ t'aya toemnikka?

Could you tell me how to get to the nearest train station?

가장 가까운 전철역이 어디에 있음니까? Kajang kakkaun chŏnch'ŏlnyŏgi ŏdie issŭmnikka?

.Where is the Line 1 station? | 1호선 전철역이 어디에 있읍니까? Ir hosŏn chŏnch'ŏlnyŏgi ŏdie issŭmnikka?

Line 2 | 2호선 I hosŏn
Line 3 | 3호선 Sam hosŏn
Line 4 | 4호선 Sa hosŏn

Which line should I take to Chamshil? | 잠실로 가려면 몇 호선을 타야 됩니까? Chamshillo karyŏmyŏn myŏt hosŏnŭl t'aya toemnikka?

Excuse me, could you help me? | 실례합니다만 좀 도와 주시겠읍니까? Shillyehamnidaman chomtowa chushigessŭmnikka?

I can't read the Korean for the fare information. | 한글을 모르기 때문에 요금을 모르겠읍니다. Han-gŭrŭl morŭgi ttaemune yogŭmŭl morŭgessŭmnida.

How much is the fare to City Hall? | 시청까지가 얼맙니까? Shich'ŏngkkajiga ŏlmamnikka?

Shinch'on | 신촌 Shinch'on

Where is the ticket machine? | 표 판매기가 어디에 있읍니까? P'yo p'anmaegiga ŏdie issŭmnikka?

Which machine should I use? | 어떤 기계를 사용해야 합니까? Ŏttŏn kigyerŭl sayonghaeya hamnikka?

Is there a subway in this city? | 이 시에 지하철이 있읍니까? I shie chihach'ŏri issŭmnikka?

Is there a subway map in English?	영어로 된 지하철 지도가 있읍니까? Yŏng-ŏro toen chiha-ch'ŏl chidoga issŭmnikka?
Where can I get a commuter train map in English?	영어로 된 전철 지도를 어디서 구할 수 있읍니까? Yŏng-ŏro toen chŏnch'ŏl chidorŭl ŏdisŏ kuhal su issŭmnikka?
When is the <u>mor-ning</u> rush hour?	아침 러시 아워는 언제입니까? Ach'im rŏshi awonŭn ŏnjeim-nikka?
evening	저녁 Chŏnyŏk
When is the ear-liest train of the day?	첫차가 언제 있읍니까? Ch'ŏtch'aga ŏnje issŭmnikka?
When does the last train depart?	막차가 언제 있읍니까? Makch'aga ŏnje issŭmnkka?
Is there a train station nearby?	근처에 전철이 있읍니까? Kŭnch'ŏe chŏnch'ŏri issŭm-nikka?

Seoul and Pusan have fast, clean, and efficient subway and commuter train systems. The latter are not quite the Western equivalent of com-muter trains. They're actually public trains crisscrossing and encircling the urban areas, and linking with the subways.

You can use the subways and commuter trains easily if you have a map or guide, and there are many available. The station signs are in Roman letters, or romacha, so you'll be

able to read them. The only difficulty you
might have will be with the ticket machines
at the entrance. But you can just buy the
cheapest ticket in order to get in. Keep it
until the end of your ride. Hand it to the
ticket taker at the exit; he'll tell you how
much you owe, and you can pay him.

TAXIS

Where can I get a taxi?	택시 어디서 타는지 아세요? T'aekshi ŏdisŏ t'anŭnji aseyo?
Can I get a cab in the street around here?	이 근처에서 택시 탈 수 있읍니까? I kŭnch'ŏesŏ t'aekshi t'al su issŭmnikka?
Would you call me a cab please?	택시 좀 불러 주시겠읍니까? T'aekshi chom pullŏ chushigessŭmnikka?
Take me to the Taehan Theater please.	대한 극장까지 가 주세요. Taehan Kŭkchangkkaji ka chuseyo.
I'd like to go near Shinch'on intersection.	신촌 로타리쪽으로 가 주세요. Shinch'on rot'aritchoguro ka chuseyo.
63 Building in Yŏŭido	여의도 63 빌딩 Yŏŭido Yuksam Pilting
Do you know where this address is?	이 주소가 어딘지 아세요? I chusoga ŏdinji aseyo?

Moving around Town

the American Embassy	미국 대사관이	Miguk taesagwani

Can I get there by <u>one</u> o'clock?

1시까지 도착할 수 있을까요?
Han<u>shi</u>kkaji toch'ak'al su issŭlkkayo?

two	2	Tu

Could you go faster, please?

더 빨리 갈 수 있읍니까?
Tŏ ppalli kal su issŭmnikka?

There's no need to hurry.

서둘 필요는 없읍니다.
Sŏdul p'iryonŭn ŏpsŭmnida.

Go straight please.

직진해 주세요.
Chikchinhae chuseyo.

How long will it take to <u>Myŏng-dong</u> by cab?

명동까지 택시로 얼마나 걸립니까?
<u>Myŏngdong</u>kkaji t'aekshiro ŏlmana kŏllimnikka?

the Chosŏn Hotel	조선 호텔	Chosŏn Hot'el

How much will it cost to go to <u>Chamshil</u> by cab?

잠실까지 택시 요금이 얼마나 나옵니까? <u>Chamshil</u>kkaji t'aekshi yogŭmi ŏlmana naomnikka?

Kyŏngbokkung	경복궁	Kyŏngbokkung

How far is it?

얼마나 멉니까?
Ŏlmana mŏmnikka?

Turn to the right at the next corner, please.

다음 코너에서 우회전 해주세요.
Taŭm k'onŏesŏ uhoejŏn hae chuseyo.

Could you go a little farther please?	조금만 더 가 주시겠어요? Chogŭmman tŏ ka chushigessŏyo?
Would you mind going back a little?	약간만 되돌아 가 주시겠어요? Yakkanman toedora ka chushigessŏyo?
I think it's around here.	이 근처인 것 같은데요. I kŭnch'ŏin kŏt kat'ŭndeyo.
Could you stop just before the next intersection?	다음 로타리 조금 못 미쳐 세워 주세요. Taŭm rot'ari chogŭm mot mich'yŏ sewo chuseyo.
Around here is fine.	됐읍니다. Twaessŭmnida.
Stop here please.	여기 세워 주세요. Yŏgi sewo chuseyo.
Please wait here for a moment.	잠시만 기다려 주세요. Chamshiman kidaryŏ chuseyo.
How much do I owe you?	얼맙니까? Ŏlmamnikka?

Cruising taxis are plentiful in cities and large towns; there are also taxi stands at train stations, near hotels, and in certain downtown districts. Meters show the fare in digits; there's a 20 percent surcharge added from 12 P.M. until 4 A.M.; you don't tip the driver unless he does something special for you, like carrying luggage or waiting while you make a stop.

The driver may not know exactly where

it is, and if he does, he's not expected to venture far from a main road unless he chooses to. If you're going someplace well known, like a hotel or train station, there's no problem. Otherwise, tell the driver the main intersection or landmark near your destination. Some drivers will help you from there; others will expect you to get out and find your own way from the main road.

MOVING AROUND

Inquiries

What would you recommend that I see here?

여기에서는 어떤 것이 볼 만합니까? Yŏgiesŏnŭn ŏttŏn kŏshi pol manhamnikka?

  in that city

그 도시에서는 Kŭ toshiesŏnŭn

Is ___ worth going to see?

_가[이] 볼 만합니까? —ga[i] pol manhamnikka?

What are the main attractions there?

그 곳에 볼 만한 것이 어떤 것이 있읍니까? Kŭ kose pol manhan kŏshi ŏttŏn kŏshi issŭmnikka?

Is it easy to get there?

그 곳에 쉽게 갈 수 있읍니까? Kŭ kose swipke kal su issŭmnikka?

Where is the tourist information center?

여행 안내소가 어디에 있읍니까? Yŏhaeng annaesoga ŏdie issŭmnikka?

the Korea National Tourist Corporation (KNTC)	한국 관광 공사가	Han-guk Kwan-gwang Kongsaga

We have <u>a half day</u> free here.	<u>오후에는</u> 한가합니다.	<u>Ohuenŭn</u> han-gahamnida.

a day	하루는	Harunŭn
a few days	며칠은	Myŏch'irŭn
a week	일 주일은	Il chuirŭn

We'd like to see the <u>aquarium</u>.	<u>수족관을</u> 보고 싶습니다.	<u>Sujokkwanŭl</u> pogo shipsŭmnida.

business district	비즈니스가를	Pijŭnisŭgarŭl
castle	성을	Sŏng-ŭl
downtown area	번화가를	Pŏnhwagarŭl
gardens	정원을	Chŏngwonŭl
harbor	항구를	Hanggurŭl
lake	호수를	Hosurŭl
market	시장을	Shijang-ŭl
museum	박물관을	Pangmulgwanŭl
old town	구시가를	Kushigarŭl
palace	궁전을	Kungjŏnŭl
park	공원을	Kongwonŭl
shrine	사당을	Sadang-ŭl
temple	사찰을	Sach'arŭl
zoo	동물원을	Tongmurwonŭl

Are there English guidebooks for <u>Seoul</u>?	영어로 된 <u>서울</u> 여행 안내서가 있읍니까 ?	Yŏng-ŏro toen <u>Seoul</u> yŏhaeng annaesŏga issŭmnikka?

Chejudo	제주도	Chejudo

Which guidebook would you recommend?	어떤 여행 안내서가 좋습니까? Ŏttŏn yŏhaeng annaesŏga chossŭmnikka?
Where can I buy the guidebook?	여행 안내서를 어디서 살 수 있읍니까? Yŏhaeng annaesŏrŭl ŏdisŏ sal su issŭmnikka?
Could you tell me the points of interest <u>here</u>?	여기 명소에 어떤 곳이 있읍니까? Yŏgi myŏngso-e ŏttŏn koshi issŭmnikka?
there	거기 Kŏgi
I'm interested in <u>antiques</u>.	<u>골동품에</u> 관심이 있읍니다. <u>Koltongp'ume</u> kwanshimi issŭmnida.

architecture	건축에	Kŏnch'uge
art	예술에	Yesure
Buddhist temples	사찰에	Sach'are
ceramics	도자기에	Tojagie
crafts	공예에	Kongyee
festivals	축제에	Ch'ukchee
folk art	민속 예술에	Minsok yesure
furniture	가구에	Kague
historic sites	유적지에	Yujŏkchie
Korean gardens	한국 정원에	Han-guk chŏngwone
Korean painting	한국 미술에	Han-guk misure

Korea is so rich in things to see and do that your only problem will be limiting yourself to those you have time for. If your tastes run to the traditional, you'll find that the Korea of yesteryear is very much alive today. There are many places where the past is preserved—cities like Seoul, for example. And in towns like Kyŏngju and Yong-in, you can see what feudal Korea was like. Throughout Korea there are homes, temples, and shrines built according to traditional Korean styles of architecture. And the centuries-old art forms are still intact: brush painting, ceramics, and woodblock prints, among others. The stylized entertainment of theatrical arts like *puch'aech'um*, *t'alch'um*, and *ch'ajŏnnori* also reflect the preservation of traditional values. The old culture is everywhere.

Do you prefer things contemporary? Then high-tech Korea is for you: the excitement and vitality of the cities, the world of Korean industry, the taste and purity of modern Korean design. You'll find sightseeing easy in Korea. The country is well-equipped to accommodate tourists, and the Koreans like foreign visitors. They'll do everything they can to help you enjoy their country.

General

Where does the tour go?	어디로 가는 관광입니까? Ŏdiro kanŭn kwan-gwang-im-nikka?
How many hours does the tour take?	관광이 몇 시간이나 걸립니까? Kwan-gwang-i myŏt shiganina kŏllimnikka?

When does the tour <u>start</u>?	관광이 언제 시작됩니까? Kwan-gwang-i ŏnje <u>shijak-toemnikka?</u>
finish	끝납니까 kkŭnnamnikka
Where does the tour start?	관광이 어디서 시작됩니까? Kwan-gwang-i ŏdisŏ shijak-toemnikka?
At which hotels do you have pick-up service?	어느 호텔에 픽업 서비스가 있읍니까? Ŏnŭ hot'ere p'ik'ŏp sŏbisŭga issŭmnikka?
Can I join the tour at the ____ Hotel?	____ 호텔에서 관광에 합류할 수 있읍니까? ____ Hot'eresŏ kwan-gwang-e hamnyuhal su issŭmnikka?
Does the all-day tour stop for lunch somewhere?	일일 관광은 점심 시간에 어디선가 섭니까? Iril kwan-gwang-ŭn chŏmshim shigane ŏdisŏn-ga sŏmnikka?
Is lunch included in the tour fare?	관광 요금에 점심이 포함됩니까? Kwan-gwang yogŭme chŏmshimi p'ohamdoemnikka?
Is there any free time for shopping?	쇼핑할 자유 시간이 있읍니까? Syop'inghal chayu shigani issŭmnikka?
How much is the fare for the tour?	관광 요금이 얼맙니까? Kwan-gwang yogŭmi ŏlmam-nikka?
I'd like <u>one ticket</u> for that tour.	그 관광표 <u>한 장</u> 부탁합니다. Kŭ kwan-gwangp'yo <u>han chang</u> put'ak'amnida.

two tickets	두 장	tu chang
three tickets	석 장	sŏk chang
four tickets	넉 장	nŏk chang

Are there sight-seeing buses in the city?

시내에 관광 버스가 있읍니까?
Shinaee kwan-gwang pŏsŭga issŭmnikka?

Are there sightseeing buses to Imjingak?

임진각 가는 관광 버스가 있읍니까? Imjin-gak kanŭn kwan-gwang pŏsŭga issŭmnikka?

Minsokch'on

민속촌　　Minsokch'on

Are there morning tours?

아침 관광이 있읍니까? Ach'im kwan-gwang-i issŭmnikka?

afternoon	오후	Ohu
evening	야간	Yagan
all-day	일일	Ir il
two-day	이일	I il

Are there group tours to Chejudo?

제주도 단체 여행이 있읍니까?
Chejudo tanch'e yŏhaeng-i issŭmnikka?

What kind of transportation do you use?

어떤 교통편을 이용합니까?
Ŏttŏn kyot'ongp'yŏnŭl iyonghamnikka?

Are the meals and lodging included in the tour fare?

관광 요금에 숙식이 포함됩니까?
Kwan-gwang yogŭme sukshigi p'ohamdoemnikka?

Are the meals Western or Korean?

식사는 양식입니까 한식입니까?
Shiksanŭn yangshigimnikka hanshigimnikka?

Is the hotel Western style?	호텔은 서양식입니까? Hot'erŭn sŏyangshigimnikka?
Is there a chance to stay at a Korean inn?	한국식 여관에 머물 기회가 있읍니까? Han-gukshik yŏgwane mŏmul kihoega issŭmnikka?

Considering how difficult driving in Korea can be for foreigners, organized sightseeing tours are a convenient way to get around. The KNTC Tourist Information Centers(TIC) or any travel agency can help you find a suitable one. You can spend a few hours seeing some major points of interest, or a few days or weeks seeing much more.

Sightseeing on Your Own

I'd like to go to ___, ___, and ___. (places)	___, ___, ___을[를] 가고 싶습니다. ___, ___, ___(r)ŭl kago shipsŭmnida.
Could you tell me how to go to ___?	___에는 어떻게 갑니까? ___enŭn ŏttŏk'e kamnikka?
Can I get to ___ by train and bus?	___에 기차와 버스를 타고 갈 수 있읍니까? ___e kich'awa pŏsŭrŭl t'ago kal su issŭmnikka?
Which line do I take to go to ___?	___에 가려면 어떤 노선을 타야 합니까? ___e karyŏmyŏn ŏttŏn nosŏnŭl t'aya hamnikka?

Where can I get the ___ line?	___선은 어디서 타야 합니까? ___sŏnŭn ŏdisŏ t'aya hamni-kka?
How far is ___ from the station?	___은(는) 역에서 멉니까? ___(n)ŭn yŏgesŏ mŏmnikka?
Can I get there from the station on foot?	역에서 걸어갈 수 있읍니까? Yŏgesŏ kŏrŏgal su issŭmni-kka?
Can I find it easily?	찾기 쉽습니까? Ch'atki swipsŭmnikka?
Can I walk from ___ to ___?	___에서 ___까지 걸어갈 수 있읍니까? ___esŏ ___kkaji kŏrŏgal su issŭmnikka?
I'd like to see a festival.	축제를 보고 싶습니다. Ch'ukcherŭl pogo shipsŭmni-da.
Is there a festival somewhere today?	오늘 어딘가에 축제가 있읍니까? Onŭl ŏdin-ga-e ch'ukchega issŭmnikka?
tomorrow	내일 Naeil
Where can I see ___?	___를(을) 어디서 볼 수 있읍니까? ___(r)ŭl ŏdisŏ pol su issŭmnikka?
Which museum would be best for seeing ___?	___을[를] 보려면 어떤 박물관이 가장 좋습니까? ___[r]ŭl po-ryŏmyŏn ŏttŏn pangmulgwani kajang chossŭmnikka?

I'd like to look around Myŏng-dong on my own.	명동을 혼자서 한 번 둘러보고 싶은 데요. Myŏngdong-ŭl honjasŏ han pŏn tullŏbogo ship'ŭndeyo.
here	여기를 Yŏgirŭl
What's the best way to spend a day sightseeing on my own?	혼자서 관광을 하며 하루를 보내는 가장 좋은 방법이 뭡니까? Honjasŏ kwan-gwang-ŭl hamyŏ harurŭl ponaenŭn kajang choŭn pangbŏbi mwomnikka?
two days	이틀 .it'ŭl
Could you tell me what sightseeing sequence I should follow?	관광 코스로는 어떤 것이 좋습니까? Kwan-gwang k'osŭronŭn ŏttŏn kŏshi chossŭmnikka?
I'd like to see traditional architecture.	전통 건축을 보고 싶습니다. Chŏnt'ong kŏnch'ugŭl pogo shipsŭmnida.

If you want to get out and see things on your own, some preliminary inquiries can help. You can use these phrases with hotel staff, tourist information center personnel, or Korean friends or acquaintances.

Tour Guides

I'd like an English speaking guide for a day.	영어 안내원이 하루 필요합니다. Yŏng-ŏ annaewoni haru p'iryohamnida.
two days	이틀 it'ŭl

How can I arrange for a guide?	관광 안내원을 어떻게 구할 수 있읍니까? Kwan-gwang annae-wonŭl ŏttŏk'e kuhal su issŭm-nikka?
Could you arrange for the guide for me?	관광 안내원을 한 사람 부탁합니다. Kwan-gwang annaewonŭl han saram put'ak'amnida.
Is a tour guide available?	관광 안내원이 있읍니까? Kwan-gwang annaewoni is-sŭmnikka?
Is there an English-speaking guide?	영어를 하는 관광 안내원이 있읍니까? Yŏng-ŏrŭl hanŭn kwan-gwang annaewoni issŭmnikka?
How much does a guide charge <u>per hour</u>?	관광 안내원은 <u>시간당</u> 얼마씩 받읍니까? Kwan-gwang annae-wonŭn shigandang ŏlmassik passŭmnikka?
per day	일당 iltang

Hotel Taxi

How much is the <u>hourly</u> rate?	<u>시간당</u> 얼맙니까? <u>Shigandang</u> ŏlmamnikka?
daily	일당 Iltang
Where can I get a hotel taxi?	호텔 택시는 어디서 구할 수 있읍니까? Hot'el t'aekshinŭn ŏdi-sŏ kuhal su issŭmnikka?
Do I need to call?	전화 해야 합니까? Chŏnhwa haeya hamnikka?

Is a hotel taxi available for sightseeing?	관광용 호텔 택시가 있읍니까? Kwan-gwangyong hot'el t'aekshiga issŭmnikka?
Is an English-speaking chauffeur available?	영어를 하는 기사가 있읍니까? Yŏng-ŏrŭl hanŭn kisaga issŭmnikka?
Is the rate <u>by the meter</u>?	요금은 미터제입니까? Yogŭmŭn mit'ŏjeimnikka?
by the hour	시간제 Shiganje

This is the Western equivalent of limousine service, but the car is not limousine-sized. It's a convenient way to get around, especially in places like Seoul, where you may want to visit several places of interest on the outskirts of town. The hot'el taxi, as the Koreans call it, has the added advantage of the driver's knowing the sights.

If he speaks some English, he can be a helpful guide. It's not as expensive as you might think, especially if a few of you share the costs.

While Sightseeing: Getting In

Am I allowed to take pictures inside?	안에서 사진 찍어도 됩니까? Anesŏ sajin tchigŏdo toemnikka?
Where is the entrance?	입구가 어딥니까? Ipkuga ŏdimnikka?

Do you have an English guidebook?	영어 안내 책자 있읍니까? Yŏng-ŏ annae ch'aekcha is-sŭmnikka?
catalog	카탈로그 k'at'allogŭ
How much is the guidebook?	안내 책자 얼맙니까? Annae ch'aekcha ŏlmamni-kka?
Do I have to take off my shoes?	신발을 벗어야 합니까? Shinbarŭl pŏsŏya hamnikka?
Can I just look around?	좀 둘러 봐도 됩니까? Chom tullŏ pwado toemnikka?
Do I have to wait for a guided tour?	안내 관광을 받으려면 기다려야 합니까? Annae kwan-gwang-ŭl padŭryŏmyŏn kidaryŏya hamnikka?
How long do we have to wait?	얼마나 기다려야 합니까? Ŏlmana kidaryŏya hamnikka?
What time does it open?	언제 문을 엽니까? Ŏnje munŭl yŏmnikka?
Is it open on Saturdays?	토요일에 문을 엽니까? T'oyoire munŭl yŏmnikka?
on Sundays	일요일에 Iryoire
Is it open now?	지금 문 열었읍니까? Chigŭm mun yŏrŏssŭmnikka?
Is it still open?	아직도 열려 있읍니까? Ajikto yŏlnyŏ issŭmnikka?

How long does it stay open?	몇 시까지 엽니까? Myŏt shikkaji yŏmnikka?
Is there an admission fee?	입장료가 있읍니까? Ipchangnyoga issŭmnikka?
How much is the admission?	입장료는 얼맙니까? Ipchangnyonŭn ŏlmamnikka?
Is there a discount for <u>students</u>?	학생 할인 됩니까? <u>Haksaeng</u> harin toemnikka?
senior citizens	노인 Noin
What's the minimum age for the discount? (senior citizens)	몇 살부터 할인 됩니까? Myŏt salbut'ŏ harin toemnikka?
What's the age limit for the discount? (children)	몇 살까지 할인 됩니까? Myŏt salkkaji harin toemnikka?

Asking about the Sights

What's the purpose of ___?	___은[는] 뭐 하는 데 쓰였읍니까? ___(n)ŭn mwo hanŭn te ssŭyŏssŭmnikka?
How long did it take to complete?	완성하는 데에 얼마나 걸렸읍니까? Wansŏnghanŭn tee ŏlmana kŏlnyŏssŭmnikka?
Is it <u>an everyday</u> object?	이건 일상 생활에 쓰이는 겁니까? Igŏn ilsang saenghware ssŭinŭn kŏmnikka?
a religious	종교 chonggyo

What was it used for?	그것은 뭣에 쓰였읍니까? Kŭgŏsŭn mwose ssŭyŏssŭmnikka?
What is it made of?	그것의 재료는 뭡니까? Kŭgŏsŭi chaeryonŭn mwomnikka?
How was it made?	그것은 어떻게 만들어진 겁니까? Kŭgŏsŭn ŏttŏk'e mandŭrŏjin kŏmnikka?
What is <u>it</u>?	이건 뭡니까? Igŏn mwomnikka?

that	저건	Chŏgŏn
that building	저 건물은	Chŏ kŏnmurŭn
that monument	저 기념비는	Chŏ kinnyŏmbinŭn

How old is it?	얼마나 오래된 겁니까? Ŏlmana oraedoen kŏmnikka?
Is it original?	원작입니까? Wonjagimnikka?
Who was the <u>architect</u>?	그 건축가는 누구입니까? Kŭ kŏnch'ukkanŭn nuguimnikka?

artist	예술가 yesulga
craftsman	공예가 kongyega
painter	화가 hwaga
sculptor	조각가 chogakka

Who made this?	이건 누가 만들었읍니까? Igŏn nuga mandŭrŏssŭmnikka?

Travelling

BY AIR

Inquiries

Is that a Korean Air Lines flight?

그건 대한 항공편입니까?
Kŭgŏn Taehan Hanggongp'yŏnimnikka?

What time does the flight to Pusan leave?

부산행이 몇 시에 있읍니까?
Pusanhaeng-i myŏt shie issŭmnikka?

to Chejudo

제주도행이 Chejudohaeng-i

What type of aircraft do they use for that flight?

그 편에 어떤 기종이 운항됩니까?
Kŭ p'yŏne ŏttŏn kijong-i unhangdoemnikka?

Is there a connecting flight to Chejudo?

제주도 연결편이 있읍니까?
Chejudo yŏn-gyŏlp'yŏni issŭmnikka?

Sokch'o

속초 Sokch'o

Is there meal service in flight?

식사 서비스가 있읍니까?
Shiksa sŏbisŭga issŭmnikka?

Should I buy my air ticket in advance?

비행기표를 미리 사야 합니까?
Pihaenggip'yorŭl miri saya hamnikka?

Can I get a ticket at the airport the day of the trip?

공항에서 당일표를 살 수 있읍니까? Konghang-esŏ tang-il-p'yorŭl sal su issŭmnikka?

Is there a flight to Chejudo?	제주도행 비행기 있읍니까? Chejudohaeng pihaenggi issŭmnikka?
to Pusan	부산행 Pusanhaeng
Is it a nonstop flight?	그건 논스톱입니까? Kŭgŏn nonsŭt'obimnikka?
Where does it stop over?	도중에 어디에서 섭니까? Tojung-e ŏdiesŏ sŏmnikka?
Is there a daily flight to Sokch'o?	속초행이 매일 있읍니까? Sokch'ohaeng-i maeil issŭmnikka?

Tickets

When is the next available flight to Pusan?	부산행 다음 비행기가 언제 있읍니까? Pusanhaeng taŭm pihaenggiga ŏnje issŭmnikka?
Is there an earlier flight than that?	그것보다 좀 이른 것 있읍니까? Kŭgŏtpoda chom irŭn kŏt issŭmnikka?
a later	나중 najung
What's the air fare to Taegu?	대구까지 항공료가 얼맙니까? Taegukkaji hanggongnyoga ŏlmamnikka?
What's the flying time to Chejudo?	제주도까지 비행 시간이 얼마나 됩니까? Chejudokkaji pihaeng shigani ŏlmana toemnikka?
Pusan	부산 Pusan

Travelling

Is there a limit on the number of bags?	가방 수에 제한이 있읍니까? Kabang sue chehani issŭmnikka?
When do I have to check in?	언제 맡겨야 합니까? Ŏnje matkyŏya hamnikka?
Do I need to reconfirm the reservation?	예약을 확인해야 합니까? Yeyagŭl hwaginhaeya hamnikka?
Can I get a ticket to Kwangju for today?	광주행 오늘표 있읍니까? Kwangjuhaeng onŭlp'yo issŭmnikka?
tomorrow	내일 naeil
I'd like a one-way ticket to Yŏsu.	여수행 편도로 부탁합니다. Yŏsuhaeng p'yŏndoro put'ak'amnida.
round trip	왕복으로 wangbogŭro
Two tickets to Chinju, please.	진주행 두 장 부탁합니다. Chinjuhaeng tu chang put'ak'amnida.
three	세 장 se chang
Is there a morning flight to Ulsan?	울산행 아침 비행기 있읍니까? Ulsanhaeng ach'im pihaenggi issŭmnikka?
afternoon evening	오후 ohu 저녁 chŏnyŏk
I'd like a ticket to Yŏsu on August 10.	8월 10일 여수행 표 있읍니까? P'arwol shibil Yŏsuhaeng p'yo issŭmnikka?

September 20   9월 20일   Kuwol ishibil
October 30   10월 30일   Shiwol
                                samshibil

Information about the Airport

How much does the <u>bus</u> to the airport cost?
공항까지 버스 요금이 얼마나 됩니까? Konghangkkaji pŏsŭ yogŭmi ŏlmana toemnikka?

     taxi   택시   t'aekshi

How long does the taxi take to the airport?
공항까지 택시로 얼마나 걸립니까? Konghangkkaji t'aekshiro ŏlmana kŏlimnikka?

Where is the airport?
공항이 어디에 있읍니까? Konghang-i ŏdie issŭmnikka?

Is the airport far?
공항이 멉니까? Konghang-i mŏmnikka?

How can I get to the airport?
공항에 어떻게 가는 편이 좋습니까? Konghang-e ŏttŏk'e kanŭn p'yŏni chossŭmnikka?

Is there a <u>train</u> to the airport?
공항 가는 전철이 있읍니까? Konhang kanŭn chŏnch'ŏri issŭmnikka?

     bus   버스가   pŏsŭga
     subway   지하철이   chihach'ŏri

At the Airport

Can I get a seat by the <u>window</u>?
창쪽 좌석 있읍니까? Ch'angtchok chwasŏk issŭmnikka?

     aisle   통로쪽   T'ongnotchok

Travelling

When is the departure?

언제 출발합니까?
Ŏnje ch'ulbarhamnikka?

What's the departure gate?

출발 게이트가 어디에 있읍니까?
Ch'ulbal keit'ŭga ŏdie issŭmnikka?

What's the arrival time?

언제 도착합니까?
Ŏnje toch'ak'amnikka?

I'd like to check in this suitcase.

이 가방 좀 맡기고 싶습니다.
I kabang chom matkigo shipsŭmnida.

This is carry-on.

이건 소지품입니다.
Igŏn sojip'umimnida.

Is a seat in the no-smoking section available?

금연석 있읍니까?
Kŭmyŏnsŏk issŭmnikka?

International Air Travel

What's the air fare to <u>Milan</u>?

<u>밀라노</u>까지 항공료가 얼맙니까?
<u>Millano</u>kkaji hanggongnyoga ŏlmamnikka?

Kuala Lumpur

쿠알라룸푸르 K'uallalump'urŭ

How long does the flight take?

비행 시간이 얼마나 됩니까?
Pihaeng shigani ŏlmana toemnikka?

Is that a lunch flight?

그 비행기 점심 서비스가 있읍니까? Kŭ pihaenggi chŏmshimsŏbisŭga issŭmnikka?

When is the departure time?	출발 시간이 언젭니까? Ch'ulbal shigani ŏnjemnikka?
arrival	도착 Toch'ak
I'd like a ticket to Hong Kong.	홍콩행으로 부탁합니다. Hongk'onghaeng-ŭro put'ak'amnida.
When is the first available flight to Jakarta?	다음 자카르타행이 언제 있읍니까? Taŭm Chak'arŭt'ahaeng-i ŏnje issŭmnikka?
Is there a direct flight to Tokyo from this airport?	이 공항에서 도쿄행 직행이 있읍니까? I konghang-esŏ Tok'yohaeng chik'aeng-i issŭmnikka?

Only one airline operates within Korea: Korean Air Lines(KAL). Although most KAL personnel know at least some English, the Korean phrases can be helpful, especially at local airports. Domestic flights are available in Seoul, Pusan, Cheju Island, Kwangju, Taegu, Yŏsu, Sokch'o and Chinju. Ticket reservations and advance sales are available from the Korean Air reservation office.

Travelling

BY TRAIN

Inquiries

Can I buy a ticket in advance?	예매표 살 수 있읍니까? Yemaep'yo sal su issŭmnikka?

Can I buy a ticket on the day of the trip?

당일표 있읍니까?
Tang-ilp'yo issŭmnikka?

Where is the ticket window/counter?

표 파는 곳이 어디에 있읍니까?
P'yo p'anŭn koshi ŏdie issŭmnikka?

ticket counter for Saemaŭrho reservations

새마을호 예매 창구가 Saemaŭrho yemae ch'angguga

Saemaŭrho ticket counter for today's trains

새마을호 당일표 발매 창구가
Saemaŭrho tang-ilp'yo palmae ch'angguga

Is there a timetable in English?

영어로 된 시간표 있읍니까?
Yŏng-ŏro toen shiganp'yo issŭmnikka?

Where can I get a timetable in English?

영어로 된 시간표를 어디서 구할 수 있읍니까? Yŏng-ŏro toen shiganp'yorŭl ŏdisŏ kuhal su issŭmnikka?

Which line do I take to go to Pusan?

부산으로 가려면 어느 차를 타야 됩니까? Pusanŭro karyŏmyŏn ŏnŭ ch'arŭl t'aya toemnikka?

Which station does the train for Taejŏn leave from?

대전행이 어느 역에서 출발합니까?
Taejŏnhaeng-i ŏnŭ yŏgesŏ ch'ulbarhamnikka?

Nonsan

논산 Nonsan

Where can I buy a ticket for the Saemaŭrho?

새마을호 표 어디서 삽니까?
Saemaŭrho p'yo ŏdisŏ samnikka?

Train Information

When is the earliest train of the day for Kyŏngju?

경주행 첫차가 몇 시에 있읍니까?
Kyŏngjuhaeng ch'ŏtch'aga myŏt shie issŭmnikka?

last

막차 makch'a

What's the difference in cost between the limited express and ordinary express?

특급과 급행의 요금차가 얼마나 됩니까? T'ŭkkŭpkwa kŭp'aeng-ŭi yogŭmch'aga ŏlmana toemnikka?

How long do I have to wait?

얼마나 기다려야 합니까?
Ŏlmana kidaryŏya hamnikka?

Does the Saemaŭr-ho stop at Taegu?

새마을호가 대구에 섭니까?
Saemaŭrhoga Taegue sŏmnikka?

Is there a sleeping car on the train?

침대차가 있읍니까?
Ch'imdaech'aga issŭmnikka?

dining car

식당차 Shiktangch'a

Are there limited express trains to Pusan?

부산행 특급 있읍니까?
Pusanhaeng t'ŭkkŭp issŭmnikka?

ordinary express

급행 kŭp'aeng

Is there a through train to Suwon?

수원행 직행 있읍니까?
Suwonhaeng chik'aeng issŭmnikka?

Do I have to change trains?

차를 갈아타야 합니까?
Ch'arŭl karat'aya hamnikka?

Where do I have to change trains?	어디서 갈아타야 합니까? Ŏdisŏ karat'aya hamnikka?
Where is the information center?	안내소가 어디에 있읍니까? Annaesoga ŏdie issŭmnikka?
I'd like to go to <u>Iri</u>.	<u>이리로</u> 가려고 합니다. <u>Iriro</u> karyŏgo hamnida.
Kyŏngju	경주로 Kyŏngju
Can I stop over?	도중 하차할 수 있읍니까? Tojung hach'ahal su issŭmnikka?

Tickets

Is there a discount for a child?	소아 할인 됩니까? Soa harin toemnikka?
We'd like <u>unreserved seats</u>.	<u>입석으로</u> 부탁합니다. <u>Ipsŏgŭro</u> put'ak'amnida.
first class seats the sleeping car	좌석으로 Chwasŏgŭro 침대차로 Ch'imdaech'aro
Can I get a seat by the window?	창문 쪽 좌석으로 부탁합니다. Ch'angmun tchok chwasŏgŭro put'ak'amnida.
How much is the fare?	요금은 얼맙니까? Yogŭmŭn ŏlmamnikka?
I'd like a <u>one-way ticket</u> to Pusan.	부산행 <u>편도로</u> 부탁합니다. Pusanhaeng <u>p'yŏndoro</u> put'ak'amnida.
round-trip ticket	왕복으로 wangbogŭro

ticket for a reserved seat	좌석표로	chwasŏkp'yoro
first-class ticket	일등표로	iltŭngp'yoro

I'd like two tickets to Pusan for today.

부산행 <u>오늘</u> 표 2 매 부탁합니다.
Pusanhaeng <u>onŭl</u> p'yo tu mae put'ak'amnida.

tomorrow   내일   naeil

Waiting for the Train

Which track does the train for Pusan leave from?

부산행이 어느 홈에서 출발합니까?
Pusanhaeng-i ŏnŭ homesŏ ch'ulbarhamnikka?

Which track does the train from Pusan arrive at?

부산발 열차가 어느 홈에 도착합니까? Pusanbal yŏlch'aga ŏnŭ home toch'ak'amnikka?

What time does the train for <u>Kyŏngju</u> leave?

<u>경주행</u>이 언제 떠납니까?
<u>Kyŏngjuhaeng</u>-i ŏnje ttŏnamnikka?

next train   다음 차가   Taŭm ch'aga

Is this the platform for the train to <u>Kyŏngju</u>?

여기가 <u>경주행</u> 홈입니까?
<u>Yŏgiga Kyŏngjuhaeng</u> homimnikka?

Kwangju   광주   Kwangju

Will the train for Taegu leave on time?

대구행이 정시에 출발합니까?
Taeguhaeng-i chŏngshie ch'ulbarhamnikka?

Where's the <u>newsstand</u>?

신문 판매대가 어디에 있읍니까?
<u>Shinmun p'anmaedaega</u> ŏdie issŭmnikka?

restaurant	식당이	Shiktang-i
toilet	화장실이	Hwajangshiri
waiting room	대합실이	Taehapshiri

Where can I find a porter?

짐꾼이 어디에 있읍니까?
Chimkkuni ŏdie issŭmnikka?

Excuse me, could you help with my baggage?

짐 좀 옮겨 주시겠어요.
Chim chom omgyŏ chushigessŏyo?

Put it down here, please.

여기 내려 주세요.
Yŏgi naeryŏ chuseyo.

How much do I owe you?

얼맘니까?
Ŏlmamnikka?

Where is the track for the Saemaŭrho?

새마을호 홈이 어딥니까?
Saemaŭrho homi ŏdimnikka?

the track for Suwon

수원행 홈이 Suwonhaeng homi

On the Train

Can I change to first class?

일등차로 바꿔 탈 수 있읍니까?
Iltŭngch'aro pakkwo t'al su issŭmnikka?

Where are we now?

여기가 어딥니까?
Yŏgiga ŏdimnikka?

What time do we arrive at Pusan?

부산에 언제 도착합니까?
Pusane ŏnje toch'ak'amnikka?

Is this seat free?

이 자리 비었읍니까?
I chari piŏssŭmnikka?

I think that's my seat.	저기가 제 자린 것 같습니다. Chŏgiga che charin kŏt kassŭmnida.
Where's the <u>dining car</u>?	식당차가 어디에 있읍니까? <u>Shiktangch'aga</u> ŏdie issŭmnikka?
telephone	전화가 Chŏnhwaga

Vendors

What kind of <u>cigarettes</u> do you have?	어떤 담배가 있읍니까? Ŏttŏn <u>tambaega</u> issŭmnikka?
juice box lunches	주스가 chusŭ 도시락이 toshiragi
What is that?	그건 뭡니까? Kŭgŏn mwomnikka?
Give me a beer, please.	맥주로 주세요. Maekchuro chuseyo.
Give me ginseng tea and a box lunch, please.	인삼차하고 도시락 하나 주세요. Insamch'ahago toshirak hana chuseyo.
How much is it?	얼맙니까? Ŏlmamnikka?
Excuse me. Do you have <u>beer</u>?	이봐요. 맥주 있읍니까? Ibwayo. <u>Maekchu</u> issŭmnikka?

candy
  cigarettes
  coffee
  cola
  ice cream
	캔디 K'aendi
	담배 Tambae
	커피 K'ŏp'i
	콜라 K'olla
	아이스크림 Aisŭk'ŭrim

Travelling

ginseng tea	인삼차	Insamch'a
Korean box lunch	도시락	Toshirak
juice	주스	Chusŭ
mandarin oranges	귤	Kyul
nuts	밤	Pam
peanuts	땅콩	Ttangk'ong
pudding	푸딩	P'uding
chŏngju	청주	Ch'ŏngju
sandwiches	샌드위치	Saendŭwich'i
tea	홍차	Hongch'a

Lost and Found

I've lost my <u>cam-era</u>.

카메라를 잃어버렸읍니다.
<u>K'amerarŭl</u> irŏbŏryŏssŭmnida.

travelers' checks

여행자 수표를 Yŏhaengja sup'yorŭl

Where is the lost and found office?

유실물 취급소가 어디에 있읍니까?
Yushilmul ch'wigŭpsoga ŏdie issŭmnikka?

There are few porters available in Korean train stations, and there are many staircases to climb. You'll do well to travel light!

Superexpress Trains

The superexpress train Saemaŭrho, operates on the Seoul–Pusan(Taejŏn, Taegu) run, Seoul–Mokp'o(Taejon, Nonsan, Iri, Kwangju) run, Seoul–Chŏnju (Taejŏn, Iri) run, and Seoul–Kyŏngju(Taejon, Taegu) run. It takes four hours and 50 minutes from Seoul to Pusan, and five hours and 50 minutes from Seoul to Mokp'o.

Other Types of Trains

High-class express	무궁화호	Mugunghwaho
Limited express	특급	t'ŭkkŭp
Ordinary express	보급	pogŭp

Ticket Reservations

Ticket reservations and advance sales are available from tourist agencies and the railroad stations. It is wise to purchase tickets in advance, especially during holidays and vacation months. Round-trip tickets are also sold.

BY BOAT

How long do we remain in port?	항구에서 얼마 동안이나 머뭅니까? Hangguesŏ ŏlma tong-anina mŏmumnikka?
I'd like a <u>first class</u> ticket.	1등표로 주세요. Iltŭngp'yoro chuseyo.
second class	2등 Idŭng
Are meals served on board?	배에서 식사가 나옵니까? Paeesŏ shiksaga naomnikka?
Can we buy something to eat on board?	배에서 먹을 것을 살 수 있읍니까? Paeesŏ mŏgŭl kŏsŭl sal su issŭmnikka?

Travelling

I don't feel well.	몸이 안 좋은데요. Momi an choŭndeyo.
Do you have something for seasickness?	멀미약 있읍니까? Mŏlmiyak issŭmnikka?
Do we have time to go ashore at this port?	이 항구에서는 뭍에 올라갈 수 있읍니까? I hangguesŏnŭn mut'e ollagal su issŭmnikka?
What time do we have to be back on board?	몇 시에 배에 돌아와야 합니까? Myŏt shie paee torawaya hamnikka?
When do we arrive at Chejudo?	제주도에 언제 도착합니까? Chejudo-e ŏnje toch'ak'amnikka?
Pusan	부산에 Pusan
Is there a cruise ship on the Halnyŏ Waterway?	한려 수도에 유람선이 있읍니까? Halnyŏ sudo-e yuramsŏni issŭmnikka?
Can I go to Chejudo by ship?	제주도에 배로 갈 수 있읍니까? Chejudo-e paero kal su issŭmnikka?
What type of ship is it?	어떤 종류의 뱁니까? Ŏttŏn chongnyuŭi paemnikka?
When does the next ship leave?	다음 배가 언제 떠납니까? Taŭm paega ŏnje ttŏnamnikka?
ferry	연락선이　　　yŏllaksŏni
hydrofoil	수중익선이　　sujung-iksŏni
hovercraft	호버크라프트가　hobŏk'ŭrap'ŭt'ŭga

Where is the har-bor?	항구가 어디에 있읍니까? Hangguga ŏdie issŭmnikka?
ticket office	매표소가 Maep'yosoga
How long does the crossing take?	건너는 데 얼마나 걸립니까? Kŏnnŏnŭn te ŏlmana kŏllim-nikka?
When do we board?	언제 탑니까? Ŏnje t'amnikka?
Do we stop at any ports?	어느 항구에서나 다 섭니까? Ŏnŭ hangguesŏna ta sŏmni-kka?

SEOUL

Royal Palaces, Myŏngdong, It'aewon

Only four of the five palaces of the Yi Dynasty remain: Kyŏngbok Palace in the north; Ch'angdŏk Palace and Ch'anggyŏng Palace in the east; and Tŏksu Palace in the south. Fortunately, they are all conveniently located within a 30- or 40-minute walk of the downtown area.

Kyŏngbok Palace was built in 1395 as the residence of the first Yi Dynasty king and symbol of dynastic power in Korea. Many pavilions and gates, including Kwanghwamun, Shinmunun, Kŏnch'unmun, and Yŏngch'umun were erected initially, and in 1412 Kyŏnghoeru and other pavilions were added, making Kyŏngbok, the Palace of Shining Happiness, truly a splendid

Travelling

and luxurious seat of power. For modern Koreans and visitors, Kyŏngbok Palace is a beautiful park with pleasant shady surroundings, a place of refuge from the hectic urban scene, and an open-air museum exhibiting intricately sculptured pagodas, relief sculptures and monuments moved here from remote historic sites around Korea.

Ch'angdŏk Palace is probably the favorate of most visitors. The main gate through which one passes, Tonhwamun, is possibly the oldest gate in Seoul, escaping the ravages of the Japanese invasion of 1592 although the major portions of the palace were burned; rebuilt in 1611 and used as the official royal residence until 1910 when the king moved to Kyŏngbok Palace.

Ch'anggyŏng Palace, the "Palace of Glorious Blessings," stands on the site of a Koryŏ palace that T'aejo used until Kyŏngbok Palace was constructed. First built as a detached palace in 1483, it has undergone many reconstructions, the most recent being from 1983 to 1986 to rebuild the structures that were destroyed to make room for a zoo and botanical garden during the Japanese colonial period.

Just a few steps to the west of City Hall and major hotel district is Tŏksu Palace that was the scene of King Sunjong's abdication of power and the end of the Yi Dynasty that coincided with Japan's annexation of the country in 1905.

Within strolling distance of the principal downtown hotels that cluster around the City Hall Plaza lies Myŏngdong, the famous shopping district. On the circumstance of this

compact area stand major department stores:
Midop'a, Shinsegye, and Lotte.

It'aewon is more than shopper's paradise.
The area is about a 10-minute taxi ride from
the city center.

How big is the palace area?	이 궁전은 면적이 얼마나 됩니까? I kungjŏnŭn myŏnjŏgi ŏlmana toemnikka?
When was it built?	언제 세워졌읍니까? Ŏnje sewojyŏssŭmnikka?
Can I go inside?	안에 들어갈 수 있읍니까? Ane tŭrŏgal su issŭmnikka?
Is Myŏngdong more expensive than other shopping areas?	명동은 다른 쇼핑가에 비해 비쌉니까? Myŏngdong-ŭn tarŭn syop'ingga-e pihae pissamnikka?
Are the stores open at night too?	가게들이 밤에도 영업을 합니까? Kagedŭri pamedo yŏng-ŏbŭl hamnikka?
Is the Shinsegye Dept. Store within walking distance from Myŏngdong?	명동에서 신세계 백화점까지 걸어갈 수 있읍니까? Myŏngdong-esŏ Shinsegye paek'wajŏmkkaji kŏrŏgal su issŭmnikka?

Travelling

A complete spectrum of 5,000 years of Korean art can be viewed in the Central National Museum, located at the northern end
of Sejongno. Its collection of over 100,000

pieces comprises prehistoric artifacts, excavated tomb ornaments including magnificent gold crowns and girdles, Buddhist sculptures, earthenware, stoneware, celadon, porcelain, paintings and ink rubbings.

Is it always crowded?	항상 붐빕니까? Hangsang pumbimnikka?
Do you think I should go to the Central National Museum?	국립 중앙 박물관 가 볼 만합니까? Kungnip chung-ang pangmulgwan ka pol manhamnikka?
What type of collection are they exhibiting now?	어떤 것들이 전시 중입니까? Ŏttŏn kŏtttŭri chŏnshi chung-imnikka?
How late is it open?	몇 시까지 합니까? Myŏt shikkaji hamnikka?

NEAR SEOUL

Minsokch'on

Located about 45 kilometers south of Seoul near the Suwon exit on the Seoul-Pusan Expressway, Minsokch'on, or the Korean Folk Village as it is known in English, is a great place to get a taste of what Korean life was like before the arrival of modernization. The re-created 19th-century village is an actual working community where traditional furniture, tools, handicrafts, arts, food and dress are utilized and displayed as they were in that era.

The visitor to Minsokch'on can observe traditionally clad craftsmen at work in a pottery, a blacksmith shop, a brass foundry and other workshops as well as watch artisans at work preparing silk and cotton for spinning and weaving and making baskets, rush mats, fans, clothing, pipes, musical instruments and paper. Visitors are also free to peek into the houses, from well-to-do scholar's mansion to the humble farmer's mud-and-thatch cottage, to see how the occupants live.

What are the special handicrafts in Minsokch'on?	민속촌에 어떤 수공예품이 있읍니까? Minsokch'one ŏttŏn sugong-yep'umi issŭmnikka?

P'anmunjŏm and Imjin-gak

Located only 60 kilometers northwest of Seoul astride the demilitarized zone (DMZ) separating South and North Korea, P'anmunjŏm is one of the world's most unusual tourist destinations. Once known for its rice, ginseng and the friendliness of its people, P'anmunjŏm, which was originally called Nŏlmun-ri, is now known as a tension-filled place where the armistice bringing the Korean War to a ceasefire was signed and representatives of the U.N. Command and the Communist side meet in an effort to maintain peace.

Along the drive to P'anmunjŏm are many monuments honoring the nations who participated in the Korean War and their fallen heros, not to mention numerous tank traps and other defenses. Just before P'anmunjŏm is Imjin-gak, the site of an anti-Communist exhibition center, an outdoor military museum, several monuments, and a few restaurants and souvenir shops.

Kanghwado

Korea's fifth largest island, Kanghwado is located about 56 kilcmeters northwest of Seoul at the mouth of the Han River. It is about an hour-and-half ride via paved roads from Seoul by way of Kimp'o, where the international airport is located.

The whole spectrum of Korea's history from the era of the nation's founding by the mythical Tan-gun to its opening to the West in the late 19th century can be observed in the dolmens, tombs, temples, shrines, forts, walls and batteries, pavilions and monuments scattered all over the island. It is where King Kojong of Koryŏ took refuge during the mid-13th century, at which time the 80,000 wood blocks comprising the Tripitaka Koreana were carved, battles were fought with a French flotilla in 1866 and an American one in 1871, and the Treaty of Kanghwa which forcibly opened the country to Japanese imperialism was signed in 1876.

OTHER AREAS

Halnyŏ Waterway

The Halnyŏ Waterway, a national park since 1968, is a shimmering expanse of placid sea stretching westward from the islands of Kŏjedo and Hansando past Ch'ungmu, a popular resort and fishing village and Namhaedo Island to the industrial port of Yŏsu. The 115 inhabited and 253 uninhabited islands scattered throughout it make for some of the most picturesque scenery in the country. Haegŭmgang, a camellia-forested rock outcropping at the southern tip of Kŏjedo, Korea's second largest island, is particularly beautiful.

Kyŏngju

Kyŏngju, 224 miles southeast of Seoul, was the capital of the Shilla Kingdom (57B.C.–935 A.D.)

Today it is literally a museum without walls, filled with historic remains of ancient Shilla. These fascinating attractions include Tumuli Park, the burial place of Shilla royalties; Ch'ŏmsŏngdae or Star Tower, a stone observatory; P'osŏkchŏng, a pleasure garden with a small pond in the shape of an abalone shell; Panwol-song Castle, the principal royal residence; and Anapchi Pond, which when drained revealed a treasure of Shilla artifacts. The Kyŏngju National Museum houses mag-

Travelling

nificent gold crowns, gold jewelry, ceramics and decorations from the great earthen tombs of the Shilla kings and queens. On the grounds of the Museum is the Emille Bell, one of the largest and most resonant of Asian bells.

Chejudo Island

Korea's only island province is just within an hour by jet from Seoul, but it takes the traveler to a different world. Cheju, 220 miles off the southern port of Pusan, enjoys a semi-tropical climate, with mild weather all year round. The plants and landscape are entirely distinct from those of the mainland, and are unique to Cheju. The beauties of the island orange from lofty Mt. Hallasan, the highest mountain in South Korea, with a huge crater of an extinct volcano on its peak, to the famed woman divers who make their living garnering seafood and other marine products from the depths of the ocean, even in winter.

There are an increasing number of modern hotels scattered over Chejudo, and a highway encircles the island for sightseers.

Driving

ASKING THE WAY AND DIRECTIONS

How far away is ____? (distance)
____이[가] 얼마나 멉니까?
____i[ga] ŏlmana mŏmnikka?

How far away is ____? (time)
____까지 몇 시간이나 가야 됩니까?
____kkaji myŏt shiga-nina kaya toemnikka?

Do you have a road map?
도로 지도 있읍니까?
Toro chido issŭmnikka?

Could you show me where ____ is on the map?
이 지도에서 ____이[가] 어디에 있는지 좀 가르쳐 주시겠읍니까?
I chido-esŏ ____i[ga] ŏdie in-nŭnji chom karŭch'yŏ chushi-gessŭmnikka?

Could you show me where I am on the map?
이 지도에서 제가 지금 있는 곳이 어디인지 말씀해 주시겠읍니까?
I chido-esŏ chega chigŭm in-nŭn koshi ŏdiinji malssŭmhae chushigessŭmnikka?

Is this the fastest way?
이 길이 가장 빠른 길입니까?
I kiri kajang pparŭn kirimni-kka?

Do I go straight?
곧바로 가야 합니까?
Kotparo kaya hamnikka?

Do I turn to the right?
오른쪽으로 돌아야 합니까?
Orŭntchogŭro toraya hamni-kka?

left	왼쪽으로 Oentchogŭro
Where is the entrance to the highway?	고속 도로 입구가 어디에 있읍니까? Kosoktoro ipkuga ŏdie issŭmnikka?
tourist information center	여행 안내소가 Yŏhaeng annaesoga
gas station	주유소가 Chuyusoga
Excuse me, but ___.	실례합니다만 ___. Shillyehamnidaman ___.
How do I get to ___?	___에 가려면 어떻게 가는 것이 좋읍니까? ___e karyŏmyŏn ŏttŏk'e kanŭn kŏshi chossŭmnikka?
I think we're lost.	길을 잃은 것 같습니다. Kirŭl irŭn kŏt kassŭmnida.
Which is the road to ___?	___(으)로 가려면 어디로 가야 합니까? ___(ŭ)ro karyŏmyŏn ŏdiro kaya hamnikka?
Is this the road to ___?	이 길이 ___(으)로 가는 길입니까? I kiri ___(ŭ)ro kanŭn kirimnikka?
What's the name of this town?	이 도시의 이름이 뭡니까? I toshiŭi irŭmi mwomnikka?
Is the next town far?	다음 도시가 여기서 멉니까? Taŭm toshiga yŏgisŏ mŏmnikka?
gas station	주유소가 chuyusoga

HIRING A CAR

What's the deposit?
보증금이 얼맙니까?
Pojŭnggŭmi ŏlmamnikka?

Do you take credit cards?
크레디트 카드 받습니까? K'ŭredit'ŭ k'adŭ passŭmnikka?

Can you deliver it to my hotel?
제 호텔까지 대 줄 수 있읍니까?
Che hot'elkkaji tae chul su issŭmnikka?

to this address
이 주소까지 I chusokkaji

Here's my International Driving Permit.
제 국제 면허증입니다. Che kukche myŏnhŏchŭng-imnida.

Please give me some emergency telephone numbers.
비상 전화 번호 좀 가르쳐 주세요.
Pisang chŏnhwa pŏnho chom karŭch'yŏ chuseyo.

Where can I rent a car?
차를 어디서 빌 수 있읍니까?
Ch'arŭl ŏdisŏ pil su issŭmnikka?

I'd like to rent a car.
차를 빌려고 합니다.
Ch'arŭl pilnyŏgo hamnida.

Do you have a small car?
소형차 있읍니까?
Sohyŏngch'a issŭmnikka?

mid-size car
중형차 Chunghyŏngch'a

May I see your list of rates?
요금표 좀 보여 주세요. Yogŭmp'yo chom poyŏ chuseyo.

I prefer a car with automatic transmission.
자동 변속 차가 좋겠읍니다.
Chadong pyŏnsok ch'aga chok'essŭmnida.

Do you have a car that's cheap and easy to handle?	싸고 운전하기 쉬운 차 있읍니까? Ssago unjŏnhagi swiun ch'a issŭmnikka?
I'd like it for <u>a day</u>.	하루 빌려고 합니다. Haru pillyŏgo hamnida.
a week	일 주일 Il chuil
What's the rate for <u>a day</u>?	일당 요금이 얼맙니까? Iltang yogŭmi ŏlmamnikka?
a week	주당 Chudang
Does the rate include mileage?	요금에 주행 요금이 포함돼 있읍니까? Yogŭme chuhaeng yogŭmi p'ohamdwae issŭmnikka?
How much is the insurance?	보험료가 얼맙니까? Pohŏmnyoga ŏlmamnikka?
Do I have to leave a deposit?	보증금이 있읍니까? Pojŭnggŭmi issŭmnikka?

ACCIDENTS AND SERVICING

The radiator is leaking.	냉각기가 샙니다. Naenggakkiga saemnida.
The keys are locked inside the car.	열쇠가 차 안에 있는데 문이 잠겼읍니다. Yŏlsoega ch'a ane innŭnde muni chamgyŏssŭmnida.
I don't have any tools.	수리 도구가 없읍니다. Suri toguga ŏpsŭmnida.

Could you lend me a flashlight?	회중 전등 좀 빌려 주시겠읍니까?	Hoejung chŏndŭng chom pil-nyŏ chushigessŭmnikka?
hammer	망치	Mangch'i
pliers	뻰찌	Ppentchi
screwdriver	드라이버	Tŭraibŏ
My car has broken down.	차가 고장났읍니다.	Ch'aga kojangnassŭmnida.
The engine won't start.	시동이 안 걸립니다.	Shidong-i an kŏllimnida.
The car doesn't go.	차가 움직이지 않읍니다.	Ch'aga umjigiji anssŭmnida.
I need an auto mechanic.	정비공이 있어야겠읍니다.	Chŏngbigong-i issŏyagessŭm-nida.
Is there a repair shop/garage near here?	이 근처에 정비소가 있읍니까?	I kŭnch'ŏe chŏngbisoga issŭm-nikka?
Do you know the phone number of a nearby garage?	근처의 정비소 전화 번호 알고 계세요?	Kŭnch'ŏŭi chŏngbiso chŏnhwa pŏnho algo kyeseyo?
Could you send a mechanic?	정비공 좀 보내 주시겠읍니까?	Chŏngbigong chom ponae chu-shigessŭmnikka?
tow truck	견인 트럭	Kyŏnin t'ŭrŏk
Could you help me?	좀 도와 주시겠읍니까?	Chom towa chushigessŭmnikka?

Driving

I have a flat tire.	빵꾸가 났읍니다. Ppangkkuga nassŭmnida.
Could you help me change the tire?	타이어를 가는 데 좀 도와 주시겠읍니까? T'aiŏrŭl kanŭn te chom towa chushigessŭmnikka?
I've run out of gas.	연료가 떨어졌읍니다. Yŏlnyoga ttŏrŏjyŏssŭmnida.
Could you give me some gas?	연료 좀 나눠 쓸 수 있읍니까? Yŏlnyo chom nanwo ssŭl su issŭmnikka?
The car is overheated.	차가 과열됐읍니다. Ch'aga kwayŏldwaessŭmnida.
Can I get some water?	물 좀 얻을 수 있읍니까? Mul chom ŏdŭl su issŭmnikka?
The car is stuck in the <u>mud</u>.	차가 진흙에 빠졌읍니다. Ch'aga chinhŭge ppajyŏssŭmnida.
ditch	도랑에 torang-e
Could you give me <u>a hand</u>?	좀 거들어 주시겠읍니까? Chom kŏdŭrŏ chushigessŭmnikka?
push it pull it	밀어 mirŏ 끌어 kkŭrŏ
The battery is dead.	배터리가 다 닳았읍니다. Paet'ŏriga ta tarassŭmnida.
Do you have a jumper cable?	점퍼 케이블 있읍니까? Chŏmp'ŏ k'eibŭl issŭmnikka?

At the Garage

Can you take a look at the car-buretor?
기화기 좀 봐 주세요.
Kihwagi chom pwa chuseyo.

   gear box
   ignition coil
   thermostat
기어 박스　Kiŏ paksŭ
점화 코일　Chŏmhwa k'oil
온도 조절 장치　Ondo chojŏl
　　　　　changch'i

What's the problem?
뭐가 잘못 됐읍니까？　Mwoga chalmot twaessŭmnikka?

Is it fixable?
고칠 수 있읍니까？
Koch'il su issŭmnikka?

Do you have the necessary parts?
필요한 부속품이 있읍니까？
P'iryohan pusokp'umi issŭmnikka?

Is it possible to get it fixed now?
지금 고칠 수 있읍니까？　Chigŭm koch'il su issŭmnikka?

   today
오늘 중에　Onŭl chung-e

How long will it take?
얼마나 걸립니까？
Ŏlmana kŏllimnikka?

Can you repair it temporarily?
임시로 좀 고쳐 주시겠읍니까？
Imshiro chom koch'yŏ chushigessŭmnikka?

Can you give me an estimate for the repair?
수리비 견적 좀 뽑아 주세요.
Suribi kyŏnjŏk chom ppoba chuseyo.

Is everything okay now?
이제 됐읍니까？
Ije twaessŭmnikka?

May I have an itemized bill and a receipt?	명세서하고 영수증 좀 부탁합니다. Myŏngsesŏhago yŏngsujŭng chom put'ak'amnida.
Thank you very much for your help.	도와 주셔서 감사합니다. Towa chusyŏsŏ kamsahamnida.
There's something wrong with my car.	차가 이상이 있읍니다. Ch'aga isang-i issŭmnida.
I don't know what's wrong with the car.	차가 어디가 이상이 있는지 모르겠 읍니다. Ch'aga ŏdiga isang-i innŭnji morŭgessŭmnida.
I think there's something wrong with the <u>battery</u>.	배터리가 이상이 있는 것 같습니다. <u>Paet'ŏriga isang-i innŭn kŏt kassŭmnida.</u>

brakes	브레이크가	Pŭreik'ŭga
clutch	클러치가	K'ŭllŏch'iga
door	문이	Muni
electrical system	전기 장치가	Chŏn-gi changch'iga
engine	엔진이	Enjini
gears	기어가	Kiŏga
headlight	헤들라이트가	Hedŭllait'ŭga
ignition	점화 장치가	Chŏmhwa changch'iga
starter	시동 장치가	Shidong chanch'iga
steering wheel	핸들이	Haendŭri
transmission	변속 장치가	Pyŏnsok changch'iga
water pump	물 펌프가	Mul p'ŏmp'ŭga

AT THE FILLING STATION

Please check the battery.	배터리 좀 봐 주세요.
	Paet'ŏri chom pwa chuseyo.

brake fluid	브레이크 오일	Pŭreik'ŭ oil
clutch fluid	클러치 오일	K'ŭllŏch'i oil
oil	엔진 오일	Enjin oil
spark plugs	스파크 플러그	Sŭp'ak'ŭ p'ullŏgŭ
tires	타이어	T'aiŏ

Add 1 liter of oil, please.	엔진 오일 1*l* 만 넣어 주세요.
	Enjin oil illitŏman nŏŏ chuseyo.

2 liters	2*l*	irit'ŏ
3 liters	3*l*	samlit'ŏ

Put distilled water in the battery, please.	배터리에 증류수 좀 넣어 주세요.
	Paet'ŏrie chŭngnyusu chom nŏŏ chuseyo.

Put water in the radiator, please.	냉각기에 물 좀 넣어 주세요.
	Naenggakkie mul chom nŏŏ chuseyo.

Charge the battery, please	배터리 충전 좀 부탁합니다.
	Paet'ŏri ch'ungjŏn chom put'ak'amnida.

Can you fix a flat tire?	빵꾸 수리합니까?
	Ppangkku surihamnikka?

Change this tire, please.	이 타이어 좀 갈아 주세요.
	I t'aiŏ chom kara chuseyo.

Tighten the fan belt, please.	팬 벨트 좀 팽팽하게 해 주세요. P'aen belt'ŭ chom p'aeng-p'aenghage hae chuseyo.
Would you clean the windshield?	앞 유리 좀 닦아 주세요. Ap yuri chom takka chuseyo.
Do you have a road map of this area?	이 지역의 도로 지도 있읍니까? I chiyŏgŭi toro chido issŭm-nikka?
Where are the rest rooms?	화장실이 어딥니까? Hwajangshiri ŏdimnikka?
Is there a gas station nearby?	근처에 주유소가 있읍니까? Kŭnch'ŏe chuyusoga issŭmni-kka?
I need some gas.	가솔린 좀 부탁합니다. Kasollin chom put'ak'amnida.
How much is a liter of <u>regular</u>?	레귤러 1*l* 에 얼맙니까? <u>Re-gyullŏ</u> il lit'ŏe ŏlmamnikka?
super diesel	수퍼 Sup'ŏ 디젤 Tijel
Give me <u>10 liters</u> of regular please.	레귤러 10*l* 부탁합니다. Regyul-lŏ <u>ship lit'ŏ</u> put'ak'amnida.
20 30	20 iship 30 samship
Give me <u>3,000</u> won worth of super, please.	수퍼 <u>3,000</u> 원 어치만 주세요. Sup'ŏ <u>samch'ŏn</u> won ŏch'iman chuseyo.
4,000 5,000	4,000 sach'ŏn 5,000 och'ŏn

Fill it up, please.	가득 채워 주세요. Kadŭk ch'aewo chuseyo.

AT THE PARKING LOT

When does the parking garage <u>open</u>?	주차장이 몇 시에 문을 <u>엽니까</u>? Chuch'ajang-i myŏt shie mu- nŭl <u>yŏmnikka</u>?
close	닫습니까 tassŭmnikka
What's the parking fee?	주차료가 얼맙니까? Chuch'aryoga ŏlmamnikka?
I'd like to park <u>for one hour</u>.	<u>1시간</u> 주차하려고 합니다. <u>Han shigan</u> chuch'aharyŏgo hamnida.

for two hours	2시간	Tu shigan
till noon	12시까지	Yŏltushikkaji
till 5 o'clock	5시 까지	Tasŏssikkaji
overnight	하룻밤	Harutpam
for a day	하루	Haru
for two days	이틀	It'ŭl

Do I leave the key in the car?	열쇠를 차 안에 놔 둡니까? Yŏlsoerŭl ch'a ane nwa tum- nikka?
Excuse me, but ___.	실례합니다만 ___. Shillyehamnidaman ___.
Can I park here?	여기에 주차할 수 있읍니까? Yŏgie chuch'ahal su issŭmni- kka?

Is it illegal to park here?	여기가 주차 금지 구역입니까? Yŏgiga chuch'a kŭmji kuyŏgimnikka?
Is there any street parking nearby?	이 근처에 도로 주차장이 있읍니까? I kŭnch'ŏe toro chuch'ajang-i issŭmnikka?
Is there a parking garage nearby?	근처에 주차장이 있읍니까? Kŭnch'ŏe chuch'ajang-i issŭmnikka?

ROAD SIGNS

서행	slow down
정지	stop
일방 통행	one way
추월 금지	no passing
비포장 도로	soft shoulder
도로 공사중	road under construction
우회로	detour
보행자 전용 도로	road strictly for pedestrians
입구	entrance
출구	exit
톨게이트	tollgate
비상 전화	emergency telephone
통행 금지	road closed

Tunnel

Danger

Slippery

Bicycles Only

Road Closed

No Entry for Vehicles

No Entry for Vehicles
or Motocycles

No Entry

No Right Turn

No Left Turn

 No U Turn	 No Passing
 No Parking No Standing	 No Parking
 Maximum Speed	 Minimum Speed
 Slow Down	 Stop

Yield

Cars Only

Bicycles Only

Traffic Circle Ahead

Sound Horn

Pedestrians Only

One Way

End of Restriction

Driving

Shopping

GENERAL

Where can I find a good ____?

어디에 좋은 ____가[이] 있읍니까?
Ŏdi-e choŭn ____ga[i] issŭmnikka?

antique shop	골동품점이	koltongp'umjŏmi
art gallery	화랑이	hwarang-i
barber shop	이발소가	ibalsoga
beauty parlor	미용실이	miyongshiri
bookstore	서점이	sŏjŏmi
camera shop	카메라점이	k'amerajŏmi
ceramics store	도자기점이	tojagijŏmi
clothing store	의류점이	ŭiryujŏmi
confectionery	제과점이	chegwajŏmi
cosmetics shop	화장품점이	hwajangp'umjŏmi
department store	백화점이	paek'wajŏmi
drugstore	약국이	yakkugi
electrical appliance store	전기 기구점이	chŏn-gi kigujŏmi
florist	꽃가게가	kkotkagega
folkware shop	민예품점이	minyep'umjŏmi
grocery store	식료품점이	shingnyop'umjŏmi
handicrafts shop	공예품점이	kong-yep'umjŏmi
jewelry store	보석방이	posŏkpang-i
liquor store	술집이	sulchibi
newsstand	신문 판매대가	shinmun p'anmaedaega

optician	안경점이	an-gyŏngjŏmi
pharmacy	약국이	yakkugi
record store	레코드 가게가	rek'odŭ kagega
restaurant	레스토랑이	resŭt'orang-i
shoe store	양화점이	yang-hwajŏmi
souvenir shop	기념품 가게가	kinyŏmp'um kagega
sporting goods store	운동구점이	undonggujŏmi
stationery store	문방구점이	munbanggujŏmi
supermarket	수퍼가	sup'ŏga
tailor	양복점이	yangbokchŏmi
tobacco shop	담배 가게가	tambae kagega
toiletries shop	화장품점이	hwajangp'um-jŏmi
toy store	완구점이	wan-gujŏmi
travel agency	여행사가	yŏhaengsaga
video equipment shop	비디오 가게가	pidio kagega
watch and clock store	시계방이	shigyepang-i

I'd like to go shopping today.	오늘 뭘 좀 살까 합니다.	**Onŭl mwol chom salkka hamnida.**
Where's the nearest ____?	가장 가까운 ____가[이] 어디에 있읍니까?	**Kajang kakkaun ____ ga[i] ŏdie issŭmnikka?**
Which do you recommend?	어느 ____가[이] 좋습니까?	**Ŏnŭ ____ ga[i] chossŭmnikka?**
Where do they sell ____?	____을[를] 어디서 팝니까?	**____ (r)ŭl ŏdisŏ p'amnikka?**

Where's the main shopping area?	큰 쇼핑가가 어디에 있읍니까? K'ŭn syop'inggaga ŏdie issŭmnikka?
I'd like to go to a shopping arcade.	쇼핑 아케이드에 가고 싶습니다. Syop'ing ak'eidŭe kago shipsŭmnida.
Is it far?	거기가 멉니까? Kŏgiga mŏmnikka?
Can you tell me how to get there?	거기까지 어떻게 가면 좋습니까? Kŏgikkaji ŏttŏk'e kamyŏn chossŭmnikka?
Where's a good place to window shop?	윈도우 쇼핑으로는 어디가 좋습니까? Windou syop'ing-ŭronŭn ŏdiga chossŭmnikka?

How often have you read or heard that Korea is a "shoppers' paradise"? It's true. Not only can you buy familiar items that you need, now you can explore the Korean decorative arts firsthand. Remember that bargaining is not always practiced in Korea.

IN A DEPARTMENT STORE

Where's the men's clothing department?	신사복 매장이 어디에 있읍니까? Shinsabok maejang-i ŏdie issŭmnikka?
women's clothing	부인복 Puinbok

shoe	구두	Kudu
housewares	가정용품	Kajŏng-yongp'um
china	도자기	Tojagi
jewelry	보석	Posŏk
notions	잡화	Chap'wa
luggage	여행 가방	Yŏhaeng kabang
handicrafts	수공예품	Sugong-yep'um

Where's the
ladies'room?

여자 화장실이 어디에 있읍니까?
Yŏja hwajangshiri ŏdie issŭm-nikka?

men's room	남자 화장실이	Namja hwajangshiri
elevator	엘리베이터가	Ellibeit'ŏga
snack bar	스낵 바가	Sŭnaek paga
escalator	에스컬레이터가	Esŭk'ŏlleit'ŏga
coffee shop	커피 숍이	K'ŏp'i syobi
restaurant	식당이	Shiktang-i

Korean department stores carry all the things
you would expect, and a lot more as well.
The folkware sections have crafts from all
over Korea: handmade dolls, toys, pottery,
paper crafts, bamboo baskets, lacquer trays,
bowls, chopsticks, handmade and dyed fabrics,
and more. You'll also find typical Korean craft
items in the housewares section in a range
from everyday pottery to expensive lacquer-
ware.

Don't miss the food section; the entire base-
ment floor is devoted to fresh and packaged
foods, both Korean- and Western-style.

AT THE JEWELER'S

I want an ame-thyst.	자수정 좀 보여 주세요.	**Chasu-jŏng** chom poyŏ chuseyo.

coral	산호	Sanho
a diamond	다이아몬드	Taiamondŭ
an emerald	에머럴드	Emŏrŏldŭ
ivory	상아	Sang-a
jade	비취	Pich'wi
pearls	진주	Chinju
cultured pearls	양식 진주	Yangshik chinju
a ruby	루비	Rubi
a sapphire	사파이어	Sap'aiŏ

How much is it?
그거 얼맙니까?
Kŭgŏ ŏlmamnikka?

Are these Korean pearls?
이거 한국 진주입니까?
Igŏ Han-guk chinjuimnikka?

The luster is won-derful.
광택이 좋군요.
Kwangt'aegi chok'unnyo.

I prefer a baroque [round] shape.
변형된 것이 [둥근 것이] 좋겠읍니다. Pyŏnhyŏngdoen kŏshi [Tunggŭn kŏshi] chok'essŭmnida.

Can you tell me how to care for them?
사용하는 데 주의할 점 좀 말씀해 주시겠읍니까? Sayonghanŭn te chuŭihal chŏm chom malssŭmhae chushigessŭmnikka?

I'd like to see <u>a</u> <u>bracelet</u>.	팔찌 좀 보여 주세요.	
	<u>P'altchi</u> chom poyŏ chuseyo.	
a brooch	브로치	Pŭroch'i
some cufflinks	커프스 단추	K'ŏp'ŭsŭ tanch'u
some earrings	귀걸이	Kwigŏri
a necklace	목걸이	Mokkŏri
a pin	핀	P'in
a ring	반지	Panji
a wristwatch	손목 시계	Sonmok shigye
Is this <u>gold</u>?	이거 금입니까?	
	Igŏ <u>kŭ</u>mimnikka?	
platinum	백금	paekkŭm
silver	은	ŭn
stainless steel	스텐레스	sŭt'enlesŭ

How many karats is it?

그거 몇 캐럿 짜리입니까?
Kŭgŏ myŏt k'aerŏt tchariimnikka?

Is it solid gold?

그거 순금입니까?
Kŭgŏt sun-gŭmimnikka?

Is it gold plated?

그거 금 도금한 겁니까? Kŭgŏ kŭm tokŭmhan kŏmnikka?

What kind of stone is that?

그것은 어떤 보석입니까?
Kŭgŏsŭn ŏttŏn posŏgimnikka?

Clock and Watches

I want a watch with <u>a calendar function</u>.

<u>날짜와 요일이 나오는</u> 시계를 사려고 합니다. <u>Naltchawa yoiri naonŭn</u> shigyerŭl sayrŏgohamnida.

an electronic alarm	전자 알람 Chŏnja allam
I'd like a clock.	시계 하나 사려고 합니다. Shigye hana saryŏgo hamnida.
I want an <u>alarm</u> clock.	알람 시계를 하나 사려고 합니다. <u>Allam</u> shigyerŭl hana saryŏgo hamnida.
a travel alarm	여행용 알람 Yŏhaeng-yong allam
I'd like a wrist-watch.	손목 시계 좀 보여 주세요. Sonmok shigye chom poyŏ chuseyo.
I want a <u>digital</u> watch.	디지털 시계를 사려고 합니다. <u>Tijit'ŏl</u> shigyerŭl saryŏgo hamnida.
quartz	수정 Sujŏng

IN THE STORE

I'm interested in something <u>inexpensive.</u>	싼 것으로 좀 보여 주세요. <u>Ssan kŏsŭro</u> chom poyŏ chuseyo.
handmade	수제품으로 Sujep'umŭro
Do you have any others?	다른 것으로는 뭐가 있읍니까? Tarŭn kŏsŭronŭn mwoga issŭmnikka?
I'd like a <u>big</u> one.	좀 큰 것으로 보여 주세요. Chom <u>k'ŭn</u> kŏsŭro poyŏ chuseyo.

small	작은	chagŭn
cheap	싼	ssan
better	더 좋은	to choŭn
good	좋은	choŭn

How much is <u>it</u>?
이거 얼맙니까?
<u>Igŏ</u> ŏlmamnikka?

that one
저거   Chŏgŏ

Could you write it down?
글로 써 주시겠읍니까?
Kŭllo ssŏ chushigessŭmnikka?

I want to spend about ___ won.
예산은 약 ___ 원입니다.
Yesanŭn yak ___ wonimnida.

Do you have something <u>less expensive</u>?
좀 싼 거 있읍니까?
Chom ssan kŏ issŭmnikka?

more expensive
좀 비싼   Chom pissan

I'll take it/this.
이걸로 주시죠.
Igŏllo chushijyo.

May I use a credit card?
크레디트 카드 받습니까?
K'ŭredit'ŭ k'adŭ passŭmnikka?

Which cards do you take?
어떤 카드를 받습니까?
Ŏttŏn k'adŭrŭl passŭmnikka?

May I have a receipt, please?
영수증 좀 부탁합니다. Yŏngsujŭng chom put'ak'amnida.

Could you send it to my hotel?
호텔로 좀 보내 주시겠읍니까?
Hot'ello chom ponae chushigessŭmnikka?

Could you send it to this address?	이 주소로 좀 보내 주시겠읍니까? I chusoro chom ponae chushigessŭmnikka?
Could you ship it overseas for me?	해외로 우송해 줍니까? Haeoero usonghae chumnikka?
How much would it cost?	우송료가 얼마나 됩니까? Usongnyoga ŏlmana toemnikka?
I'd also like to see ____.	____도 좀 보여 주세요. ____ d[t]o chom poyŏ chuseyo.
That's all, thank you.	됐읍니다. 감사합니다. Twaessŭmnida. Kamsahamnida.
I'd like to ex- change this.	이것을 바꾸려고 합니다. Igŏsŭl pakkuryŏgo hamnida.
return	반품하려고 panp'umharyŏgo
May I have a refund, please?	환불해 주시겠읍니까? Hwanburhae chushigessŭmnikka?
Here's my receipt.	영수증 여기 있읍니다. Yŏngsujŭng yŏgi issŭmnida.
Thank you for your help.	도와 주셔서 감사합니다. Towa chusyŏsŏ kamsahamnida.
Excuse me.	실례합니다. Shillyehamnida.
Can you help me?	좀 도와 주시겠읍니까? Chom towa chushigessŭmnikka?

I'd like to see some ___.	___ 좀 보여 주세요. ___ chom poyŏ chuseyo.
Do you have any ___?	___ 있읍니까? ___ issŭmnikka?
I'm just looking, thank you.	그냥 둘러보고 있는 중입니다. 감사합니다. Kŭnyang tullŏbogo innŭn chung-imnida. Kamsahamnida.
I'd like something for a child.	애에게 뭘 사주려고 합니다. Aege mwol sajuryŏgo hamnida.
a 5-year-old boy	5살 된 남자애 Tasŏt sal toen namjaae
I'd like to see that one.	저것 좀 보여 주세요. Chŏgŏt chom poyŏ chuseyo.
the one in the window	진열장에 있는 것 Chinyŏlchang-e innŭn kŏt
I'd like to replace this ___.	이 ___을[를] 바꾸려고 합니다. I ___ (r)ŭl pakkuryŏgo hamnida.

THE SALESCLERK

I'm sorry; we don't accept credit cards.	미안합니다. 크레디트 카드는 받지 않습니다. Mianhamnida. K'ŭredit'ŭ k'adŭnŭn patchi anssŭmnida.
We accept Diners Club.	다이너스 클럽을 받습니다. Tainŏsŭ K'ŭllŏbŭl passŭmnida.

American Express	아메리칸 익스프레스를 Ame-rik'an Iksŭp'ŭresŭrŭl
Visa	비자를 Pijarŭl
Master Card	마스터 카드를 Masŭt'ŏ K'adŭrŭl

Here's your receipt.

영수증 여기 있읍니다.
Yŏngsujŭng yŏgi issŭmnida.

Thank you.

감사합니다. Kamsahamnida.

Come again.

또 오세요. Tto oseyo.

Welcome.

어서 오십시오.
Ŏsŏ oshipshio.

What are you looking for?

뭘 찾으십니까?
Mwol ch'ajŭshimnikka?

What color do you want?

어떤 색깔을 찾으세요?
Ŏttŏn saekkarŭl ch'ajŭseyo?

size

사이즈를 saijŭrŭl

I'm sorry. We don't have it/any.

미안합니다. 그건 없는데요.
Mianhamnida Kŭgŏn ŏmnŭn-deyo.

Would you like us to order it for you?

주문해 드릴까요?
Chumunhae tŭrilkkayo?

Please write your name and phone number.

성함과 전화 번호 좀 적어 주세요.
Sŏnghamgwa chŏnhwa pŏnho chom chŏgŏ chuseyo.

It should be here in a few days.

며칠 내에 도착될 겁니다.
Myŏch'il nae-e toch'aktoel kŏmnida.

next week	다음주 중에	Taŭmchu chung-e

We'll call you when it's here.	도착하면 연락 드리겠읍니다.	Toch'ak'amyŏn yŏllak tŭrigessŭmnida.

That will be ___ won, please.	___ 원 되겠읍니다.	___ won toegessŭmnida.

These are some things that you'll hear while you're shopping. If you're not quite sure what's being said, you can ask the clerk to point to the phrase in the book.

IN A GIFT SHOP

Could you show me your selection of bamboo baskets?	대바구니 좀 보여 주세요.	Taebaguni chom poyŏ chuse-yo.

carved objects	조각품	Chogakp'um
ceramics	도자기	Tojagi
cloisonné	칠보 자기	Ch'ilbo chagi
fans	부채	Puch'ae
Korean chests of drawers	문갑	Mun-gap
Korean dolls	한국 인형	Han-guk inhyŏng
kites	연	Yŏn
lacquerware	칠기	Ch'ilgi
masks	가면	Kamyŏn
porcelain	자기	Chagi

| Is this handmade? | 이거 수제품입니까? |
| | Igŏ sujep'umimnikka? |

| Where in Korea is it from? | 이거 어느 지방산입니까? |
| | Igŏ ŏnŭ chibangsanimnikka? |

| I'd like a nice gift. | 좋은 선물 하나 사려고 합니다. |
| | Choŭn sŏnmul hana saryŏgo hamnida. |

a small gift	작은 선물 하나
	Chagŭn sŏnmul hana
a souvenir	기념품 하나
	Kinyŏmp'um hana

| It's for ____. | ____에게 줄 겁니다. |
| | ____ege chul kŏmnida. |

| I don't want to spend more than ____ won. | ____ 원 이하의 것으로 하고 싶습니다. |
| | ____ won ihaŭi kŏsŭro hago shipsŭmnida. |

| Could you suggest something? | 어떤 것이 좋습니까? |
| | Ŏttŏn kŏshi chossŭmnikka? |

Allow yourself time to browse in Korean-style gift shops. You're sure to see something you like. Korean shopkeepers will wrap purchases beautifully.

AT THE TOBACCONIST

| Do you have American cigarettes? | 양담배 있읍니까? |
| | Yangdambae issŭmnikka? |

What brands?	어떤 종류가 있읍니까? Ŏttŏn chongnyuga issŭmnikka?
Please give me some matches too.	성냥도 좀 주세요. Sŏngnyangdo chom chuseyo.
Do you sell <u>chewing tobacco</u>?	씹는 담배 팝니까? <u>Ssimnŭn tambae p'amnikka?</u>

cigarette holders	담뱃갑	Tambaetkap
flints	라이터 돌	Lait'ŏ tol
lighter fluid [gas]	라이터 기름[가스]	Lait'ŏ kirŭm[kasŭ]
lighters	라이터	Lait'ŏ
pipes	파이프	P'aip'ŭ

A pack of cigarettes, please.	담배 한 갑 주세요. Tambae han kap chuseyo.
I'd like <u>filtered</u> cigarettes.	필터가 있는 담배 한 갑 주세요. <u>P'ilt'ŏga innŭn</u> tambae han kap chuseyo.

king size	킹 사이즈	K'ing saijŭ
mild	순한	Sunhan
low tar	니코틴이 적은	Nik'ot'ini chŏgŭn

Are these cigarettes strong[mild]?	이 담배 독합니까[순합니까]? I tambae tok'amnikka [sunhamnikka]?

Smoking

Do you mind if I smoke?	담배 피워도 되겠읍니까? Tambae p'iwodo toegessŭmnikka?
I don't mind if you smoke.	네, 피우세요. Ne, p'iuseyo.

Would you mind putting out the cigarette?	담배 좀 꺼 주시겠읍니까? Tambae chom kkŏ chushige-ssŭmnikka?
Would you like a cigarette?	담배 피우시겠읍니까? Tambae p'iushigessŭmnikka?
May I trouble you for a cigarette?	담배 있으면 좀 부탁합니다. Tambae issŭmyŏn chom pu-t'ak'amnida.
light	불 Pul
No thanks, I don't smoke.	감사합니다만 담배 안 피웁니다. Kamsahamnidaman tambae an p'iumnida.
I've given it up.	끊었읍니다. Kkŭnŏssŭmnida.

TOILETRIES

Is there a store that carries American [European] toiletries?	미제[유럽제] 화장품을 파는 가게가 있읍니까? Mije[Yurŏp-che] hwajangp'umŭl p'anŭn kagega issŭmnikka?
Do you have after-shave lotion?	애프터 세이브 로션 있읍니까? Aep'ŭt'ŏ syeibŭ losyŏn issŭm-nikka?
bobby pins	머리 핀 Mŏri p'in
body lotion	바디 로션 Padi losyŏn
brushes	솔 Sol
combs	빗 Pit
eye liner	아이 라이너 Ai lainŏ
eye pencil	아이 펜슬 Ai p'ensŭl
eye shadow	아이 세도우 Ai syedou

hand lotion	핸드 로션	Haendŭ losyŏn
lipstick	립스틱	Lipsŭt'ik
mascara	마스카라	Masŭk'ara
mirrors	거울	Kŏul
nail clippers	손톱 깎이	Sont'op kkakki
perfume	향수	Hyangsu
razors	면도기	Myŏndogi
razor blades	면도날	Myŏndonal
rouge, blusher	루즈	Rujŭ
safety pins	핀	P'in
shampoo	샴푸	Syamp'u
shaving lotion	세이빙 로션	Syeibing losyŏn
soap	비누	Pinu
sponges	스폰지	Sŭp'onji
toothbrush	칫솔	Ch'issol
toothpaste	치약	Ch'iyak

IN A MUSIC-RELATED SHOP

Do you have an LP album?	LP 앨범 있읍니까? Elp'i aelbŏm issŭmnikka?	
a 33 RPM	33 회전	Samship-sam hoejŏn
a 45 RPM	45 회전	Saship-o hoejŏn
Where is the American music section?	미국 음악이 어디에 있읍니까? Miguk ŭmagi ŏdie issŭmnikka?	
classical music	클래식이	K'ŭllaeshigi
jazz	재즈가	Chaejŭga
latest hits	최근 히트곡이	Ch'oegŭn hit'ŭgogi
opera	오페라가	Op'eraga
pop music	팝송이	P'apsong-i

Can I listen to this record?	이 레코드 좀 들어 볼 수 있읍니까? I rek'odŭ chom tŭrŏ pol su issŭmnikka?
Do you have any records[tapes] by ___?	___ 레코드[테이프] 있읍니까? ___ rek'odŭ[t'eip'ŭ] issŭmnikka?
Is there a record shop around here?	근처에 레코드 가게 있읍니까? Kŭnch'ŏe rek'odŭ kage issŭmnikka?
Do you sell <u>cartridges</u>?	카트리지 있읍니까? <u>K'at'ŭriji</u> issŭmnikka?
cassettes	카세트	K'aset'ŭ
records	레코드	Rek'odŭ

CLOTHES

Items

I want something in <u>black</u>.	검은색으로 좀 보여 주세요. <u>Kŏmŭnsaegŭro</u> chom poyŏ chuseyo.

blue	하늘색으로	Hanŭlsaegŭro
brown	갈색으로	Kalsaegŭro
gray	회색으로	Hoesaegŭro
green	녹색으로	Noksaegŭro
pink	분홍색으로	Punhong-saegŭro
purple	보라색으로	Porasaegŭro
red	빨간색으로	Ppalgansaegŭro
white	흰색으로	Hŭinsaegŭro
yellow	노란색으로	Noransaegŭro

I'd like a solid color.	무지로 좀 보여 주세요. Mujiro chom poyŏ chuseyo.
a print	날염포로 Naryŏmp'oro
stripes	줄무늬로 Chulmunŭiro
checks	체크 무늬로 Ch'ek'ŭ munŭiro

| I'd like a darker color. | 더 어두운 색으로 좀 보여 주세요. Tŏ ŏdu-un saegŭro chom poyŏ chuseyo. |

| Do you have anything to match this? | 여기에 어울리는 것으로 어떤 것이 있읍니까? Yŏgie ŏullinŭn kŏsŭro ŏttŏn kŏshi issŭmnikka? |

| Do you have something in cotton? | 면으로 된 것으로 어떤 것이 있읍니까? Myŏnŭro toen kŏsŭro ŏttŏn kŏshi issŭmnikka? |

wool	울로	Ullo
silk	실크로	Shilk'ŭro
polyester	폴리에스터로	P'olliesŭt'ŏro
leather	가죽으로	Kajugŭro
vinyl	비닐로	Pinillo
nylon	나일론으로	Naillonŭro

| Could you please show me some belts. | 벨트 좀 보여 주세요. Pelt'ŭ chom poyŏ chuseyo. |

blouses	블라우스	Pŭllausŭ
dresses	드레스	Tŭresŭ
gloves	장갑	Changgap
handkerchiefs	손수건	Sonsugŏn
hats	모자	Moja
jeans	청바지	Ch'ŏngbaji
overcoats	오바	Oba
pants	바지	Paji

raincoats	레인코트	Reink'ot'ŭ
scarves	스카프	Sŭk'ap'ŭ
shirts	와이 샤쓰	Wai syassŭ
shorts(briefs)	반바지	Panbaji
skirts	치마	Ch'ima
slips	속옷	Sogot
socks	양말	Yangmal
stockings	스타킹	Sŭt'ak'ing
suits	양복	Yangbok
sweaters	스웨터	Sŭwet'ŏ
swim suits	수영복	Suyŏngbok
tee shirts	티 샤쓰	T'i syassŭ
ties	넥타이	Nekt'ai
undershirts	내의	Nae-ŭi
wallets	지갑	Chigap

Is there a special sale today?
오늘 세일합니까?
Onŭl seirhamnikka?

I'd like the ____ with long/short sleeves.
소매가 긴/짧은 ____ 좀 보여 주세요.
Somaega kin/tchalbŭn ____ chom poyŏ chuseyo.

Do you have anything else?
다른 것 있읍니까?
Tarŭn kŏt issŭmnikka?

larger	더 큰	Tŏ k'ŭn
smaller	더 작은	Tŏ chagŭn
cheaper	더 싼	Tŏ ssan
of better quality	더 좋은	Tŏ choŭn
longer	더 긴	Tŏ kin
shorter	더 짧은	Tŏ tchalbŭn

I'd prefer a different color.
다른 색으로 좀 보여 주세요.
Tarŭn saegŭro chom poyŏ chuseyo.

style	스타일로	sŭt'aillo

Shopping for clothing in Korea yields basic styles as well as designs, patterns, and fabrics unavailable anywhere else. Some Korean designers have boutiques in the department stores and elsewhere; they feature lines of clothing more affordable than you may expect, both high fashion items and simple, well-made sportswear. And don't overlook traditional Korean clothing. A silk or cotton *hanbok* (한복) makes a stylish gift perhaps for yourself!

Sizes

Where's the dressing room?	옷은 어디서 입습니까?	Osŭn ŏdisŏ ipsŭmnikka?
Do you have a mirror?	거울 있읍니까?	Kŏul issŭmnikka?
It's too long.	너무 긴데요.	Nŏmu kindeyo.
short	짧은데요	tchalbŭndeyo
loose	헐렁한데요	hŏllŏnghandeyo
Can you alter it?	이것을 고칠 수 있읍니까?	Igŏsŭl koch'il su issŭmnikka?
The zipper doesn't work.	지퍼가 고장났읍니다.	Chip'ŏga kojangnassŭmnida.
There's a button missing.	여기 단추가 없읍니다.	Yŏgi tanch'uga ŏpsŭmnida.
It doesn't fit me.	이건 맞지 않는데요.	Igŏn matchi annŭndeyo.

It fits very well.	이거 잘 맞습니다. Igo chal massŭmnida.
I'll take it.	이걸로 하죠. Igŏllo hajyo.
Please take my measurements.	제 치수 좀 재 주세요. Che ch'isu chom chae chuseyo.
My size is <u>small</u>.	내 사이즈는 <u>스몰</u>입니다. Nae saijŭnŭn sŭmorimnida.
medium	미디엄입니다 midiŏm- imnida
large	라지입니다 lajiimnida
May I try it on?	입어 봐도 됩니까? Ibŏ pwado toemnikka?

You may try on Korean clothing before you buy it. Although you can find a good fit in most items, some may be short-waisted for Westerners, and some sleeves may also be short.

IN A BOOKSTORE

Where can I find <u>detective stories</u>?	<u>탐정 소설</u>이 어디에 있읍니까? <u>T'amjŏng sosŏri</u> ŏdie issŭm-nikka?
history books novels	역사책이 Yŏksach'aegi 소설이 Sosŏri
Do you have English translations of <u>Korean classics</u>?	영문판 <u>한국 고전</u> 있읍니까? Yŏngmunp'an <u>Han-guk kojŏn</u> issŭmnikka?

English	Korean	Romanization
modern Korean novels	근대 소설	kŭndae sosŏl
current Korean novels	현대 소설	hyŏndae sosŏl

Do you have English translations of Yi Kwang-su's books?
영문판 <u>이 광수</u> 작품 있읍니까?
Yŏngmunp'an <u>Yi Kwang-su</u> chakp'um issŭmnikka?

| Kim Ŭn-guk's | 김 은국 | Kim Ŭn-guk |
| Ch'oe In-ho's | 최 인호 | Ch'oe In-ho |

I'm looking for a copy of ____.
____ 있읍니까?
____ issŭmnikka?

The title of the book is ____.
제목은 ____입니다.
Chemogŭn ____imnida.

The author of the book is ____.
저자는 ____입니다.
Chŏjanŭn ____imnida.

I don't know the title/author.
제목은/저자는 잘 모르겠읍니다.
Chemogŭn/chŏjanŭn chal morŭgessŭmnida.

I'll take these books.
이 책 좀 부탁합니다.
I chaek chom put'ak'amnida.

Do you have books in <u>English</u>?
<u>영문</u> 서적 있읍니까?
<u>Yŏngmun</u> sŏjŏk issŭmnikka?

| French | 불어 | Purŏ |
| German | 독어 | Togŏ |

Where are the books in English?
영문 서적이 어디에 있읍니까?
Yŏngmun sŏjŏgi ŏdie issŭmnikka?

I want <u>a guide-book</u>.	가이드북을 사고 싶습니다.	<u>Kaidŭbugŭl</u> sago shipsŭmnida.
a map of this city	이 도시의 지도를	I toshi-ŭi chidorŭl
a map of Korea	한국 지도를	Han-guk chidorŭl
a pocket dictionary	포켓판 사전을	P'ok'etp'an sajŏnŭl
an English-Korean dictionary	영한 사전을	Yŏnghan sajŏnŭl
a book for learning Korean	한국어 학습서를	Han-gugŏ haksŭpsŏrŭl

Bookstores, newsstands and stationery stores are usually separate in Korea, although some bookstores do sell newspapers. At bookstores and newsstands in large tourist hotels you can find some American and European newspapers, and also weekly news magazines, usually international or Far East editions. You can also buy English-language newspapers written and published in Korea. If you don't see them, ask the vendor. Some bookstores have good selections of books in English.

NEWSPAPERS AND MAGAZINES

Do you have news magazines?	뉴스 관계 잡지 있읍니까?	Nyusŭ kwan-gye chapchi i-ssŭmnikka?
I'd like these.	이것 좀 부탁합니다.	Igŏt chom put'ak'amnida.

How much are they?	이거 얼맙니까?
	Igŏ ŏlmamnikka?

Do you carry newspapers[magazines] in English?	영어 신문[잡지] 있읍니까?
	Yŏng-ŏ shinmun[chapchi] issŭmnikka?

I'd like an English language newspaper.	영어 신문 하나 주세요. Yŏng-ŏ shinmun hana chuseyo.

May I see what you have, please?	어떤 것이 있는지 좀 보여 주세요. Ŏttŏn kŏshi innŭnji chom poyŏ chuseyo.

STATIONERY

I want to buy <u>a ballpoint pen</u>.	<u>볼펜 하나</u> 주세요.
	<u>Polp'en hana</u> chuseyo.
a fountain pen	만년필 하나 Mannyŏnp'il hana
a deck of cards	트럼프 하나 T'ŭrŏmp'ŭ hana
some envelopes	봉투 좀 Pongt'u chom
an eraser	지우개 하나 Chiugae hana
some glue	접착제 하나 Chŏpch'akche hana
a notebook	노트 하나 Not'ŭ hana
some pencils	연필 좀 Yŏnp'il chom
a pencil sharpener	연필깎이 하나 Yŏnp'ilkkakki hana
some rubber bands	고무 밴드 좀 Komu paendŭ chom
some Scotch tape	스카치 테이프 하나 Sŭk'ach'i t'eip'ŭ hana

some typing paper	타이프 용지 좀	T'aip'ŭ yongji chom
some wrapping paper	포장지 좀	P'ojangji chom
a writing pad	필기 용지 한 권	P'ilgi yongji han kwon
some writing paper	필기 용지 좀	P'ilgi yongji chom

ELECTRICAL APPLIANCES

What voltage does this take?	이것은 몇 V용입니까? Igosŭn myŏt polt'ŭ yong-im-nikka?
Do you have one suitable for <u>A-merican</u> voltage?	미국 전압에 맞는 거 있읍니까? <u>Miguk</u> chŏnabe mannŭn kŏ issŭmnikka?
South American European	남미 Nammi 유럽 Yurŏp
Is there a 110 volt one?	110V용 있읍니까? Paek ship polt'ŭyong issŭmnikka?

100 volts	paek polt'ŭ
110 volts	paek ship polt'ŭ
220 volts	ibaek iship polt'ŭ

| This is out of order/broken. | 이것이 고장났읍니다. Igoshi kojangnassŭmnida. |
| How much is this? | 이거 얼맙니까? Igo ŏlmamnikka? |

It's rather expensive.
좀 비싸군요.
Chom pissagunnyo.

It's more than I expected.
생각했던 것보다 비싸군요.
Saenggak'aettŏn kŏtpoda pissagunnyo.

That's not a final price, is it?
확정 가격은 아니죠?
Hwakchŏng kagyŏgŭn anijyo?

Can't you come down a little?
좀 깎아 주시죠.
Chom kkakka chushijyo.

How about ____ won?
____ 원에 해 주세요.
____ wone hae chuseyo.

Where can I buy electrical appliances?
전기 제품을 어디서 살 수 있읍니까?
Chŏn-gi chep'umŭl ŏdisŏ sal su issŭmnikka?

I want to buy <u>a battery</u>.
<u>전지 하나</u> 사러 왔읍니다.
<u>Chŏnji hana</u> sarŏ wassŭmnida.

a blender	믹서 하나	Miksŏ hana
a cassette recorder	카세트 하나	K'aset'ŭ hana
an electric razor	전기 면도기 하나	Chŏn-gi myŏndogi hana
a hair dryer	헤어 드라이어 하나	Heŏ tŭraiŏ hana
a microcassette recorder	소형 카세트 하나	Sohyŏng k'aset'ŭ hana
a miniature TV	소형 TV 하나	Sohyŏng t'ibi hana
a minicalculator	계산기 하나	Kyesan-gi hana

a portable compo-nent stereo system	휴대용 콤포넌트 시스템 하나 Hyudaeyong k'omp'onŏnt'ŭ shisŭt'em hana
a portable radio	휴대용 라디오 하나 Hyudaeyong radio hana
a record player	전축 하나 Chŏnch'uk hana
a tape recorder	테이프 리코더 하나 T'eip'ŭ rik'odŏ hana
a television set	TV 하나 T'ibi hana

IN A FOOD SHOP

I'd like ___.	___ 주세요. ___ chuseyo.
a bag of sugar	설탕 한 포 Sŏlt'ang han p'o
a bar of chocolate	초콜렛 하나 Ch'ok'ollet hana
a bottle of ketchup	케첩 한 병 K'ech'ŏp han pyŏng
a bottle of juice	주스 한 병 Chusŭ han pyŏng
a box of candy	캔디 한 박스 K'aendi han paksŭ
a box of chocolate	초콜렛 한 박스 Ch'ok'ollet han paksŭ
a box of crackers	크래커 한 박스 K'ŭraek'ŏ han paksŭ
a box of raisins	건포도 한 박스 Kŏnp'odo han paksŭ
a can of tuna	참치 캔 하나 Ch'amch'i k'aen hana
a half kilo of cheese	치즈 500 g Ch'ijŭ obaek kŭram

English	Korean	Romanization
a half kilo of tangerines	귤 500 g	Kyul obaek kŭram
a jar of instant coffee	인스턴트 커피 한 병	Insŭt'ŏnt'ŭ k'ŏp'i han pyŏng
a jar of jam	잼 한 병	Chaem han pyŏng
a jar of mayon-naise	마요네즈 한 병	Mayonejŭ han pyŏng
a jar of pepper	후추 한 병	Huch'u han pyŏng
a jar of salt	소금 한 병	Sogŭm han pyŏng
a kilo of apples	사과 1 kg	Sagwa il k'illo
a kilo of bananas	바나나 1 kg	Panana il k'illo
a kilo of ham	햄 1 kg	Haem il k'illo
a liter of milk	우유 1*l*	Uyu il lit'ŏ
a package of candy	캔디 한 봉지	K'aendi han pongji

AT A SHOEMAKER'S

There's a pair in the window that I like.	저기 진열장에 있는 것이 마음에 듭니다.	Chŏgi chinyŏlchang-e innŭn kŏshi maŭme tŭmnida.
Do they come in <u>another color</u>?	다른 색깔 있읍니까?	<u>Tarŭn saekkal</u> issŭmnikka?
calf	송아지 가죽	Song-aji kajuk
suede	양 가죽	Yang kajuk
patent leather	에나멜 가죽	Enamel kajuk

Can you measure my size?	제 사이즈 좀 잴 수 있읍니까? Che saijŭ chom chael su i-ssŭmnikka?
These are too <u>narrow</u>.	이건 너무 <u>좁은데요</u>. Igŏn nŏmu chobŭndeyo.

wide	넓은데요	nŏlbŭndeyo
loose	헐렁한데요	hŏllŏnghandeyo
tight	끼이는데요	kki-inŭndeyo.

They fit fine.	꼭 맞읍니다. Kkok massŭmnida.
I'll take them.	이걸로 하죠. Igŏllo hajyo.
Do you have shoe-laces here?	여기서 구두끈 팝니까? Yŏgisŏ kudukkŭn p'amnikka?
I'd like to see a pair of <u>shoes</u>.	구두 좀 보여 주세요. <u>Kudu</u> chom poyŏ chuseyo.

boots	부츠	Puch'ŭ
casual shoes	캐주얼화	K'aejuŏrhwa
high-heeled shoes	하이힐	Haihil
low-heeled shoes	굽이 낮은 구두	Kubi najŭn kudu
running shoes	러닝화	Rŏninghwa
sandals	샌달	Saendal

PHOTOGRAPHY

I'd like some film for this camera.	이 카메라에 넣을 필름 좀 주세요. I k'amera-e nŏŭl p'illŭm chom chuseyo.

I'd like 20 exposures.	20장 짜리로 주세요. Sǔmu chang tchariro chuseyo.
36 exposures	36장 짜리로 Sǒrǔn yǒsǒt chang tchariro
I'd like to buy a camera.	카메라 하나 사러 왔읍니다. K'amera hana sarǒ wassǔmnida.
I'd like to buy an expensive/inexpensive camera.	고급/싼 카메라 하나 사려고 합니다. Kogǔp/ssan k'amera hana saryǒgo hamnida.
I want an exposure meter.	노출계 하나 사려고 합니다. Noch'ulgye hana saryǒgo hamnida.
some flash bulbs	플래시 전구 몇 개 P'ǔllaeshi chǒngu myǒt kae
a filter	필터 하나 P'ilt'ǒ hana
a lens cap	렌즈 캡 하나 Lenjǔ k'aep hana
a telescopic lens	망원 렌즈 하나 Mangwon lenjǔ hana
a zoom lens	줌 렌즈 하나 Chum lenjǔ hana
Where is there a camera shop?	카메라점이 어디에 있읍니까? K'amerajǒmi ǒdie issǔmnikka?
Do you develop film here?	필름 현상합니까? P'illǔm hyǒnsanghamnikka?
How much does it cost to develop a roll?	필름 한 통 현상하는 데 얼맙니까? P'illǔm han t'ong hyǒnsanghanǔn te ǒlmamnikka?

I have <u>one roll</u>.	한 통 있읍니다. <u>Han t'ong</u> issŭmnida.
two rolls	두 통 Tu t'ong
I want one print of each.	한 장씩 뽑아 주세요. Han changssik ppoba chuseyo.
I want an enlargement.	확대해 주세요. Hwaktaehae chuseyo.
I want a print with a <u>glossy</u> finish.	광택 있게 해 주세요. Kwangt'aek <u>itke</u> hae chuseyo.
matte	없이 ŏpshi
I want a roll of <u>color</u> film.	컬러 필름 한 통 주세요. <u>K'ŏllŏ</u> p'illŭm han t'ong chuseyo.
black and white	흑백 Hŭkpaek
I want a roll of film for slides.	슬라이드용 필름 한 통 주세요. Sŭllaidŭyong p'illŭm han t'ong chuseyo.
I want a film pack, number ___.	___번 필름 하나 주세요. ___ pŏn p'illŭm hana chu- seyo.

Meeting People

WITH LOCALS

I'm planning to go to ____, ____, and ____.
ㅡㅡ, ㅡㅡ, ㅡㅡ을[를] 들를 예정입니다. ____, ____, ____[r]ŭl tŭllŭl yejŏng-imnida.

What do you think about my itinerary here?
저의 여행 일정을 어떻게 생각하십니까? Chŏŭi yŏhaeng ilchŏng-ŭl ŏttŏk'e saenggak'ashimnikka?

Is there anything not on my itinerary that you would recommend?
저의 여정 이외에 어디 갈 만한 곳 없읍니까? Chŏŭi ilchŏng ioee ŏdi kal manhan kot ŏpsŭmnikka?

Could you explain a little about ____?
ㅡㅡ에 대해서 좀 설명해 주시겠읍니까? ____e taehaesŏ chom sŏlmyŏnghae chushigessŭmnikka?

Would you recommend a nice place to eat?
어디 좋은 식당 하나 소개해 주시겠읍니까? Ŏdi choŭn shiktang hana sogaehae chushigessŭmnikka?

Where's a good place for souvenir shopping?
기념품을 사려는데 어디가 좋습니까? Kinyŏmp'umŭl saryŏnŭnde ŏdiga chossŭmnikka?

Do you live here?
여기서 사십니까? Yŏgisŏ sashimnikka?

in Seoul	서울에서	Sŏuresŏ
in Pusan	부산에서	Pusanesŏ

I've always wanted to come here.

여길 한번 꼭 오고 싶었읍니다.
Yŏgil hanbŏn kkok ogo ship'ŏssŭmnida.

It's a wonderful place.

정말 좋은 곳이군요. Chŏngmal choŭn koshigunnyo.

I've really been enjoying it here.

여기 있는 동안 정말 즐거웠읍니다.
Yŏgi innŭn tong-an chŏngmal chŭlgŏwossŭmnida.

I've been to ____, ____, and ____.

지금까지 ____, ____, ____을[를] 다녀 왔읍니다.
Chigŭmkkaji ____, ____, ____ (r)ŭl tanyŏ wassŭmnida.

As you travel around seeing the sights, you'll have many opportunities to meet Korean people. Although as a rule Koreans prefer formal introductions, sightseeing does provide various situations where you can strike up a casual conversation. You may have questions about the places you're visiting, and Koreans are by nature hospitable; most would try to assist you. This section will help you get the conversation started—and to continue it if it seems appropriate! You can use these phrases with local Korean people, and with those from out of town too. Koreans enjoy sightseeing, you'll probably meet a lot of Korean tourists. For more information on Korean customs in social situations, see "Korea and Its People."

WITH OUT-OF-TOWN PEOPLE

Are you with <u>a tour group</u>?	관광단과 함께 오셨읍니까? Kwan-gwangdan-gwa hamkke osyŏssŭmnikka?
your family a friend	가족과 Kajokkwa 친구와 Ch'in-guwa
Are you on your own?	혼자 오셨읍니까? Honja osyŏssŭmnikka?
How long will you be staying here?	여기서 얼마나 계실 겁니까? Yŏgisŏ ŏlmana kyeshil kŏmnikka?
Where are you staying?	어디에 머물고 계십니까? Ŏdie mŏmulgo kyeshimnikka?
Where are you from?	어디서 오셨읍니까? Ŏdisŏ osyŏssŭmnikka?
I hear it's nice there.	거기가 좋다면서요? Kŏgiga chot'amyŏnsŏyo?
What's ____ famous for?	____은[는] 무엇으로 유명합니까? ____(n)ŭn muŏsŭro yumyŏnghamnikka?
What's the special local food in ____?	____에는 어떤 특별한 음식이 있읍니까? ____ enŭn ŏttŏn t'ŭkpyŏrhan ŭmshigi issŭmnikka?
What's a good hotel to stay at in ____?	____에서는 어떤 호텔이 좋습니까? ____esŏnŭn ŏttŏn hot'eri chossŭmnikka?

Could you tell me a good place to eat?	좋은 식당 있으면 좀 가르쳐 주시 겠읍니까? Choŭn shiktang issŭmyŏn chom karŭch'yŏ chushigessŭmnikka?
Do you live here?	여기 사십니까? Yŏgi sashimnikka?
Are you here for sightseeing, or on business?	관광차 오셨읍니까, 사업차 오셨읍 니까? Kwan-gwangch'a osyŏssŭmnikka, saŏpch'a osyŏssŭmnikka?
When did you come here?	여기 언제 오셨읍니까? Yŏgi ŏnje osyŏssŭmnikka?
How do you like it here?	여기 어떻습니까? Yŏgi ŏttŏssŭmnikka?
What have you seen here?	여기서 어떤 것들을 보셨읍니까? Yŏgisŏ ŏttŏn kŏttŭrŭl posyŏssŭmnikka?
I've been to ____, ____, and ____.	전 ____, ____, ____을[를] 다녀왔 읍니다. Chŏn ____, ____, ____ (r)ŭl tanyŏ wassŭmnida.
Have you been to ____?	____ 가 보셨읍니까? ____ ka posyŏssŭmnikka?
I recommend that you go to ____.	____ 한번 가 보세요. ____ hanbŏn ka poseyo.
I ate at ____, and it was wonderful.	____에서 식사를 하니까 참 좋더군 요. ____esŏ shiksarŭl hanikka ch'am chot'ŏgunnyo.

Follow-up

I'm a <u>student</u>.	전 학생입니다. Chŏn <u>haksaeng</u>-imnida.	
doctor	의사	ŭisa
lawyer	변호사	pyŏnhosa
I'm a businessman.	사업을 하나 하고 있읍니다. ŏbŭl hana hago issŭmnida.	Sa-
I'm from <u>the United States</u>.	전 <u>미국에서</u> 왔읍니다. Chŏn <u>Migugesŏ</u> wassŭmnida.	
Canada	캐나다에서	K'aenada-esŏ
Italy	이태리에서	It'aerieso
I live in <u>New York</u>.	전 <u>뉴욕에서</u> 살고 있읍니다. Chŏn <u>Nyuyok-esŏ</u> salgo issŭmnida.	
Hong Kong	홍콩에서	Hongk'ong-esŏ
Cairo	카이로에서	K'airo-esŏ
I'm here for <u>sight- seeing</u>.	여기에 <u>관광차</u> 왔읍니다. Yŏgi-e <u>kwan-gwangch'a</u> wa- ssŭmnida.	
business	사업차	saŏpch'a
I've been in Korea for <u>two days</u>.	한국에 온 지 <u>이틀</u> 됐읍니다. Han-guge on chi <u>it'ŭl</u> twae- ssŭmnida.	
three days	사흘	sahŭl
four days	나흘	nahŭl
one week	일 주일	il chuil
I came here <u>today</u>.	전 <u>오늘</u> 왔읍니다. Chŏn <u>ŏnŭl</u> wassŭmnida.	

yesterday	어제	ŏje
two days ago	이틀 전에	it'ŭl chŏne
three days ago	사흘 전에	sahŭl chŏne

What do you think of ____?

____ 어떻습니까?
____ ŏttŏssŭmnikka?

Do you like ____?

____ 좋습니까?
____ chossŭmikka?

I think ____ is very <u>beautiful</u>.

____ 정말 <u>좋다고</u> 생각합니다.
____ chŏngmal <u>chot'ago</u> saeng-gak'amnida.

interesting	흥미롭다고	hŭngmiroptago
magnificent	웅장하다고	ungjanghadago
wonderful	좋다고	chot'ago

By the way, let me introduce myself.

참, 인사드리겠읍니다.
Ch'am, insadŭrigessŭmnida.

My name is ____.

제 이름은 ____입니다.
Che irŭmŭn ____imnida.

I'm here <u>alone</u>.

저 <u>혼자</u> 왔읍니다.
Chŏ <u>honja</u> wassŭmnida.

with my wife	집사람과 같이	Chipsaram-gwa kach'i
with my husband	남편과 같이	Namp'yŏn-gwa kach'i
with my friend	친구와 같이	Ch'in-guwa kach'i
with my colleague	동료와 같이	Tongnyowa kach'i

These are pictures of my family.

이것이 제 가족 사진입니다.
Igŏshi che kajok sajinimnida.

Would you like to see them?	한번 만나 보시겠읍니까? Hanbŏn manna poshigessŭmnikka?
Are you a student?	학생입니까? Haksaeng-imnikka?
What are you studying?	지금 뭘 공부하고 있읍니까? Chigŭm mwol kongbuhago issŭmnikka?
What do you do?	지금 뭘 하십니까? Chigŭm mwol hashimnikka?
Are you <u>single</u>?	<u>독신</u>입니까? <u>Tokshin</u>imnikka?
married	결혼했음 Kyŏrhonhaessŭm
Do you have any children?	애들이 있으십니까? Aedŭri issŭshimnikka?
How many children do you have?	애들은 몇이나 됩니까? Aedŭrŭn myŏch'ina toemnikka?
How old are they?	애들은 몇 살이나 됐읍니까? Aedŭrŭn myŏt sarina toessŭmnikka?
Is your <u>family</u> here?	<u>가족</u>은 여기에 있읍니까? <u>Kajog</u>ŭn yŏgie issŭmnikka?
wife husband	부인은 Puinŭn 남편은 Namp'yŏnŭn
Do you have any pictures of your <u>family</u>?	<u>가족</u> 사진 갖고 계십니까? <u>Kajok</u> sajin katko kyeshimnikka?
children	애들 Aedŭl

It's my first time in <u>Korea</u>.	<u>한국엔</u> 처음입니다.
	<u>Han-gugen</u> ch'ŏŭmimnida.

| Chejudo | 제주도엔 | Chejudo-en |
| Pusan | 부산엔 | Pusanen |

I'll stay here <u>overnight</u>.	여기서 <u>하루</u> 묵을 겁니다.
	Yŏgisŏ <u>haru</u> mugŭl kŏmnida.

| for a few days | 며칠 | myŏch'il |
| for a week | 일 주일 | il chuil |

I'm staying at the ___ Hotel.	전 ___ 호텔에서 머물 겁니다.
	Chŏn ___ Hot'eresŏ mŏmul kŏmnida.

I'm <u>single</u>.	전 <u>독신입니다</u>.
	Chŏn <u>tokshinimnida</u>.

| married | 결혼했읍니다 | kyŏrhon-haessŭmnida |

I have a family.	전 가족이 있읍니다.
	Chŏn kajogi issŭmnida.

I have no children.	애들은 없읍니다.
	Aedŭrŭn ŏpsŭmnida.

I have <u>one</u> child (ren).	애가 <u>하나</u> 있읍니다.
	Aega <u>hana</u> issŭmnida.

| two | 둘 | tul |
| three | 셋 | set |

Taking Pictures

Don't move.	움직이지 마세요.
	Umjigiji maseyo.

| Smile | 웃으세요. | Usŭseyo. |

That's it.	됐읍니다. Twaessŭmnida.
Would you take a picture of me, please?	사진 좀 찍어 주시겠읍니까? Sajin chom tchigŏ chushigessŭmnikka?
Thank you.	감사합니다. Kamsahamnida.
Would you like me to take a picture for you?	제가 한 장 찍어 드릴까요? Chega han chang tchigŏ tŭrilkkayo?
May I take your picture?	사진 한 장 찍어도 되겠읍니까? Sajin han chang tchigŏdo toegessŭmnikka?
Stand here.	여기 서 계세요. Yŏgi sŏ kyeseyo.

APPOINTMENTS

May I call you?	전화해도 되겠읍니까? Chŏnhwahaedo toegessŭmnikka?
Are you doing anything <u>this afternoon</u>?	<u>오늘 오후에</u> 특별한 일 있읍니까? <u>Onŭl ohu-e</u> t'ŭkpyŏrhan il issŭmnikka?
this evening	오늘 저녁에 Onŭl chŏnyŏge
Are you free this evening?	오늘 저녁에 시간 있읍니까? Onŭl chŏnyŏge shigan issŭmnikka?
What about <u>dinner</u> together?	<u>저녁이나</u> 함께 하시죠. <u>Chŏnyŏgina</u> hamkke hashijyo.

| drinks | 약주나 | Yakchuna |
| sightseeing | 관광이나 | Kwan-gwang-ina |

I'd like to invite you for <u>cocktails.</u>

칵테일에 초대하고 싶습니다.
<u>K'akt'eire</u> ch'odaehago ship-sŭmnida.

| dinner | 저녁 식사에 | Chŏnyŏk shiksa-e |
| a show | 쇼에 | Syo-e |

I hope you can come.

오셨으면 합니다.
Osyŏssŭmyŏn hamnida.

Where shall I meet you?

어디서 만날까요?
Ŏdisŏ mannalkkayo?

Shall I meet you at <u>my hotel lobby?</u>

제가 묵고 있는 호텔 로비에서 만날까요? <u>Chega mukko innŭn hot'el lobiesŏ</u> mannalkkayo?

your hotel lobby

묵고 계시는 호텔 로비에서
Mukko kyeshinŭn hot'el lobiesŏ

the restaurant

레스토랑에서 Resŭt'orang-esŏ

the cocktail lounge

칵테일 라운지에서 K'akt'eil launjiesŏ

Shall I come to pick you up?

차로 모시러 올까요?
Ch'aro moshirŏ olkkayo?

Could I see you again?

또 뵐 수 있을까요?
Tto poel su issŭlkkayo?

Here's my name, hotel, telephone number, and extension.

이것이 제 이름, 호텔, 전화 번호입니다. Igŏshi che irŭm, hot'el, chŏnhwa pŏnhoimnida.

Will you call me if you have time?	시간 있으면 전화 주시겠읍니까? Shigan issŭmyŏn chŏnhwa chushigessŭmnikka?
Could you give me your telephone number?	전화 번호 하나 주시겠읍니까? Chŏnhwa pŏnho hana chushigessŭmnikka?
What time shall we meet?	몇 시에 만날까요? Myŏt shie mannalkkayo?
Is <u>six</u> covenient for you?	<u>6시</u> 괜찮겠읍니까? <u>Yŏsŏssi</u> kwaench'ank'essŭmnikka?
six-thirty seven	6시 반 Yŏsŏssi pan 7시 Ilgopshi
See you then.	그럼 그때 뵙겠읍니다. Kŭrŏm kŭttae poepkessŭmnida.

SAYING GOOD-BYE

I hope I'll see you again.	또 뵙겠읍니다. Tto poepkessŭmnida.
Nice talking to you.	말씀 재미있었읍니다. Malssŭm chaemiissŏssŭmnida.
Good-bye. Good morning. Good afternoon. Good evening. Good night.	안녕히 계세요. Annyŏnghi kyeseyo (leaving someone who remains). 안녕히 가세요. Annyŏnghi kaseyo (seeing someone off).

Eating and Drinking Out

IN A RESTAURANT

General Inquiries

Can you recommend a <u>nice</u> restaurant?

<u>좋은</u> 레스토랑 하나 소개해 주시겠
읍니까? <u>Chŏŭn</u> resŭt'orang hana sogaehae chushigessŭmnikka?

small	작은	Chagŭn
fancy	멋있는	Mŏdinnŭn
first class	일급	Ilgŭp

I'd like to have <u>American</u> food.

미국 음식을 먹고 싶습니다.
<u>Miguk</u> ŭmshigŭl mŏkko shipsumnida.

Chinese	중국	Chungguk
French	프랑스	P'ŭrangsŭ
German	독일	Togil
Indian	인도	Indo
Italian	이태리	It'aeri
Japanese	일본	Ilbon
Korean	한국	Han-guk
Spanish	스페인	Sŭp'ein

How much would it be per person?

일인분이 얼맙니까?
Irinbuni ŏlmamnikka?

Do they take credit cards?

크레디트 카드 받습니까? K'ŭredit'ŭ k'adŭ passŭmnikka?

Are they open for <u>lunch</u>?	점심 시간에 문 엽니까? **Chŏmshim** shigane mun yŏm-nikka?
dinner breakfast	저녁 Chŏnyŏk 아침 Ach'im
What are their hours?	영업 시간이 어떻게 됩니까? Yŏng-ŏp shigani ŏttŏk'e toem-nikka?
Do you have the telephone number?	여기 전화 번호가 어떻게 됩니까? Yŏgi chŏnhwa pŏnhoga ŏttŏ-k'e toemnikka?
Is there a restaurant nearby?	근처에 레스토랑이 있읍니까? Kŭnch'ŏe resŭt'orang-i issŭm-nikka?
Is there a restaurant that is <u>still</u> open?	아직도 문을 닫지 않은 레스토랑이 있읍니까? **Ajikto munŭl tatchi anŭn** resŭt'orang-i i-ssŭmnikka?
already	지금쯤 문을 연 Chigŭmtchŭm munŭl yŏn
Is there a <u>Mac-Donald's</u> around here?	이 근처에 맥도날드가 있읍니까? I kŭnch'ŏe <u>Maektonaldŭga</u> i-ssŭmnikka?
Kentucky Fried Chicken Shakey's Mr. Donut	켄터키 프라이드 치킨이 K'en-t'ŏk'i p'ŭraidŭ ch'ik'ini 세이키가 Syeik'iga 미스터 도나스가 Misŭt'ŏ Tonasŭga

Baskin-Robbins	배스킨 로빈즈가
	Paesŭk'in Robinjŭga

Do you know <u>a good</u> restaurant?
좋은 레스토랑 아는 데 있읍니까?
Choŭn resŭt'orang anŭn te issŭmnikka?

an inexpensive	싼	Ssan
a quiet	조용한	Choyonghan
the nearest	제일 가까운	Cheil kakkaun
the best	최고로 좋은	Ch'oegoro choŭn

Reservation

<u>Two people</u> at 12, please.
12시 2명입니다.
Yŏltushi <u>tu myŏng</u>-imnida.

Three people	3명	se myŏng
Four people	4명	ne myŏng
Five people	5명	tasŏn myŏng
Six people	6명	yŏsŏn myŏng
Seven people	7명	ilgom myŏng
Eight people	8명	yŏdŏl myŏng

Two people at <u>12 : 30</u>, please.
12시 반 2명입니다.
Yŏltushi pan tu myŏng-imnida.

1 : 00	1시	Hanshi
1 : 30	1시 반	Hanshi pan
2 : 00	2시	Tushi
6 : 00	6시	Yŏsŏssi
6 : 30	6시 반	Yŏsŏssi pan
8 : 00	8시	Yŏdŏlshi

My name is ___.
제 이틈은 ___입니다.
Che irŭmŭn ___ imnida.

Do I need to make a reservation?	예약을 해야 합니까? Yeyagŭl haeya hamnikka?
Do you take reservations?	예약 받습니까? Yeyak passŭmnikka?
I'd like to make a reservation for <u>dinner tonight</u>.	<u>오늘 저녁을</u> 예약하려고 합니다. Onŭl chŏnyŏgŭl yeyak'aryŏgo hamnida.

lunch today	오늘 점심을	Onŭl chŏmshimŭl
lunch tomorrow	내일 점심을	Naeil chŏmshimŭl
dinner tomorrow	내일 저녁을	Naeil chŏnyŏgŭl

Arriving

We'd like to sit at the counter.	카운터에 앉겠읍니다. K'aunt'ŏe ankessŭmnida.
Can we get a table now?	지금 테이블 있읍니까? Chigŭm t'eibŭl issŭmnikka?
Do we have to wait?	기다려야 합니까? Kidaryŏya hamnikka?
How long do we have to wait?	얼마나 기다려야 합니까? Ŏlmana kidaryŏya hamnikka?
Good morning. Good afternoon./ Good evening.	수고하십니다. Sugohashimnida.
I have a reservation for 8 o'clock. My name is ___.	8시에 예약했읍니다. 이름은 ___ 입니다. Yŏdŏlshie yeyak'aessŭmnida. Irŭmŭn ___imnida.

| I'd like a table for four. | 4사람 앉을 테이블 있읍니까?
Ne saram anjŭl t'eibŭl issŭm-nikka? |

At the Table

We'd like to order drinks first.	먼저 마실 것 좀 부탁해요. Mŏnjŏ mashil kŏt chom put'ak'eyo.
I'd like some <u>pea-nuts</u>.	땅콩 좀 부탁합니다. **Ttang-**k'ong chom put'ak'amnida.
potato chips	감자 튀김 Kamja t'wigim
No drinks, thank you.	술은 놔두세요. Surŭn nwaduseyo.
Give us a menu, please.	메뉴판 좀 갖다 주세요. Menyu-p'an chom katta chuseyo.

Questions

What would you recommend?	어떤 것이 좋습니까? Ŏttŏn kŏshi chossŭmnikka?
Can we order now?	지금 주문해도 됩니까? Chigŭm chumunhaedo toem-nikka?
We'll take some more time before ordering.	잠시만 있다 오세요. Chamshiman itta oseyo.
Could you bring some bread and butter?	버터 바른 빵 좀 부탁합니다. Pŏt'ŏ parŭn ppang chom put'ak'amnida.

Water, please.	물 좀 갖다 주세요. Mul chom katta chuseyo.
What's the specialty of the house?	이 집 전문이 뭡니까? I chip chŏnmuni mwomnikka?
Is there a special today?	오늘 특식이 뭡니까? Onŭl t'ŭkshigi mwomnikka?
What's good today?	오늘은 뭐가 좋습니까? Onŭrŭn mwoga chossŭmnikka?

Ordering

I'd like to have two orders of ___.	___ 2인분 부탁합니다. ___ i inbun put'ak'amnida.
three orders four orders	3인분 sam inbun 4인분 sa inbun
Bring me ___ later.	나중에 ___ 좀 부탁합니다. Najung-e ___ chom put'ak'amnida.
May I change <u>A</u> to <u>B</u>?	<u>A</u> 을(를) <u>B</u> (으)로 바꿀 수 있 읍니까? <u>A</u> (r)ŭl <u>B</u> (ŭ)ro pakkul su issŭmnikka?
I like my steak <u>rare</u>.	스테이크는 <u>설익혀</u> 주세요. Sŭt'eik'ŭnŭn <u>sŏrik'yŏ</u> chuseyo.
medium	보통으로 익혀 pot'ong-ŭro ik'yŏ
well-done	잘 익혀 chal ik'yŏ
I'd like it cooked without <u>salt</u>.	<u>소금은</u> 넣지 말고 해 주세요. <u>Sogŭmŭn</u> noch'i malgo hae chuseyo.

butter or oil	버터나 기름은	Pŏt'ŏna kirŭmŭn
red pepper	고추는	Koch'unŭn
MSG	조미료는	Chomiryonŭn

Does it take long?	오래 걸립니까? Orae kŏllimnikka?
I'd like ___. I'll have ___.	___로 주세요. ___(ŭ)ro chuseyo.
Do you have___?	___ 있읍니까? ___ issŭmnikka?
I'd like to have some ___ first.	먼저 ___ 좀 부탁합니다. Mŏnjŏ ___ chom put'ak'am-nida.
I'd like to have ___, ___, and ___.	___, ___, ___(으)로 갖다 주세요. ___, ___, ___(ŭ)ro katta chu-seyo.

SNACKS

biscuits	비스켓	pisŭk'et
cake	케이크	k'eik'ŭ
candy	캔디	k'aendi
cocoa	코코아	k'ok'oa
coffee	커피	k'ŏp'i
coke	콜라	k'olla

cookies	쿠키	k'uk'i
crackers	크래커	k'ŭraek'ŏ
French toast	프렌치 토스트	P'ŭrench'i t'osŭt'ŭ
ham	햄	haem
hamburger	햄버거	haembŏgŏ
hard boiled eggs	삶은 계란	salmŭn kyeran
sandwich	샌드위치	saendŭwich'i
toast	토스트	t'osŭt'ŭ

FOOD

Meat

bacon	베이컨	peik'ŏn
beef	쇠고기	soegogi
beefsteak	비프스테이크	pip'ŭsŭt'eik'ŭ
corned beef	콘 비프	k'on pip'ŭ
ground beef	그라운드 비프	kŭraundŭ pip'ŭ
ground pork	그라운드 포크	kŭraundŭ p'ok'ŭ
ham	햄	haem
hamburger steak	햄버거 스테이크	haembŏgŏ sŭt'eik'ŭ

kidneys	콩팥	k'ongp'at
liver	간	kan
meatballs	미트볼	mit'ŭbol
ox tail	쇠꼬리	soekkori
pork	돼지고기	twaejigogi
pork chop	포크 찹	p'okŭ ch'ap
roast beef	로스트 비프	rosŭt'ŭ pip'ŭ
roast pork	로스트 포크	rosŭt'ŭ p'ok'ŭ
sausage	소시지	soshiji
steak	스테이크	sŭt'eik'ŭ
stew meat	스튜 미트	sŭt'yu mit'ŭ
T-bone steak	티본 스테이크	t'ibon sŭt'eik'ŭ
tongue	텅	t'ŏng
veal	송아지 고기	song-aji kogi

Bread

We'd like some bread, please.	빵으로 주세요. Ppang-ŭro chuseyo.	
French bread	프랑스 빵	P'ŭrangsŭ ppang
Italian bread	이태리 빵	It'aeri ppang
rolls	롤 빵	Rol ppang
rye	호밀 빵	Homil ppang
toast	토스트	T'osŭt'ŭ

Fish and Shellfish

English	Korean	Romanization
abalone	전복	chŏnbok
clams	대합	taehap
cod	대구	taegu
crab	게	ke
croaker	굴비	kulbi
flounder	넙치	nŏpch'i
herring	청어	ch'ŏng-ŏ
lobster	대하	taeha
mackerel	고등어	kodŭng-ŏ
mussels	홍합	honghap
oysters	굴	kul
porgy	도미	tomi
salmon	연어	yŏnŏ
sardines	정어리	chong-ŏri
shrimp	새우	sae-u
skate	홍어	hong-ŏ
spanish mackerel	삼치	samch'i
trout	송어	song-ŏ
tuna	참치	ch'amch'i
yellowtail	방어	pang-ŏ

Main Course Dishes

I'd like it <u>baked</u>.	구워 주세요.	**Kuwo** chuseyo.
boiled	끓여	Kkŭryŏ
broiled	불에 구워	Pure kuwo
fried	튀겨	T'wigyŏ
grilled	석쇠에 구워	Sŏksoe-e kuwo
roasted	로스트로 해	Rosŭt'ŭro hae
sautéed	살짝 튀겨	Saltchak t'wigyŏ
rare	설익혀	Sŏrik'yŏ
medium	중간으로 해	Chungganŭro hae
well-done	잘 익혀	Chal ik'yŏ

Soup

chicken soup	치킨 수프	ch'ik'in sup'ŭ
consommé	콩소메	k'ongsome
corn soup	콘 수프	k'on sup'ŭ
cream soup	크림 수프	k'ŭrim sup'ŭ
onion soup	어니언 수프	ŏniŏn sup'ŭ
tomato soup	토마토 수프	t'omat'o sup'ŭ
vegetable soup	야채 스프	yach'ae sup'ŭ

Appetizers

| caviar | 캐비아 | k'aebia |

celery and olives	셀러리 올리브	sellŏri ollibŭ
cheese	치즈	ch'ijŭ
clams on the half-shell	대합	taehap
crabmeat	게살	kesal
ham	햄	haem
herring	청어	ch'ŏng-ŏ
lobster	대하	taeha
mushrooms	버섯	pŏsŏt
melon	멜런	mellŏn
oysters on the half-shell	굴	kul
salami	살라미	sallami
sardines	정어리	chŏng-ŏri
sausage	소시지	soshiji

Fowl

chicken	치킨	ch'ik'in
chicken thigh	닭 다리	tak tari
duck	오리	ori
quail	메추라기	mech'uragi
rabbit	토끼	t'okki
turkey	칠면조	ch'ilmyŏnjo

radish	무우	mu-u
red pepper	고추	koch'u
spring onion	실파	shilp'a
spinach	시금치	shigŭmch'i
string beans	강남콩	kangnamk'ong
tomato	토마토	t'omat'o
turnip	순무	sunmu

Nuts

almonds	아몬드	amondŭ
chestnuts	밤	pam
peanuts	땅콩	ttangk'ong
walnuts	호도	hodo

Pasta, Rice, and Potatoes

baked potato	군 감자	kun kamja
boiled potato	찐 감자	tchin kamja
French fries	프렌치 프라이	P'ŭrench'i p'ŭrai
macaroni	마카로니	mak'aroni
mashed potatoes	매쉬트 퍼테이토	maeshit'ŭ p'ŏt'eit'o
rice	밥	pap
spaghetti	스파게티	sŭp'aget'i

Salad and Dressing

green salad	그린 샐러드	kŭrin saellŏdŭ
tomato salad	토마토 샐러드	t'omat'o saellŏdŭ

Vegetables

broccoli	브라컬리	pŭrak'ŏlli
cabbage	양배추	yangbaech'u
carrot	당근	tanggŭn
cauliflower	콜러플라워	k'ollŏp'ŭllawo
celery	셀러리	sellŏri
corn	콘	k'on
cucumber	오이	oi
eggplant	가지	kaji
endive	꽃상치	kkotsangch'i
garlic	마늘	manŭl
green pepper	피망	p'imang
leek	부추	puch'u
lettuce	상치	sangch'i
onion	양파	yangp'a
parsley	파슬리	p'asŭlli
potato	감자	kamja

Accompaniments

butter	버터	pŏt'ŏ
cream	크림	k'ŭrim
honey	꿀	kkul
jam	잼	chaem
ketchup	케첩	k'ech'ŏp
lemon	레먼	lemŏn
margarine	마가린	magarin
marmalade	마멀레이드	mamŏlleidŭ
mayonnaise	마요네즈	mayonejŭ
mustard	겨자	kyŏja
oil	기름	kirŭm
olive oil	올리브유	olibŭyu
pepper	후추	huch'u
salt	소금	sogŭm
sugar	설탕	sŏlt'ang
syrup	시럽	shirŏp
vinegar	식초	shikch'o

Desserts

cake	케이크	k'eik'ŭ

chocolate cake	초콜렛 케이크	Ch'ok'ollet k'eik'ǔ
cookies	쿠키	k'uk'i
custard	카스테라	k'asǔt'era
ice cream	아이스크림	aisǔk'ǔrim
coffee ice cream	커피 아이스 크림	k'ǒp'i aisǔ k'ǔrim
chocolate sundae	초콜렛 선데이	ch'ok'ollet sǒndei
vanilla ice cream	바닐라 아이스 크림	panilla aisǔ k'ǔrim
pastry	페이스트리	p'eisǔt'ǔri
chestnut tart	체스넛 타트	ch'esǔnǒt t'at'ǔ
cream puff	슈크림	syuk'ǔrim
fruit tart	프루트 타트	p'ǔrut'ǔ t'at'ǔ
pie	파이	p'ai
apple pie	애플 파이	aep'ǔl p'ai
lemon meringue	레몬 머랭	lemon mǒraeng
pudding	푸딩	p'uding
sherbet	셔빗	syǒbit
melon sherbet	멜런 셔빗	mellǒn syǒbit
orange sherbet	오렌지 셔빗	orenji syǒbit
pineapple sher-bet	파인애플 셔빗	p'ainaep'ǔl syǒbit
soufflé	수플레이	sup'ǔllei

chocolate soufflé	초콜렛 수플레이
	ch'ok'ollet sup'ŭllei
grapefruit soufflé	그레이프프루트 수플레이
	kŭreip'ŭp'ŭrut'ŭ sup'ŭllei

Cheese

What kind of cheese do you have?	치즈는 어떤 종류가 있읍니까?
	Ch'ijŭnŭn ŏttŏn chongnyuga issŭmnikka?
Do you have a cheese tray?	치즈 담는 쟁반 있읍니까?
	Chijŭ tamnŭn chaengban i-ssŭmnikka?
Can I see them (the cheeses)?	좀 볼 수 있읍니까?
	Chom pol su issŭmnikka?
Give me some blue cheese, please.	블루 치즈로 부탁합니다.
	Pŭllu ch'ijŭro put'ak'amnida.

| Edam cheese | 이덤으로 | Idŏmŭro |
| Swiss cheese | 스위스 치즈로 | Sŭwisŭ ch'ijŭro |

| Please bring some crackers, too. | 크래커도 좀 부탁합니다. |
| | K'ŭraek'ŏdo chom put'ak'amnida. |

Fruit

apple	사과	sagwa
banana	바나나	panana
grapes	포도	p'odo
kiwi	키위	k'iwi

melon	멜런	mellŏn
orange	오렌지	orenji
papaya	파파야	p'ap'aya
peach	복숭아	poksung-a
Korean pear	배	pae
persimmon	감	kam
pineapple	파인애플	p'ainaep'ŭl
strawberries	딸기	ttalgi
tangerine	귤	kyul

Eating and Drinking Out

DRINKS

Non-Alcoholic

| Is the juice fresh? | 주스 신선한 겁니까? Chusŭ shinsŏnhan kŏmnikka? |
| Do you have diet soda? | 다이어트 음료 있읍니까? Taiŏt'ŭ ŭmnyo issŭmnikka? |

Coca Cola	코카 콜라	K'ok'a K'olla
iced coffee	냉커피	naengk'ŏp'i
fruit juice	과일 주스	kwail chusŭ
apple juice	사과 주스	sagwa chusŭ
grape juice	포도 주스	p'odo chusŭ
orange juice	오렌지 주스	orenji chusŭ
pineapple juice	파인애플 주스	p'ainaep'ŭl chusŭ

tomato juice	토마토 주스	t'omat'o chusŭ
ginger ale	진저 에일	chinjŏ eil
milk	밀크	milk'ŭ
mineral water	미네랄 워터	mineral wot'ŏ
Pepsi Cola	펩시 콜라	P'epshi K'olla
tea	홍차	hongch'a
tea with lemon	레먼차	lemŏnch'a
iced tea	냉홍차	naenghongch'a
tonic water	토닉 워터	t'onik wot'ŏ

Alcoholic

beer	맥주	maekchu
draught beer	생맥주	saengmaekchu
light beer	라이트 비어	lait'ŭ piŏ
brandy	브랜디	pŭraendi
cognac	코냑	k'onyak
bourbon	버번	pŏbŏn
bourbon and soda	버번 하이볼	pŏbŏn haibol
bourbon and water	버번 워터	pŏbŏn wot'ŏ
bourbon on the rocks	버번 온 더 락	pŏbŏn on tŏ rak

straight bourbon	버번 스트레이트	pŏbŏn sŭt'ŭreit'ŭ
Mai Tai	마이 타이	Mai T'ai
Manhattan	맨해턴	Maenhaet'ŏn
martini	마티니	mat'ini
port	포트 와인	p'ot'ŭ wain
rum	럼	rŏm
gin	진	chin
gin and tonic	진 토닉	chin t'onik
gin fizz	진 피즈	chin p'ijŭ
gin on the rocks	진 온 더 락	chin on tŏ rak
screwdriver	스크루드라이버	sŭk'ŭrudŭraibŏ
scotch	스카치	sŭk'ach'i
scotch and soda	스카치 하이볼	sŭk'ach'i haibol
scotch and water	스카치 워터	sŭk'ach'i wot'ŏ
scotch on the rocks	스카치 온 더 락	sŭk'ach'i on tŏ rak
straight scotch	스카치 스트레이트	sŭk'ach'i sŭt'ŭreit'ŭ
sherry	세리	syeri
vodka	보드카	pŏdŭk'a

vodka and tonic	보드카 토닉	podŭk'a t'onik
vodka on the rocks	보드카 온 더 락	podŭk'a on tŏ rak

Do you have wine?
포도주 있읍니까?
P'odoju issŭmnikka?

whiskey
위스키 Wisŭk'i

I want it straight, please.
스트레이트로 주세요.
Sŭt'ŭreit'ŭro chuseyo.

Make it double, please.
더블로 주세요.
Tŏbŭllo chuseyo.

With lemon please.
레먼을 넣어 주시죠.
Lemŏnŭl nŏŏ chushijyo.

an olive
올리브를 Ollibŭrŭl

Ordering Wine

Do you recommend anything in particular?
어떤 것이 좋습니까?
Ŏttŏn kŏshi chossŭmnikka?

Where is it from?
어디 산입니까?
Ŏdi sanimnikka?

What's the name of it?
이거 무슨 술입니까?
Igŏ musŭn surimnikka?

What's the vintage?
몇 년 산입니까?
Myŏn nyŏn sanimnikka?

How much is a bottle of ____?
____ 한 병에 얼맙니까?
____ han pyŏng-e ŏlmamnikka?

I'll try this.	이것으로 해 보죠. Igŏsŭro hae pojyo.
Can we order by the glass?	글래스로 주문해도 됩니까? Kŭllaesŭro chumunhaedo toemnikka?
I'd like a glass of white wine.	백포도주로 한 잔 주세요. Paekp'odojuro han chan chuseyo.
Bring me a bottle, please.	한 병 부탁합니다. <u>Han pyŏng</u> put'ak'amnida.
a half bottle	반 병 Pan pyŏng
Do you have a wine list?	와인 리스트 좀 보여 주세요. Wain lisŭt'ŭ chom poyŏ chuseyo.
Do you have French wine?	프랑스산 포도주 있읍니까? <u>P'ŭrangsŭsan</u> p'odoju issŭmnikka?
American Italian Japanese	미국산 Miguksan 이태리산 It'aerisan 일본산 Ilbonsan
We'll have white wine.	백포도주로 주세요. <u>Paekp'odojuro</u> chuseyo.
red wine	레드 와인으로 Redŭ wainŭro
rose	로제로 Rojero
Do you have anything dry?	드라이 와인 있읍니까? Tŭrai wain issŭmnikka?
Is it dry?	이거 드라이입니까? Igŏ tŭraiimnikka?

| Do you have a house wine? | 이 집의 특별 와인 있읍니까? I chibŭi t'ŭkpyŏl wain issŭmnikka? |

ADDITIONAL REQUESTS

| Could you bring me some more water, please? | 여기 물 좀 더 주세요. Yŏgi mul chom tŏ chuseyo. |

bread	빵	ppang
butter	버터	pŏt'ŏ
wine	술	sul

| Could you bring me another bottle of wine, please? | 여기 술 한 병 더 주세요. Yŏgi sul han pyŏng tŏ chuseyo. |

| another glass of wine | 술 한 잔 sul han chan |

| Show me the menu again, please. | 메뉴 좀 다시 가져와 보세요. Menyu chom tashi kajyŏwa poseyo. |

| Waiter/Waitress! | 이봐요! Ibwayo! |

| Could you bring me a knife, please? | 나이프 좀 갖다 주세요. Naip'ŭ chom katta chuseyo. |

a fork	포크	P'ok'ŭ
a spoon	스푼	Sŭp'un
a glass	글래스	Kŭllaesŭ
a plate	접시	Chŏpshi
a bowl	대접	Taejŏp
a napkin	냅킨	Naepk'in
some toothpicks	이쑤시개	Issushigae

COMPLAINTS

This is overcooked.	이거 요리가 너무 익었어요. Igŏ yoriga nŏmu igŏssŏyo.
This isn't hot.	이거 덥지가 않아요. Igŏ tŏpchiga anayo.
Would you get the manager, please?	매니저 좀 불러 오세요. Maenijŏ chom pullŏ oseyo.
It's not what I ordered.	이건 내가 주문한 게 아닙니다. Igŏn naega chumunhan ke animnida.
The meat is too rare.	고기가 너무 설익었어요. Kogiga nŏmu sorigŏssŏyo.
The meat is too well done.	고기가 너무 익었어요. Kogiga nŏmu igŏssŏyo.
This is undercooked.	이거 요리가 덜 됐어요. Igŏ yoriga tŏl twaessŏyo.

CHECKS

Is this correct?	이거 정확한 겁니까? Igŏ chŏnghwak'an kŏmnikka?
I don't think the bill is right.	이 계산서 틀린 것 같은데요. I kyesansŏ t'ŭllin kŏt kat'ŭndeyo.
What are these charges for?	이건 무슨 대금입니까? Igŏn musŭn taegŭmimnikka?

I didn't order this.
이건 주문하지 않았는데요. Igŏn chumunhaji anannŭndeyo.

May I have a receipt, please?
영수증 좀 부탁해요. Yŏngsujŭng chom put'ak'aeyo.

Check, please.
여기 계산서 좀 가져오세요. Yŏgi kyesansŏ chom kajyŏoseyo.

Separate checks, please.
계산서는 개인별로 부탁합니다. Kyesansŏnŭn kaeinbyŏllo put'ak'amnida.

Do you take credit cards?
크레디트 카드 받습니까? K'ŭredit'ŭ k'adŭ passŭmnikka?

Which credit cards do you take?
어떤 크레디트 카드를 받습니까? Ŏttŏn k'ŭredit'ŭ k'adŭrŭl passŭmnikka?

Are the tax and service charge included?
세금과 서비스료가 포함된 겁니까? Segŭmgwa sŏbisŭryoga p'ohamdoen kŏmnikka?

Dining is one of the most pleasurable aspects of visiting Korea. You have a choice of good Western-style restaurants, and an almost endless variety of Korean food to explore. If you crave American fast food, you can even get that. You won't go hungry in Korea!

Korean-style eating is unlike Western style. You use chopsticks, the food is different, and table manners are different as well. Therefore, we have separate sections for the two styles.

Tipping

You may not tip in most Korean hotels and restaurants. A service charge will be added to your bill

Towels

Whenever and wherever you drink or dine in Korea, you'll begin with a refreshing hot or cold damp towel for your hands and face.

KOREAN FOOD AND DRINKS

General Inquiries

Would you recommend a good *hoe* restaurant?	좋은 횟집 하나 소개해 주시겠읍니까? Choŭn hoetchip hana sogaehae chushigessŭmnikka?
the best	최고 Ch'oego
an inexpensive	비싸지 않은 Pissaji anŭn
How much will it cost per person?	일인분에 얼마나 합니까? Irinbune ŏlmana hamnikka?
I'd like to have *pulgogi*?	불고기로 주세요. Pulgogiro chuseyo.
Is there a *naengmyŏn* restaurant neaby?	이 근처에 냉면집 있읍니까? I kŭnch'ŏe naengmyŏnchip issŭmnikka?

I'd like to go to a *haejangkuk* restaurant.	해장국집에 가고 싶습니다. Haejangkukchibe kago shipsŭmnida.

Arriving

We'll wait till a table is available.	기다렸다 테이블에 앉겠읍니다. Kidaryŏtta t'eibŭre ankessŭmnida.
How long do we have to wait?	얼마나 기다려야 합니까? Ŏlmana kidaryŏya hamnikka?
Either a Korean room or a table is fine.	방이나 테이블이나 다 좋습니다. Pang-ina t'eibŭrina ta chossŭmnida.
Could you seat us now?	이제 앉아도 됩니까? Ije anjado toemnikka?
Good afternoon./ Good evening.	수고하십니다. Sugohashimnida.
My name is ___. I have a reservation at 6.	___(이)라고 합니다. 6시에 예약을 했읍니다. ___(i)rago hamnida. Yŏsŏtshie yeyagŭl haessŭmnida.
Is a table <u>available</u>?	테이블 있읍니까? <u>T'eibŭl</u> issŭmnikka?
Korean room	방 Pang

At the Table

What's good today?	오늘은 뭐가 좋습니까? Onŭrŭn mwoga chossŭmnikka?

Do you serve anything special for this region?	이 지방 특식 있읍니까? I chi-bang t'ŭkshik issŭmnikka?
Is it <u>raw</u>?	이건 <u>날것입니까</u>? Igŏn <u>nalgŏshimnikka</u>?
cooked	익힌 겁니까 ik'in kŏmnikka
hot(spicy)	매운 겁니까 maeun kŏmnikka
salty	소금기가 있는 겁니까 sogŭm-kiga innŭn kŏmnikka
How is it cooked?	그건 어떻게 요리한 겁니까? Kŭgŏn ŏttŏk'e yorihan kŏm-nikka?
I'll have this.	이걸로 부탁합니다. Igŏllo put'ak'amnida.
Can you make an assorted dish?	모듬 요리 됩니까? Modŭm yori toemnikka?
Give us <u>two</u> large bottles of beer, please.	맥주 큰 잔으로 <u>두 개</u> 부탁해요. Maekchu kŭn chanŭro <u>tu kae</u> put'ak'aeyo.
three	세 개 se kae
four	네 개 ne kae
five	다섯 개 tasŏt kae
Give me <u>whiskey and water</u>, please.	<u>위스키 워터</u>로 부탁합니다. <u>Wisŭk'i wot'ŏro</u> put'ak'am-nida.
makkŏlli	막걸리 Makkŏlli
soju	소주 Soju

tongdongju　　　동동주　Tongdongju

Give us two bottles of <u>hot</u> *ch'ŏngju*, please.
데운 청주로 2병 부탁합니다.
<u>Teun</u> ch'ŏngjŭro tu pyŏng put'ak'amnida.

cold　　　　　찬　Ch'an

Do you have non-alcoholic drinks?
알콜분 없는 음료 있읍니까?
Alk'olbun ŏmnŭn ŭmnyo issŭmnikka?

Could you bring something to eat with drinks?
뭐 안주 될 만한 것 좀 가져오세요.
Mwo anju toel manhan kŏt chom kajyŏooseyo.

What kinds of appetizers do you have?
반주로 어떤 것이 있읍니까?
Panjuro ŏttŏn kŏshi issŭmnikka?

Could you bring us something good?
좋은 것으로 좀 갖다 주세요.
Choŭn kŏsŭro chom katta chuseyo.

Do you have a set meal/table d'hote?
정식 됩니까?
Chŏngshik toemnikka?

Is there a menu in English?
영어로 된 메뉴 있읍니까?
Yŏng-ŏro toen menyu issŭmnikka?

No drinks, thank you.
술은 놔두세요. 감사합니다.
Surŭn nwaduseyo. Kamsahamnida.

<u>Ginseng tea</u>, please.
인삼차로 주세요.
<u>Insamch'aro</u> chuseyo.

water　　　　물 좀　mul chom

What kinds of drinks do you serve?	어떤 술이 있읍니까? Ŏttŏn suri issŭmnikka?

Bring us *ch'ŏngju*, please.	청주로 주세요. Ch'ŏngjuro chuseyo.
beer	맥주 maekchu
whiskey	위스키 wisŭk'i

Give us one large bottle of beer, please.	맥주 큰 잔으로 하나 부탁해요. Maekchu k'ŭn chanŭro hana put'ak'aeyo.
small bottle	작은 잔으로 chagŭn chanŭro

Some Basic Food

cooked rice	밥	pap
pickled vegetables	김치	kimch'i
soy sauce	간장	kanjang
hot pepper paste	고추장	koch'ujang
red pepper	고춧가루	koch'utkaru
pepper	후추	huch'u

Korean cuisine is characterized by freshness, presentation, and variety. Some restaurants offer a selection of different kinds of dishes. Others specialize in one type of food or style of cooking, sometimes prepared in front of you at your table or on a grill. Many (though not all) Korean eateries display replicas of their offerings outside the front door in glass cases. The dishes look quite real and may tempt you to enter. It makes ordering easy: just point to what you want. You can't do this everywhere, but sometimes it works quite well!

Rice(밥, *Pap*) is the main dish, followed by *kimch'i*(김치), a pungent, fermented dish generally comprising cabbage or turnips seasoned with salt, garlic, leeks, ginger, red pepper and shellfish. Soup(국, *Kuk*), spicy or bland and generally containing meat, fish or seaweed, is also a vital part of almost every meal. Some of the most popular are made of soybean paste and curd. Rounding out the meal are a number of dishes called *panch'an*(반찬) that generally include parboiled vegetables, herbs and roots that are seasoned with sesame oil, garlic, soy sauce and ground and toasted sesame seeds. A seafood or meat dish is often included.

There are a number of holiday foods as well as special dishes that are a must for important celebrations. These include *ttŏk*(떡), rice cakes dusted with roasted soy, barley or millet or embellished with aromatic mugwort leaves, and *ttŏkkuk*(떡국) a rice-dumpling soup that is a must on New Year's Day. Dishes called *anju* (안주) always accompany liquor or *sul*(술). These generally consist of meat, sea food, or dried fish, nuts and fruit.

Beef, pork and fish courses are usually grilled over burning charcoal. *Pulgogi*(불고기), marinated beef slices grilled over burning charcoal, is probably the best known meat dish in Korea.

At an elegant Korean dinner, the first course might be *kujŏlp'an*(구절판) which is somewhat similar to the French hors-d'oeuvre trays. The cooked meat and vegetables are arranged on a large platter in a circle of contrasting color. In the center of the platter is a mound of paper-thin pancakes. The guest picks up one of the pancakes with his chopsticks, selects some of the meat and vegetables, places them on the pancake, rolls up the pancake and pops it into his mouth.

One of the main courses could be *shinsŏllo* (신선로), or angel's brazier, a mixture of meat, fish and vegetables and bean curd over which beef broth has been poured. All this cooks and bubbles in a brass bowl enclosed in a brazier filled with blazing charcoal.

Chopsticks are easy! Rest one at the base of the thumb and index finger and between the ends of the ring and middle finger. That chopstick remains stationary. Grasp the other between the ends of the thumb and the first two fingers, and enjoy your food.

SOME POPULAR KOREAN FOODS

Meals

iced noodles	냉면	*naengmyŏn*
kimch'i stew	김치 찌개	*kimch'i tchigae*
three-ply pork	삼겹살	*samgyŏpsal*
rib	갈비	*kalbi*
sirloin	등심	*tŭngshim*
sliced raw fish	회	*hoe*

Liquors

distilled spirits	소주	*soju*
raw rice wine	막걸리	*makkŏlli*
similar to Japanese sake	청주	*ch'ŏngju*

SOMETHING DIFFERENT

The *yojŏng* (요정) is a traditional Korean restaurant in a building all its own, usually in a garden. You dine in private Korean-style rooms, with waitresses at your table throughout the meal to assist you. Food is served in many small courses, on exquisite ceramics and lacquer. If requested, *kisaeng*, Korean geisha, may entertain. It's an elegant, extremely expensive way to dine. Many *yojŏng* require an introduction from another customer before giving you a reservation. A good way to experience the *yojŏng* is with a Korean friend or host!

Personal Services

REPAIRS

Camera

There's a problem with the <u>exposure counter</u>.	<u>필름 카운터가</u> 고장났읍니다. <u>P'illŭm kaunt'ŏga</u> kojangna-ssŭmnida.
light meter	노출계가 Noch'ulgyega
range finder	거리계가 Kŏrigyega
shutter	셔터가 Syŏt'ŏga
How much will it cost to fix it?	고치는 데 얼마나 듭니까? Koch'inŭn te ŏlmana tŭmnikka?
I'd like it as soon as possible.	되도록이면 빨리 고치면 좋겠읍니다. Toedorogimyŏn ppalli koch'imyŏn chok'essŭmnida.
When will it be ready?	언제쯤 됩니까? Ŏnjetchŭm toemnikka?
There's something wrong with this camera.	카메라에 이상이 있는 것 같습니다. K'amera-e isang-i innŭn kŏt kassŭmnida.
Can you fix it?	이거 고칠 수 있읍니까? Igŏ koch'il su issŭmnikka?

Watch

It's stopped.	가질 않아요. Kajil anayo.

| I need a crystal. | 유리 좀 끼워 주세요.
Yuri chom kkiwo chuseyo. |

an hour hand	시침	Shich'im
a minute hand	분침	Punch'im
a screw	나사	Nasa
a second hand	초침	Ch'och'im
a spring	스프링	Sŭp'ŭring

| When will it be ready? | 언제쯤 됩니까?
Ŏnjetchŭm toemnikka? |

| May I have a receipt? | 영수증 좀 부탁합니다. Yŏngsu-jŭng chom put'ak'amnida. |

| I need a battery for this watch. | 이 시계 전지 좀 갈아 주세요.
I shigye chŏnji chom kara chuseyo. |

| Can you fix this watch/clock? | 이 시계 좀 고쳐 주세요.
I shigye chom koch'yŏ chuseyo. |

| Can you look at it? | 이것 좀 봐 주시겠어요?
Igŏt chom pwa chushigessŏyo? |

| Can you clean it? | 이거 청소 좀 해 주세요. Igŏ ch'ŏngso chom hae chuseyo. |

| I dropped it. | 떨어뜨렸어요. Ttŏrŏttŭryŏssŏyo. |

| It doesn't run well. | 잘 안 가요. Chal an kayo. |

| It's slow. | 느려요. Nŭryŏyo. |
| fast | 빨라요 Ppallayo |

| The chain is broken. | 줄이 끊어졌읍니다.
Churi kkŭnŏjyŏssŭmnida. |

Shoes

I want these shoes repaired.	이 구두 좀 고쳐 주세요. I kudu chom koch'yŏ chuseyo.
I need new <u>heels</u>.	힐 좀 갈아 주세요. <u>Hil</u> chom kara chuseyo.
soles heels and soles	창 Ch'ang 힐하고 창 Hirhago ch'ang
Would you polish them, too?	그리고 좀 닦아 주세요. Kŭrigo chom takka chuseyo.
When will they be ready?	언제쯤 되죠? Ŏnjetchŭm toejyo?
The heel of my high-heeled shoes <u>came off</u>.	힐이 떨어져 나갔읍니다. Hiri ttŏrŏjyŏ <u>nagassŭmnida</u>.
broke	부러졌읍니다 purŏjyŏ- ssŭmnida
Can you fix it while I wait?	기다릴 동안에 고칠 수 있읍니까? Kidaril tong-ane koch'il su issŭmnikka?

LAUNDRY/DRY-CLEANING

I want this washed.	이것 좀 세탁해 주세요. Igŏt chom set'ak'ae chuseyo.
When will it be ready?	언제쯤 될까요? Ŏnjetchŭm toelkkayo?

Personal Services

I need it for to-night.

오늘 밤에 필요합니다.
Onŭl pame p'iryohamnida.

tomorrow
the day after tomorrow

내일 Naeil
모레 More

Could you do it as soon as possible?

가능하면 빨리 좀 해 주세요.
Kanŭnghamyŏn ppalli chom hae chuseyo.

Can you get the stain out?

이 얼룩 뺄 수 있어요?
I ŏlluk ppael su issŏyo?

Can you sew this button on?

이 단추 좀 달아 주세요.
I tanch'u chom tara chuseyo.

I want my shirts boxed.

와이셔츠는 상자에 좀 넣어 놔 주세요. Waisyŏch'ŭnŭn sangja-e chom nŏŏ nwa chuseyo.

folded
on hangers

좀 접어 chom chŏbŏ
옷걸이에 좀 걸어 ŏtkŏrie chom kŏrŏ

What time shall I come for them?

언제 오면 될까요?
Ŏnje omyŏn toelkkayo?

Do you have laundry service in this hotel?

이 호텔 세탁 서비스 있읍니까?
I hot'el set'ak sŏbisŭ issŭmnikka?

Do you have dry cleaning service in this hotel?

이 호텔 드라이클리닝 서비스 있읍니까? I hot'el tŭrai k'ŭllining sŏbisŭ issŭmnikka?

Where is the nearest laundry?

제일 가까운 세탁소가 어디에 있읍니까? Cheil kakkaun set'aksoga ŏdie issŭmnikka?

dry cleaner	드라이 클리닝 센터가 tŭrai k'ŭllining sent'ŏga
I want this dry cleaned.	이것 좀 드라이 해 주세요. Igŏt chom tŭrai hae chuseyo.
I want this ironed /pressed.	이것 좀 다려 주세요. Igŏt chom taryŏ chuseyo.
I want this mended.	이것 좀 고쳐 주세요. Igŏt chom koch'yŏ chuseyo.

AT THE HAIRDRESSER

Can you give me a color rinse?	염색 좀 부탁합니다. Yŏmsaek chom put'ak'amnida.
haircut	커트 K'ŏt'ŭ
permanent	파마 P'ama
I want auburn.	갈색으로 해 주세요. Kalsaegŭro hae chuseyo.
blond	금발로 Kŭmballo
brunette	흑색으로 Hŭksaegŭro
a darker color	더 진한 색으로 Tŏ chinhan saegŭro
a lighter color	더 연한 색으로 Tŏ yŏnhan saegŭro
the same color	같은 색으로 Kat'ŭn saegŭro
Don't apply any hair spray.	헤어 스프레이는 쓰지 마세요. Heŏ sŭp'ŭreinŭn ssŭji maseyo.
Not too much hair spray.	헤어 스프레이를 너무 많이 쓰지 마세요. Heŏ sŭp'ŭreirŭl nŏmu mani ssŭji maseyo.

I want bangs.

단발로 해 주세요.
Tanballo hae chuseyo.

a bun
it curly
it wavy

뒤로 묶어   Twiro mukkŏ
복아   Pokka
웨이브로   Weibŭro

Is it done?

됐읍니까?   Twaessŭmnikka?

Thank you very much.

감사합니다.   Kamsahamnida.

How much do I owe you?

얼맙니까?   Ŏlmamnikka?

Is there a beauty parlor(hairdresser) <u>near</u> the hotel?

호텔 근처에 미용실이 있읍니까?
Hot'el kŭnch'ŏe miyongshiri issŭmnikka?

in

안에   ane

Do you know where a good beauty parlor (hairdresser) is?

미용실은 어디가 좋습니까? Miyongshirŭn ŏdiga chossŭmnikka?

What are the business hours?

몇 시부터 몇 시까지 합니까?
Myŏt shibut'ŏ myŏt shikkaji hamnikka?

Are they used to foreigners' hair?

외국인 머리를 많이 해 본 곳입니까? Oegugin mŏrirŭl mani hae pon koshimnikka?

Is it an expensive place?

거기 비쌉니까?
Kŏgi pissamnikka?

Do I have to wait long?

오래 기다려야 합니까?
Orae kidaryŏya hamnikka?

AT THE BARBER

Just a trim, please.	다듬어만 주세요. Tadŭmŏman chuseyo.
Short in back, long in front.	뒤는 짧게, 앞은 길게 해 주세요. Twinŭn tchalke, ap'ŭn kilge hae chuseyo.
Leave it long.	좀 길게 해 주세요. Chom kilge hae chuseyo.
I want it (very) short.	짧게 잘라 주세요. Tchalke challa chuseyo.
You can cut a little <u>in back</u>.	<u>뒤만</u> 좀 잘라 주세요. <u>Twiman</u> chom challa chuseyo.

in front	앞만	Amman
off the top	위만	Wiman
on the sides	옆만	Yŏmman

I part my hair <u>on the left</u>.	가리마는 <u>왼쪽에</u> 타·주세요. Karimanŭn <u>oentchoge</u> t'a chuseyo.
on the right	오른쪽에 orŭntchoge
I comb my hair straight back.	머리는 뒤로 바로 넘겨 주세요. Mŏrinŭn twiro paro nŏmgyŏ chuseyo.
Cut a little bit more here.	여기 좀 더 잘라 주세요. Yŏgi chom tŏ challa chuseyo.
Use the scissors only.	가위로만 잘라 주세요. Kawiroman challa chuseyo.

Please trim my beard.	턱수염 좀 다듬어 주세요. T'ŏksuyŏm chom tadŭmŏ chuseyo.
mustache sideburns	콧수염 K'ossuyŏm 구레나룻 Kurenarut
Thank you very much.	감사합니다. Kamsahamnida.
How much do I owe you?	얼맙니까? Ŏlmamnikka?
It's fine that way.	그러니까 좋군요. Kŭrŏnikka chok'unnyo.
I don't want tonic.	양모제는 바르지 마세요. Yangmojenŭn parŭji maseyo.
I don't want grease.	기름은 바르지 마세요. Kirŭmŭn parŭji maseyo.
I don't want hair spray.	헤어 스프레이는 쓰지 마세요. Heŏ sŭp'ŭreinŭn ssŭji maseyo.
Does this hotel have a barber?	이 호텔에 이발소가 있읍니까? I hot'ere ibalsoga issŭmnikka?
Do you know where a good barbershop is?	좋은 이발소가 어디에 있는지 아십니까? Choŭn ibalsoga ŏdie innŭnji ashimnikka?
Do I have to wait long?	오래 기다려야 합니까? Orae kidaryŏya hamnikka?
How muh does a haircut cost there?	거기 이발 요금이 얼맙니까? Kŏgi ibal yogŭmi ŏlmamnikka?
Whose turn is it?	누구 차례입니까? Nugu ch'aryeimnikka?

I don't have much time.

시간이 얼마 없읍니다.
Shigani ŏlma ŏpsŭmnida.

I want a haircut.

이발 좀 부탁합니다.
Ibal chom put'ak'amnida.

I want a shave.

면도 좀 해주세요.
Myŏndo chom haechuseyo.

Don't cut it too short, please.

너무 짧게 깎지 마세요. Nŏmu tchalke kkakchi maseyo.

Money Exchange

BANKING TERMS

amount	금액	kŭmaek
banker	은행가	ŭnhaengga
bill	지폐	chip'ye
to borrow	빌다	pilda
capital	자본	chabon
cashier	출납원	ch'ullabwon
check	수표	sup'yo
to endorse	이서하다	isŏhada
income	수입	suip
interest rate	이율	iyul
investment	투자	t'uja
to lend	대출하다	taech'urhada
loss	손실	sonshil
to make change	잔돈으로 바꾸다	chandonŭro pakkuda
mortgage	저당	chŏdang
to open an account	계좌를 개설하다	kyejwarŭl kaesŏrhada

premium	프리미엄	p'ŭrimiŏm
profit	이윤	iyun
secretary	비서	pisŏ
safe	금고	kŭmgo
signature	서명〔사인〕	sŏmyŏng〔sain〕

AIRPORT MONEY EXCHANGE

I'd like to change dollars into <u>won</u>.

달러를 원화로 바꾸고 싶습니다.
<u>Tallŏrŭl</u> wonhwaro pakkugo shipsŭmnida.

    pounds

파운드를   P'aundŭrŭl

What's today's dollar-won exchange rate?

오늘 달러 환율이 얼맙니까?
Onŭl tallŏ hwannyuri ŏlmamnikka?

I'd like to change <u>100</u> dollars to won.

100 달러를 원화로 바꾸고 싶습니다. <u>Paek tallŏrŭl</u> wonhwaro pakkugo shipsŭmnida.

200	Ibaek
300	Sambaek
400	Sabaek
500	Obaek
600	Yukpaek
700	Ch'ilbaek
800	P'albaek
900	Kubaek

Do I need to fill out a form?

서식에 기재해야 합니까?
Sŏshige kijaehaeya hamnikka?

| Here's my passport. | 제 여권[패스포트]입니다. |
| | Che yŏkwon[p'aesŭp'ot'ŭ]imnida. |

I'd like the money in <u>large</u> bills.	고액권으로 부탁합니다.
	Koaekkwonŭro put'ak'amnida.
small	소액권으로 Soaekkwonŭro

| I want some change, too. | 잔돈도 좀 부탁합니다. Chandondo chom put'ak'amnida. |

| Give me one 10,000 won, two 5,000 won, and three 1,000 won bills, please. | 10,000원권 1장, 5,000원권 2장, 1,000원권 3장으로 부탁합니다. |
| | Manwonkwon han chang, och'ŏnwonkwon tu chang, ch'ŏnwonkwon sŏk chang-ŭro put'ak'amnida. |

| Where can I change <u>money</u>? | 돈 바꾸는 곳이 어디에 있읍니까? |
| | Ton pakkunŭn koshi ŏdie issŭmnikka? |

dollars	달러	Tallŏ
traveler's checks	여행자 수표	Yŏhaengja sup'yo
a personal check	개인용 수표	Kaeinnyong sup'yo

| Is there a hotel nearby where I can change my traveler's checks to won? | 이 근처에 여행자 수표를 원화로 바꿀 수 있는 호텔이 있읍니까? |
| | I kŭnch'ŏe yŏhaengja sup'yorŭl wonhwaro pakkul su innŭn hot'eri issŭmnikka? |

| Can I change foreign currency into won at the front desk? | 프론트에서 외화를 원화로 바꿀 수 있읍니까? P'ŭront'ŭesŏ oehwarŭl wonhwaro pakkul su issŭmnikka? |

Where is a bank?	은행이 어디에 있읍니까? Ŭnhaeng-i ŏdie issŭmnikka?
the American Express office	아메리칸 익스프레스 사무실이 Amerik'an Iksŭp'ŭresŭ samushiri
the Diners Club office	다이너스 클럽 사무실이 Ta-inŏsŭ k'ŭllŏp samushiri
the Master Card office	마스터 카드 사무실이 Masŭt'ŏ k'adŭ samushiri
the Visa office	비자 사무실이 Pija samushiri
Where's the money exchange?	환전소가 어디에 있읍니까? Hwanjŏnsoga ŏdie issŭmnikka?
Is the money exchange open?	환전소 열었읍니까? Hwanjŏnso yŏrŏssŭmnikka?
May I cash traveler's checks?	여행자 수표를 현금으로 바꿀 수 있읍니까? Yŏhaengja sup'yorŭl hyŏn-gŭmŭro pakkul su issŭmnikka?
Which window do I use to change foreign money to won?	외화를 원화로 바꾸려 하는데 어느 창구를 이용해야 합니까? Oehwarŭl wonhwaro pakkuryŏ hanŭnde ŏnŭ ch'anggurŭl iyonghaeya hamnikka?
traveler's checks	여행자 수표 Yŏhaengja sup'yo

Money Exchange

Communications

TELEPHONING

I want to make a <u>local call</u>.	시내 전화 좀 부탁합니다. <u>Shinae chŏnhwa</u> chom put'ak'amnida.
long distance call	장거리 전화 Changgŏri chŏnhwa
person-to-person call	지명 통화 Chimyŏng t'onghwa
collect call	수화인 지불 통화 Suhwain chibul t'onghwa
Please tell me how to call this number.	이 번호에 거는 방법 좀 가르쳐 주세요. I pŏnho-e kŏnŭn pangbŏp chom karŭch'yŏ chuseyo.
Can I dial direct?	다이얼을 직접 돌릴 수 있읍니까? Taiŏrŭl chikchŏp tollil su issŭmnikka?
Do I need an operator's assistance?	교환을 통해야 합니까? Kyohwanŭl t'onghaeya hamnikka?
Is there an operator who speaks English?	영어를 하는 교환이 있읍니까? Yŏng-ŏrŭl hanŭn kyohwani issŭmnikka?
What's the number for the operator?	교환 번호가 몇 번입니까? Kyohwan pŏnhoga myot pŏnimnikka?

Where is a <u>public telephone</u>?	공중 전화가 어디에 있읍니까? Kongjung chŏnhwaga ŏdie issŭmnikka?
telephone booth	전화 박스가 Chŏnhwa paksŭga
Is there an English telephone directory?	영어 전화 번호부가 있읍니까? Yŏng-ŏ chŏnhwa pŏnhobuga issŭmnikka?
I'd like to make a phone call. Could you give me some change?	전화 좀 걸려고 하는데 잔돈 좀 바꿔 주시겠읍니까? Chŏnhwa chom kŏllyŏgo hanŭnde chandon chom bakkwo chushigessŭmnikka?
May I use your phone?	전화 좀 써도 됩니까? Chŏnhwa chom ssŏdo toemnikka?

With the Other Party

Is this (company name)?	___입니까? ___imnikka?
I want extension ___.	___번 부탁합니다. ___pŏn put'ak'amnida.
Is Mr./Mrs./Miss /Ms. ___ in?	___씨 계십니까? ___ssi kyeshimnikka?
Hello! Is this ___?	여보세요. ___[이]죠? Yŏboseyo. ___[i]jyo?
___ speaking.	___입니다. ___imnida.
Hello!	여보세요. Yŏboseyo.

Is this Mr./Mrs./ Miss/Ms.___'s residence?	___씨 댁입니까? ___ssi taegimnikka?
May I speak to ___? (Mr.)	___씨 좀 부탁합니다. ___ssi chom put'ak'amnida.

With the Telephone Operator

I want Seoul 735-1268.	서울 735-1268번 부탁합니다. Seoul ch'ilsamo-e illiyukp'al pŏn put'ak'amnida.
I want this to be a person-to-person call.	지명 통화로 해 주세요. Chimyŏng t'onghwaro hae chuseyo.
collect call	수화인 지불 통화로 Suhwain chibul t'onghwaro
The name of the person I want to talk to is ___.	수화인은 ___입니다. Suhwainŭn ___imnida.
Would you tell me the cost when I'm finished?	통화가 끝나면 요금 좀 가르쳐 주시겠읍니까? T'onghwaga kkŭnnamyŏn yogŭm chom karŭch'yŏ chushigessŭmnikka?

If the Person Isn't There

Would you tell him/her to call me?	저에게 전화 좀 해 달라고 전해 주세요. Chŏege chŏnhwa chom hae tallago chŏnhae chuseyo.
My phone number is ___.	제 전화 번호는 ___입니다. Che chŏnhwa pŏnhonŭn ___imnida.

| My extension is ____. | 교환은 ____ 번입니다.
Kyohwanŭn ____ pŏnimnida. |

Please tell him/her to leave a message if I'm not here.
제가 없으면 메모를 남기라고 전해 주세요. Chega ŏpsŭmyŏn memorŭl namgirago chŏnhae chuseyo.

I'll call him/her again.
다시 전화하겠읍니다.
Tashi chŏnhwahagessŭmnida.

Thank you very much. Goodbye.
감사합니다. 수고하세요.
Kamsahamnida. Sugohaseyo.

When will he/she be back?
언제 돌아오십니까?
Ŏnje toraoshimnikka?

Will you tell him/her that ____ called?
____이[가] 전화했다고 전해 주세요.
____i[ga] chŏnhwahaettago chŏnhae chuseyo.

Communications

AT THE POST OFFICE

I'd like 5 aerograms.
항공 엽서 5통만 주세요. Hanggong yŏpsŏ tasŏt t'ongman chuseyo.

I want pretty stamps.
예쁜 우표 있읍니까?
Yeppŭn up'yo issŭmnikka?

I'd like to send this parcel.
이 소포를 좀 부치려고 합니다.
I sop'orŭl chom puch'iryŏgo hamnida.

Is there a big difference in price between airmail and sea mail?
항공편과 선편의 가격차가 많이 납니까? Hanggongp'yŏn-gwa sŏnp'yŏnŭi kagyŏkch'aga mani namnikka?

arrival time	도착 시간에 차가	toch'ak shigane ch'aga
How much will it be by <u>air</u>?	항공편은 얼맙니까?	<u>Hanggong-p'yŏnŭn</u> ŏlmamnikka?
<u>sea</u>	선편은	Sŏnp'yŏnŭn
Do I need to fill out a customs declaration form?	세관 신고서에 기입해야 합니까?	Segwan shin-gosŏe kiip'aeya hamnikka?
I want to mail a letter.	편지 하나 부치려고 합니다.	P'yŏnji hana puch'iryŏgo hamnida.
Where is a <u>mail-box</u>?	우체통이 어디에 있읍니까?	<u>Uch'et'ong-i</u> ŏdie issŭmnikka?
<u>post office</u>	우체국이	Uch'egugi
Which window sells stamps?	어느 창구에서 우표를 팝니까?	Ŏnŭ ch'angguesŏ up'yorŭl p'amnikka?
What's the postage for a <u>letter</u> to the United States?	미국까지 편지 요금이 얼맙니까?	Migukkaji <u>p'yŏnji</u> yogŭmi ŏlmamnikka?
an airmail letter	항공 편지	hanggong p'yŏnji
a registered letter	등기 편지	tŭnggi p'yŏnji
a special delivery letter	속달 편지	soktal p'yŏnji
a postcard	엽서	yŏpsŏ

TELEGRAPHING

I'd like to send a
telegram/cable to
___.

___에 전보를 치려고 합니다.
___e chŏnborŭl ch'iryŏgo
hamnida.

I'd like to send an
urgent telegram/
cable to ___.

___에 지급 전보를 치려고 합니다.
___e chigŭp chŏnborŭl ch'i-
ryŏgo hamnida.

How much is it
per letter?

한 자에 얼맘니까?
Han cha-e ŏlmamnikka?

I want to send it
collect.

수취인 지불로 치고 싶습니다.
Such'wiin chibullo ch'igo
shipsŭmnida.

When will it ar-
rive?

언제 도착합니까?
Ŏnje toch'ak'amnikka?

Where can I send
a telegram/cable?

전보를 어디서 칠 수 있읍니까?
Chŏnborŭl ŏdisŏ ch'il su i-
ssŭmnikka?

Where's the tele-
graph office?

전보 취급소가 어디에 있읍니까?
Chŏnbo ch'wigŭpsoga ŏdie
issŭmnikka?

How <u>early</u> is it
open?

몇 시에 <u>문을 엽니까</u>?
Myŏt shie <u>munŭl yŏmnikka</u>?

late

까지 합니까   kkaji
                hamnikka

Health & Fitness

WITH THE OPTICIAN

I'd like a new pair of eyeglasses.
안경 하나 하러 왔읍니다.   An-gyŏng hana harŏ wassŭmnida.

Can you give me a new prescription?
도수 좀 재 주시겠읍니까?   To-su chom chae chushigessŭm-nikka?

I'd like the lenses tinted.
렌즈는 약간 색이 있는 것으로 해 주세요.   Lenjŭnŭn yakkan saegi innŭn kŏsŭro hae chu-seyo.

Do you sell <u>contact lenses</u>?
<u>콘택트 렌즈</u> 있읍니까?   <u>K'on-t'aekt'ŭ lenjŭ</u> issŭmnikka?

  soft contact lenses
소프트 렌즈 Sop'ŭt'ŭ lenjŭ

Do you sell sun glasses?
선 글래스 있읍니까?   Sŏn kŭllaesŭ issŭmnikka?

Can you repair these glasses for me?
안경 좀 고쳐 주시겠읍니까?   An-gyŏng chom koch'yŏ chu-shigessŭmnikka?

I've broken a lens.
렌즈가 깨졌어요.   Lenjŭga kkaejyŏssŏyo.

I've broken the frame.
테가 망가졌어요.   T'ega manggajyŏssŏyo.

Can you put in a new lens?	새 렌즈로 좀 갈아 주세요. Sae lenjŭro chom kara chuseyo.
Can you get the prescription from the old lens?	이 렌즈가 몇 도인지 알 수 있읍니까? I renjŭga myŏt toinji al su issŭmnikka?
Can you tighten the screw?	나사 좀 조여 주시겠읍니까? Nasa chom choyŏ chushigessŭmnikka?
I need the glasses as soon as possible.	안경 빨리 좀 부탁합니다. An-gyŏng ppalli chom put'ak'amnida.
I don't have any others.	다른 안경이 없읍니다. Tarŭn an-gyŏng-i ŏpsŭmnida.

EMERGENCIES

I've fallen.	떨어졌읍니다. Ttŏrŏjyŏssŭmnida.
I was knocked down.	구타당했읍니다. Kut'adanghaessŭmnida.
I've had a heart attack.	심장병이 있읍니다. Shimjangpyŏng-i issŭmnida.
I burned myself.	화상을 입었읍니다. Hwasang-ŭl ibŏssŭmnida.
I'm bleeding.	출혈이 있읍니다. Ch'urhyŏri issŭmnida.
I've lost a lot of blood.	피를 많이 흘렸읍니다. P'irŭl mani hŭllyŏssŭmnida.

Health & Fitness

The wrist is sprained.	손목이 삐었읍니다. Sonmogi ppiŏssŭmnida.
I can't bend my <u>elbow</u>.	<u>팔꿈치를</u> 굽힐 수 없읍니다. <u>P'alkkumch'irŭl</u> kup'il su ŏp-sŭmnida.
knee	무릎을 Murŭbŭl
I can't move my <u>arm</u>.	<u>팔을</u> 움직일 수 없읍니다. <u>P'arŭl</u> umjigil su ŏpsŭmnida.
leg	다리를 Tarirŭl
I think the bone is <u>broken</u>.	뼈가 <u>부러진</u> 것 같습니다. Ppyŏ-ga <u>purŏjin</u> kŏt kassŭmnida.
dislocated	삔 ppin
The leg is swollen.	다리가 부었읍니다. Tariga puŏssŭmnida.
Hello. It's an emergency!	여보세요. 아주 급합니다. Yŏboseyo. Aju kŭp'amnida.
<u>I'm</u> hurt.	<u>제가</u> 다쳤읍니다. <u>Chega</u> tach'yŏssŭmnida.
My husband's My wife's My child's	남편이 Namp'yŏni 아내가 Anaega 애가 Aega
Can you send an ambulance immediately?	구급차 좀 빨리 보내 주시겠읍니까? Kugŭpch'a chom ppalli ponae chushigessŭmnikka?
We're located at ___.	여긴 ___입니다. Yŏgin ___imnida.
Help!	도와 주세요! Towa chuseyo!

Help me, somebody!	누군가 좀 도와 주세요. Nugun-ga chom towa chuseyo.
Get a doctor, quick!	빨리 의사 좀 불러 주세요. Ppalli ŭisa chom pullŏ chuseyo.
Call an ambulance!	구급차 좀 불러 주세요. Kugŭpch'a chom pullŏ chuseyo.
I need first aid.	응급 처치 좀 해 주세요. Ŭnggŭp ch'ŏch'i chom hae chuseyo.

Finding a Doctor

Do I need to make an appointment?	약속을 해야 됩니까? Yaksogŭl haeya toemnikka?
What's the telephone number of the office?	진료소 전화 번호가 어떻게 됩니까? Chillyoso chŏnhwa pŏnhoga ŏttŏk'e toemnikka?
hospital	병원 Pyŏngwon
I want to see an internist.	내과에 가려고 합니다. Naekwa-e karyŏgo hamnida.
an ear, nose, and throat specialist	이비 인후과에 Ibi inhukwa-e
a dermatologist	피부과에 P'ibukwa-e
a gynecologist	부인과에 Puinkwa-e
an obstetrician	산과에 Sankwa-e
an ophthalmologist	안과에 Ankwa-e
an orthopedic specialist	정형 외과에 Chŏnghyŏng oekwa-e
Do you know a doctor who speaks English?	영어 할 줄 아는 의사 아는 분 계세요? Yŏng-ŏ hal chul anŭn ŭisa anŭn pun kyeseyo?

Health & Fitness

Do you know an American doctor?	미국 의사 아는 분 계세요? Miguk ŭisa anŭn pun kyeseyo?
Where is the <u>office</u>?	<u>진료소가</u> 어디에 있읍니까? <u>Chillyosoga</u> ŏdie issŭmnikka?
hospital	병원이 Pyŏngwoni
What are the office hours?	진료 시간이 몇 시부터 몇 시까지 입니까? Chillyo shigani myŏt shibut'ŏ myŏt shikkajiimnikka?
Can I just walk in?	약속 없이 가도 됩니까? Yaksok ŏpshi kado toemnikka?

WITH THE DOCTOR

Telling the Doctor

My <u>ankle</u> hurts.	<u>발목이</u> 아픕니다. <u>Palmogi</u> ap'umnida.
arm	팔이 P'ari
back	허리가 Hŏriga
chest	가슴이 Kasŭmi
ear	귀가 Kwiga
elbow	팔꿈치가 P'alkkumch'iga
eye	눈이 Nuni
face	얼굴이 Ŏlguri
finger	손가락이 Sonkaragi
foot	발이 Pari
hand	손이 Soni
head	머리가 Mŏriga
leg	다리가 Tariga
muscle	근육이 Kŭnyugi
neck	목이 Mogi
nose	코가 K'oga

skin	피부가	P'ibuga
stomach	위가	Wiga
throat	목구멍이	Mokkumŏng-i
toe	발가락이	Palkaragi
tongue	혀가	Hyŏga
wrist	팔목이	P'almogi

I had a heart attack ___ years ago.

___ 년 전에 심장 마비가 있었읍니다. ___ nyŏn chŏne shimjang mabiga issŏssŭmnida.

I'm a diabetic.

당뇨병이 있읍니다. Tangnyopyŏng-i issŭmnida.

I'm taking this medicine.

이 약을 먹고 있읍니다. I yagŭl mŏkko issŭmnida.

I'm allergic to antibiotics.

항생제에는 과민합니다. Hangsaengjeenŭn kwaminhamnida.

aspirin
penicillin

아스피린에는 Asŭp'irinenŭn
페니실린에는 P'enishillinenŭn

There's a history of ___ in my family.

우리 집안에는 ___의 병력이 있읍니다. Uri chibanenŭn ___ŭi pyŏngnyŏgi issŭmnida.

There's no history of ___ in my family.

우리 집안에는 ___의 병력이 없읍니다. Uri chibanenŭn ___ŭi pyŏngnyŏgi ŏpsŭmnida.

Do you know what's wrong with me?

어디가 잘못됐읍니까? Ŏdiga chalmottwaessŭmnikka?

Do I have ___?

___가[이] 있읍니까? ___ga[i] issŭmnikka?

Is it ___?	___입니까? ___imnikka?
Is it serious?	심각합니까? Shimgak'amnikka?
Is it contagious?	전염됩니까? Chŏnyŏmdoemnikka?
Do I have to stay in bed?	누워 있어야 합니까? Nuwo issŏya hamnikka?
How long do I have to stay in bed?	얼마나 오래 누워 있어야 합니까? Ŏlmana orae nuwo issŏya hamnikka?
Do I have to go to the hospital?	병원에 가야 합니까? Pyŏngwone kaya hamnikka?
Are you going to give me a prescription?	처방전이 있읍니까? Ch'ŏbangjŏni issŭmnikka?
What kind of medicine is it?	어떤 약입니까? Ŏttŏn yagimnikka?
Will it make me sleepy?	그걸 먹으면 졸음이 옵니까? Kŭgŏl mŏgŭmyŏn chorŭmi omnikka?
How often must I take this medicine?	이 약을 하루에 몇 번 먹어야 합니까? I yagŭl harue myŏt pŏn mŏgŏya hamnikka?
When can I continue my trip?	언제 여행을 계속할 수 있읍니까? Ŏnje yŏhaeng-ŭl kyesok'al su issŭmnikka?
Thank you very much.	감사합니다. Kamsahamnida.

Where do I pay?	어디서 계산합니까? Ŏdisŏ kyesanhamnikka?
I have a headache.	두통이 있읍니다. Tut'ong-i issŭmnida.
I have indigestion.	소화가 안됩니다. Sohwaga andoemnida.
I have an infection.	곪은 데가 있읍니다. Kolmŭn tega issŭmnida.
I have an insect bite.	벌레가 물었읍니다. Pŏllega murŏssŭmnida.
I have a lump.	혹이 났읍니다. Hogi nassŭmnida.
I have a sore throat.	목구멍이 아픕니다. Mokkumŏng-i ap'ŭmnida.
I have a stomachache.	위통이 있읍니다. Wit'ong-i issŭmnida.
I have a swelling.	부은 데가 있읍니다. Puŭn tega issŭmnida.
I have a wound.	상처를 입었읍니다. Sangch'ŏrŭl ibŏssŭmnida.
I think I have a broken bone/fracture.	뼈가 부러진 것 같습니다. Ppyŏga purŏjin kŏt kassŭmnida.

dysentery
  the flu
 	
  a stomach ulcer
	이질이 있는 Ijiri innŭn
	유행성 감기가 있는 Yuhaengsŏng kamgiga innŭn
	위궤양이 있는 Wigweyang-i innŭn

I've had this pain since <u>this morning</u>.	오늘 아침부터 아팠읍니다.	<u>Onŭl ach'imbut'ŏ</u> ap'assŭmnida.
last night	어제 저녁부터	Ŏje chŏnyŏkput'ŏ
yesterday	어제부터	Ŏjebut'ŏ
I'm having chest pain.	흉통이 있읍니다.	Hyungt'ong-i issŭmnida.
I have an abscess.	종기가 났읍니다.	Chonggiga nassŭmnida.
I have a bee sting.	벌에 쏘였읍니다.	Pŏre ssoyŏssŭmnida.
I have a bruise.	타박상을 입었읍니다.	T'abaksang-ŭl ibŏssŭmnida.
I have a burn.	데었읍니다.	Teŏssŭmnida.
I have the chills.	몸이 으스스합니다.	Momi ŭsŭsŭhamnida.
I have <u>a cold</u>.	감기에 걸렸읍니다.	<u>Kamgie</u> kŏllyŏssŭmnida.
a chest cold	기침 감기에	Kich'im kamgie
a head cold	코감기에	K'ogamgie
I'm constipated.	변비가 있읍니다.	Pyŏnbiga issŭmnida.
I have cramps.	복통이 있읍니다.	Pokt'ong-i issŭmnida.
I have a cut.	베였읍니다.	Peyŏssŭmnida.
I have diarrhea.	설사가 있읍니다.	Sŏlsaga issŭmnida.

I have a fever.	열이 있읍니다. Yŏri issŭmnida.
I don't feel well.	몸이 별로 안 좋습니다. Momi pyŏllo an chossŭmnida.
I feel sick.	몸이 아픈 것 같습니다. Momi ap'ŭn kŏt kassŭmnida.
I'm dizzy.	현기증이 납니다. Hyŏn-gichŭng-i namnida.
I feel weak.	몸이 약해진 것 같습니다. Mom- i yak'aejin kŏt kassŭmnida.
It hurts me here.	여기가 아픕니다. Yŏgiga ap'ŭmnida.
My whole body hurts.	온몸이 아파요. Onmomi ap'ayo.
I feel faint.	어지러워요. Ŏjirŏwoyo.
I feel nauseated.	메스꺼워요. Mesŭkkŏwoyo.
I feel a chill.	<u>으스스해요.</u> Ŭsŭsŭhaeyo.
I've been vomiting	계속 토합니다. Kyesok t'ohamnida.
I'm pregnant.	임신 중입니다. Imshin chung-imnida.
I want to sit down for a while.	잠시 앉았으면 합니다. Chamshi anjassŭmyŏn hamnida.
My temperature is normal (98.6°F, 37°C).	체온은 정상입니다. Ch'eonŭn chŏngsang-imnida.
I feel all right now.	지금은 괜찮습니다. Chigŭmŭn kwaench'anssŭmnida.

I feel better.	많이 나아졌읍니다. Mani naajyŏssŭmnida.
I feel worse.	더 악화된 것 같습니다. Tŏ a- k'wadoen kŏt kassŭmnida.

What the Doctor Says

You've had a mild heart attack.	가벼운 심장 마비가 있었읍니다. Kabyŏun shimjang mabiga i- ssŏssŭmnida.
Are you allergic to ___ ?	___에 알레르기 체질입니까? ___e allerŭgi ch'ejirimnikka?
Are you allergic to any medicines?	알레르기 반응을 일으키는 약이 있 읍니까? Allerŭgi panŭng-ŭl irŭk'inŭn yagi issŭmnikka?
I'm giving you an injection of peni-cillin.	페니실린을 주사하겠읍니다. P'enishillinŭl chusahagessŭm- nida.
I'm prescribing an antibiotic.	항생제를 처방하겠읍니다. Hang- saengjerŭl ch'ŏbanghagessŭm- nida.
I'm giving you some medicine to take.	약을 좀 드리겠읍니다. Yagŭl chom tŭrigessŭmnida.
I'm writing a pre-scription for you.	처방전을 써 드리겠읍니다. Ch'ŏ- bangjŏnŭl ssŏ tŭrigessŭmnida.
We don't use ___ in Korea.	한국에서는 ___을[를] 사용하지 않습니다. Han-gugesŏnŭn ___ (r)ŭl sayonghaji anssŭmnida.

This is quite similar to ____.	이건 ____와[과] 아주 흡사하군요. Igŏn ____ (g)wa aju hŭpsahagunnyo.
Take ____ teaspoons of this medicine at a time.	이 약을 한 번에 ____ 스푼씩 드십시오. I yagŭl han pŏne ____ sŭp'unssik tŭseyo.
Take it every ____ hours.	____ 시간마다 드세요. ____ shiganmada tŭseyo.
Take ____ tablets with a glass of water.	____ 정씩 물로 드세요. ____ chŏngssik mullo tŭseyo.
Take it ____ times a day.	하루에 ____ 번 드세요. Harue ____ pŏn tŭseyo.
Take it after meals.	식후마다 드세요. Shik'umada tŭseyo.
Take it before meals.	식전마다 드세요. Shikchŏnmada tŭseyo.
Take it in the morning.	아침마다 드세요. Ach'immada tŭseyo.
Take it at night.	밤마다 드세요. Pammada tŭseyo.
Use an ice pack on it.	얼음 주머니 찜질을 하세요. Ŏrŭm chumŏni tchimjirŭl haseyo.
Use wet heat on it.	온습포 찜질을 하세요. Onsŭpp'o tchimjirŭl haseyo.
I want you to come back after ____ day(s).	____ 일 후에 다시 오세요. ____ il hue tashi oseyo.

I think it's ___.	___인 것 같습니다.
	___in kŏt kassŭmnida.

an allergy	알레르기	Allerŭgi
appendicitis	맹장염	Maengjangnyŏm
a bacterial infection	세균성 염증	Segyunsŏng yŏmchŭng-
a bladder infection	방광염	Panggwangnyŏm
bronchitis	기관지염	Kigwanjiyŏm
a common cold	보통 감기	Pot'ong kamgi
conjunctivitis	결막염	Kyŏlmangnyŏm
dysentery	이질	Ijil
gastroenteritis	위장염	Wijangnyŏm
hepatitis	간염	Kannyŏm
influenza	유행성 감기	Yuhaengsŏng kamgi
pneumonia	폐렴	P'yeryŏm
an ulcer	궤양	Kweyang-
a urinary infection	요도염	Yodoyŏm

It's acute.	급성입니다.	Kŭpsŏng-imnida.
It's infected.	곪았읍니다.	Kolmassŭmnida.
It's broken.	부러졌읍니다.	Purŏjyŏssŭmnida.
It's sprained.	삐었읍니다.	Ppiŏssŭmnida.
It's dislocated.	탈구됐읍니다.	T'algudwaessŭmnida.
It's inflamed.	염증입니다.	Yŏmchŭng-imnida.
I'll have to take stitches.	께매야겠읍니다.	Kkwemaeyagessŭmnida.

I'll have to lance it.	째야겠읍니다. Tchaeyagessŭmnida.
I'll have to tape it.	테이프로 고정해야겠읍니다. T'eip'ŭro kojŏnghaeyage-ssŭmnida.
You can't travel until ___.	___까지는 돌아다닐 수 없읍니다. ___kkajinŭn toradanil su ŏp-sŭmnida.
I want you to go to the hospital for some tests.	병원에서 몇 가지 검사를 받아야겠읍니다. Pyŏngwonesŏ myot kaji kŏmsarŭl padayagessŭm-nida.
I want you to go to the hospital for treatment.	병원에서 치료를 받아야겠읍니다. Pyŏngwonesŏ ch'iryorŭl pada-yagessŭmnida.
I want you to go to the hospital for surgery.	병원에서 수술을 받아야겠읍니다. Pyŏngwonesŏ susurŭl padaya-gessŭmnida.
Shall I make the arrangements for you to go to the hospital?	병원 수속을 밟아 놓을까요? Pyŏngwon susogŭl palba no-ŭlkkayo?
Where were you before you came to Korea?	한국에 오기 전에 어디에 계셨읍니까? Han-guge ogi chŏne ŏdie kyesyŏssŭmnikka?
I'm going to take your temperature.	체온을 재 보겠읍니다. Ch'eonŭl chae pogessŭmnida.
I'm going to take your blood pressure.	혈압을 재 보겠읍니다. Hyŏrabŭl chae pogessŭmnida.

Open your mouth, please.	입을 벌리세요. Ibŭl pŏlliseyo.
Stick out your tongue, please.	혀를 내밀어 보세요. Hyŏrŭl naemirŏ poseyo.
Cough, please.	기침 좀 해 보세요. Kich'im chom hae poseyo.
Breathe deeply, please.	숨을 깊이 쉬어 보세요. Sumŭl kip'i swiŏ poseyo.
Roll up your sleeve, please.	소매를 걷어 보세요. Somaerŭl kŏdŏ poseyo.
Take off your clothing to the waist, please.	웃옷을 벗어 보세요. Udosŭl pŏsŏ poseyo.
Remove your <u>trousers/skirt</u> and underwear, please.	바지/치마하고 속옷을 벗어 보세요. <u>Paji/Ch'imahago</u> sogosŭl pŏsŏ poseyo.
Lie down, please.	누워 보세요. Nuwo poseyo.
Does it hurt when I press here?	여길 누르면 아픕니까? Yŏgil nurŭmyŏn ap'ŭmnikka?
Stand up, please.	일어나세요. Irŏnaseyo.
Get dressed, please.	옷을 입으세요. Osŭl ibŭseyo.
Have you ever had this before?	전에 이런 적이 있읍니까? Chŏne irŏn chŏgi issŭmnikka?
Are you having shortness of breath?	숨이 찹니까? Sumi ch'amnikka?
Do you have any numbness here?	여기가 감각이 둔합니까? Yŏgiga kamgagi tunhamnikka?

What medicine have you been taking?	어떤 약을 먹어 왔읍니까? Ŏttŏn yagŭl mŏgŏ wassŭmnikka?
What dosage of insulin do you take?	인슐린 취하는 양이 1회에 어느 정도입니까? Insyullin ch'ihanŭn yang-i irhoee ŏnŭ chŏngdoimnikka?
Is it by injection, or oral?	주사를 놓읍니까, 먹읍니까? Chusarŭl nossŭmnikka, mŏksŭmnikka?
What treatment have you been having?	어떤 치료를 받아 왔읍니까? Ŏttŏn ch'iryorŭl pada wassŭmnikka?
Is there a history of ___ in your family?	집안에 ___ 병력이 있읍니까? Chibane ___ pyŏngnyŏgi issŭmnikka?
When is your baby due?	출산 예정일이 언젭니까? Ch'ulsan yejŏng-iri ŏnjemnikka?
I want a <u>urine</u> sample.	<u>소변</u> 검사를 해야겠읍니다. <u>Sobyŏn</u> kŏmsarŭl haeyagessŭmnida.
stool blood	대변 Taebyŏn 혈액 Hyŏraek
I want you to have an X ray.	X 레이를 찍어야겠읍니다. Eksŭ reirŭl tchigŏyagessŭmnida.
When was your last tetanus shot?	파상풍 예방 주사를 최근에 언제 맞으셨읍니까? P'asangp'ung yebang chusarŭl ch'oegŭne ŏnje majŭsyŏssŭmnikka?

I'm going to send you to a specialist.	<u>전문의에게</u> 한번 가 보십시오. <u>Chŏnmunŭiege</u> hanbŏn ka po-shipshio.

a dermatologist	피부과에	P'ibukwa-e
an ear, nose, and throat specialist	이비 인후과에	Ibi inhukwa-e
a gynecologist	부인과에	Puinkwa-e
an ophthalmologist	안과에	Ankwa-e
an orthopedist	정형 외과에	Chŏnghyŏng oekwa-e

It's minor.	대단치 않습니다. Taedanch'i anssŭmnida.

AT THE CHEMIST

Is a prescription needed for the medicine?	처방전이 필요합니까? Ch'ŏbangjŏni p'iryohamnikka?
Can you fill this prescription for me now?	이 처방전에 기입 좀 해 주시겠읍니까? I ch'ŏbangjŏne kiip chom hae chushigessŭmnikka?
It's an emergency.	급합니다. Kŭp'amnida.
Can I wait for it?	기다릴 수 있읍니까? Kidaril su issŭmnikka?
How long will it take?	얼마나 걸립니까? Ŏlmana kŏllimnikka?
When can I come for it?	언제 오면 되겠읍니까? Ŏnje omyŏn toegessŭmnikka?

Do you have contact lens care products for soft lenses?	소프트 렌즈 보호용품 있읍니까? Sop'ŭt'ŭ lenjŭ poho yongp'um issŭmnikka?
May I see what you have?	어떤 건지 좀 보여 주시겠읍니까? Ŏttŏn kŏnji chom poyŏ chushigessŭmnikka?
I need a carrying case for <u>hard lenses</u>.	<u>하드 렌즈</u> 케이스 하나 주세요. <u>Hadŭ lenjŭ</u> k'eisŭ hana chuseyo.
soft lenses	소프트 렌즈 Sop'ŭt'ŭ lenjŭ
I would like <u>some adhesive tape</u>.	<u>반창고</u> 좀 주세요. <u>Panch'anggo</u> chom chuseyo.

some alcohol	알콜	Alk'ol
an antacid	제산제	Chesanje
an antiseptic	소독약	Sodongnyak
some aspirin	아스피린	Asŭp'irin
an aspirin-free pain-killer	아스피린 성분이 없는 진통제	Asŭp'irin songbuni ŏmnŭn chint'ongje
some bandages	붕대	Pungdae
some bandaids	밴드	Paendŭ
some corn plasters	티눈 고약	T'inun koyak
some cotton	약솜	Yaksom
some cough drops	진해정	Chinhaejŏng
some cough syrup	진해 시럽	Chinhae shirŏp
some (disposable) diapers	기저귀	Kijŏgwi
some eye drops	안약	Anyak
a firstaid kit	구급 상자	Kugŭp sangja
some gauze	가제	Kaje

some insect repellent	방충제	Pangch'ungje
some iodine	옥도 정기	Okto chŏngki
a laxative	하제	Haje
an ointment	고약	Koyak
a razor	면도기	Myŏndogi
some razor blades	면도날	Myŏndonal
some sanitary napkins	생리대	Saengnidae
some sleeping pills	수면제	Sumyŏnje
some supposi- tories	좌약	Chwayak
a thermometer	체온계	Ch'eon-gye
some tissues	티슈	T'isyu
some toilet paper	화장지	Hwajangji
a toothbrush	칫솔	Ch'issol
some toothpaste	치약	Ch'iyak
some tranquillizers	진정제	Chinjŏngje
some vitamins	비타민	Pit'amin

Where is the nearest pharmacy?   제일 가까운 약국이 어디에 있읍니까?   Cheil kakkaun yakkugi ŏdie issŭmnikka?

Is there an all-night pharmacy?   철야로 영업하는 약국이 있읍니까?   Ch'ŏryaro yŏng-ŏp'anŭn yakkugi issŭmnikka?

Where is the all-night pharmacy?   철야로 영업하는 약국이 어디에 있읍니까?   Ch'ŏryaro yŏng-ŏp'anŭn yakkugi ŏdie issŭmnikka?

What time does the pharmacy o-pen?   약국이 언제 문을 엽니까?   Yakkugi ŏnje munŭl yŏmnikka?

Is there a pharmacy that carries American/European products?	미제/유럽제를 파는 약국이 있읍니까? Miie/Yurŏpcherŭl p'anŭn yakkugi issŭmnikka?
I need something for a burn.	화상약 좀 주세요. Hwasangnyak chom chuseyo.

a cold	감기약	Kamgiyak
constipation	변비약	Pyŏnbiyak
a cough	기침약	Kich'imnyak
diarrhea	설사약	Sŏlsayak
a fever	해열제	Haeyalche
a headache	두통약	Tut'ongnyak
insomnia	불면증약	Pulmyŏnchŭngnyak
nausea	멀미약	Mŏlmiyak
a toothache	치통약	Ch'it'ongnyak
an upset stomach	배탈약	Paet'alnyak

WITH THE DENTIST

Patient

I've lost a filling.	충전재가 없어졌어요. Ch'ungjŏnjaega ŏpsŏjyŏssŏyo.
I've broken a tooth.	이가 부러졌어요. Iga purŏjyŏssŏyo.
I can't chew.	씹을 수가 없어요. Ssibŭl suga ŏpsŏyo.
My gums hurt.	잇몸이 아파요. Inmomi ap'ayo.

Can you give me a temporary filling? | <u>임시</u> 충전 좀 해 주세요. <u>Imshi</u> ch'ungjŏn chom hae chuseyo.

a silver | 은 | Ŭn
a gold | 금 | Kŭm
a porcelain | 자기제 | Chagije

Can you fix this <u>bridge</u>? | 이 <u>브리지</u> 좀 고쳐 주세요. I <u>puriji</u> chom koch'yŏ chuseyo.

denture | 틀니 | t'ŭlni

I have to go to a dentist. | 치과에 가야겠읍니다. Ch'ikwa-e kayagessŭmnida.

Can you recommend a dentist? | 치과 의사 한 분 소개해 주실 수 있읍니까? Ch'ikwa ŭisa han pun sogaehae chushil su issŭmnikka?

I'd like an appointment with the dentist. | 치과에 예약을 하고 싶은데요. Ch'ikwa-e yeyagŭl hago ship'ŭndeyo.

I need to see the dentist immediately. | 치과에 빨리 가봐야겠어요. Ch'ikwa-e ppalli kabwayagessŏyo.

I have a really bad toothache. | 이가 굉장히 아파요. Iga koengjanghi ap'ayo.

I think I have <u>a cavity</u>. | <u>충치가</u> 있는 것 같아요. <u>Ch'ungch'iga</u> innŭn kŏt kat'ayo.

an abscess | 농양이 | Nongyang-i

Dentist

Does this hurt? | 아픕니까? | Ap'ŭmnikka?

Is it tender?	느낌이 부드럽습니까? Nŭkkimi pudŭrŏpsŭmnikka?
I'm giving you a prescription.	처방전을 드리겠읍니다. Ch'ŏbangjŏnŭl tŭrigessŭmnida.
Rinse with this ___ times daily.	하루에 ___ 번씩 씻어내세요. Harue ___ pŏnssik ssisŏnaeseyo.
This is an antibio-<u>tic</u>.	이건 항생제입니다. Igŏn hangsaengjeimnida.
a pain-killer	진통제 chint'ongje
Take ___ tablets/ capsules at a time.	한 번에 ___ 알씩 드세요. Han pŏne ___ alssik tŭseyo.
Take it/them every ___ hours.	이걸 ___ 시간마다 드십시오. Igŏl ___ shiganmada tushipshio.
I see the problem.	어디가 나쁜지 알겠읍니다. Ŏdiga nappŭnji algessŭmnida.
I want to take an X ray.	X레이를 찍어야겠읍니다. Eksŭ reirŭl tchigŏyagessŭmnida.
We should do it now.	지금 해야겠읍니다. Chigŭm haeyagessŭmnida.
It can wait until you get home.	귀국할 때까지는 괜찮을 겁니다. Kwiguk'al ttaekkajinŭn kwaench'anŭl kŏmnida.
I'm going to give you a <u>temporary</u> filling.	임시 충전을 하겠읍니다. <u>Imshi</u> ch'ungjŏnŭl hagessŭmnida.
silver	은 Ŭn
gold	금 Kŭm

TRADITIONAL THERAPY

With the Acupressurist

It's too hard.	너무 센데요. Nŏmu sendeyo.
Can you do it more gently?	좀 약하게 해 주세요. Chom yak'age hae chuseyo.
I can take it harder.	좀 세게 해도 됩니다. Chom sege haedo toemnida.

With the Acupressurist or Acupuncturist

My problem is here.	여기가 이상합니다. Yŏgiga isanghamnida.
My <u>neck</u> is (are) stiff.	<u>목이</u> 뻣뻣합니다. <u>Mogi</u> ppŏtppŏt'amnida.
shoulders	어깨가 Ŏkkaega
back	허리가 Hŏriga
My <u>head</u> ache(s).	<u>머리가</u> 아파요. <u>Mŏriga</u> ap'ayo.
arms	팔이 P'ari
waist	허리가 Hŏriga

General

Where can I get <u>acupressure</u>?	<u>지압을</u> 어디서 받을 수 있읍니까? <u>Chiabŭl</u> ŏdisŏ padŭl su issŭmnikka?
acupuncture	침 치료를 Ch'im ch'iryorŭl
Do you know a good acupressurist?	좋은 지압사 아는 분 계세요? Choŭn chiapsa anŭn pun kyeseyo?

Does he/she come to my place?	집에서 받을 수 있읍니까? Chibesŏ padŭl su issŭmnikka?
How much is it for an hour?	시간당 얼맙니까? Shigandang ŏlmamnikka?
Do I need to make an appointment?	예약을 해야 합니까? Yeyagŭl haeya hamnikka?
Could you get me one?	예약 좀 해 주시겠읍니까? Yeyak chom hae chushigessŭmnikka?

Although most Westerners think of acupuncture as Chinese, it's also widely practiced in Korea. You can have acupuncture or acupressure treatment at the therapist's office, or where you're staying.

LEISURE ACTIVITIES

Tennis

Is there a hotel with a tennis court?	테니스 코트가 있는 호텔이 있읍니까? T'enisŭ k'ot'ŭga innŭn hot'eri issŭmnikka?
Is the hotel tennis court for guests only?	호텔 테니스 코트는 숙박객 전용입니까? Hot'el t'enisŭ k'ot'ŭnŭn sukpakkaek chŏnyong-imnikka?
Can guests use the hotel tennis court free?	숙박객은 호텔 테니스 코트를 무료로 이용할 수 있읍니까? Sukpak-kaegŭn hot'el t'enisŭ k'ot'ŭrŭl muryoro iyonghal su issŭmnikka?

Is there a discount for hotel guests?	호텔 숙박객에게는 할인해 줍니까? Hot'el sukpakkaegegenŭn harinhae chumnikka?
Is it difficult to make a reservation for a <u>public tennis court?</u>	<u>공공 테니스 코트를</u> 예약하기가 힘듭니까? <u>Konggong t'enisŭ k'ot'ŭrŭl</u> yeyak'agiga himdŭmnikka?
hotel tennis court	호텔 테니스 코트를 Hot'el t'enisŭ k'ot'ŭrŭl
Is the fee by the hour?	요금은 시간제입니까? Yogŭmŭn shiganjeimnikka?
Can I rent a racket?	라케트를 빌 수 있읍니까? Rak'et'ŭrŭl pil su issŭmnikka?
I love to play tennis.	전 테니스를 아주 좋아합니다. Chŏn t'enisŭrŭl aju choahamnida.
Do you play tennis?	테니스 치십니까? T'enisŭ ch'ishimnikka?
Where do you play tennis?	테니스를 어디서 치십니까? T'enisŭrŭl ŏdisŏ ch'ishimnikka?
Could you tell me where I can play tennis?	어디서 테니스를 칠 수 있는지 가르쳐 주시겠읍니까? Ŏdisŏ t'enisŭrŭl ch'il su innŭnji karŭch'yŏ chushigessŭmnikka?

Bicycling

| Where can I rent a bike? | 자전거를 어디서 빌 수 있읍니까? Chajŏn-gŏrŭl ŏdisŏ pil su issŭmnikka? |

How much is the fee?	요금이 얼맙니까? Yogŭmi ŏlmamnikka?
deposit	보증금이 Pojŭnggŭmi

Is the fee by the hour?	요금이 시간제입니까? Yogŭmi shiganjeimnikka?

Does the law require a helmet?	헬멧을 써야 하는 것이 법에 규정 되어 있읍니까? Helmesŭl ssŏya hanŭn kŏshi pŏbe kyujŏng-doeŏ issŭmnikka?

Is there a bicycling course nearby?	근처에 자전거 코스가 있읍니까? Kŭnch'ŏe chajŏn-gŏ k'osŭga issŭmnikka?

Skiing

Health & Fitness

How is the snow quality?	눈의 질은 어떻습니까? Nunŭi chirŭn ŏttŏssŭmnikka?

Is the snow powdery?	눈은 가루형입니까? Nunŭn karuhyŏng-imnikka?
wet	습합니까 sŭp'amnikka

How much is the snow accumulation?	적설량은 얼마나 됩니까? Chŏk-sŏllyang-ŭn ŏlmana toemni-kka?

Do they have a ski lift?	리프트가 있읍니까? Lip'ŭt'ŭga issŭmnikka?

How long do I have to wait?	얼마나 기다려야 합니까? Ŏlmana kidaryŏya hamnikka?

Should I make a reservation for a hotel?	호텔을 예약해야 합니까? Hot'erŭl yeyak'aeya hamni-kka?

yǒgwan   여관을   Yǒgwanŭl

Can I rent ski e-
quipment at the
ski resort?

스키 용품을 스키장에서 빌 수 있
읍니까?   Sŭk'i yongp'umŭl
sŭk'ijang-eso pil su issŭmnikka?

Can I rent <u>skis</u>?

스키를 빌 수 있읍니까?   <u>Sŭk'i-
rŭl</u> pil su issŭmnikka?

ski shoes   스키화를   Sŭk'ihwarŭl
poles   스틱을   Sŭt'igŭl

Do you like ski-
ing?

스키 좋아합니까?
Sŭk'i choahamnikka?

Where do you go
for skiing?

스키 타러 어디로 가십니까? Sŭ-
k'i t'arǒ ǒdiro kashimnikka?

Is this the ski
season?

지금이 스키 시즌입니까?
Chigŭmi sŭk'i shijŭnimnikka?

Where can I ski
now?

지금 어디서 스키를 탈 수 있읍
니까?   Chigŭm ǒdisǒ sŭk'irŭl
t'al su issŭmnikka?

Where is a nearby
ski resort?

가까운 스키장이 어디에 있읍니까?
Kakkaun sŭk'ijang-i ǒdie i-
ssŭmnikka?

How can I get
there?

거기에 어떻게 가면 좋습니까?
Kǒgie ǒttǒk'e kamyǒn cho-
ssŭmnikka?

Is there a <u>train</u>
that goes there?

거기 가는 기차가 있읍니까? Kǒgi
kanŭn <u>kich'aga</u> issŭmnikka?

bus   버스가   pǒsŭga

How long does it take to get there?	거기까지 얼마나 걸립니까? Kŏgikkaji ŏlmana kŏllimnikka?
Is the ski resort crowded?	스키장이 붐빕니까? Sŭk'ijang-i pumbimnikka?
Is the ski slope difficult?	경사가 타기에 힘듭니까? Kyŏngsaga t'agie himdŭmikka?

Swimming

Is the water <u>cold</u>?	물이 찹니까? Muri ch'amnikka?
clean	깨끗합 kkaekkŭt'am
calm	잔잔합 chanjanham
Is the beach sandy?	해변에 백사장이 있읍니까? Haebyŏne paeksajang-i issŭmnikka?
Are there·big waves?	큰 파도가 입니까? K'ŭn p'adoga imnikka?
Is it safe for children?	애들에게 안전합니까? Aedŭrege anjŏnhamnikka?
Are there lifeguards on duty?	구조원이 있읍니까? Kujowoni issŭmnikka?
Are there <u>jellyfish</u>?	해파리가 있읍니까? <u>Haep'ariga</u> issŭmnikka?
sharks	상어가 Sang-ŏga
Can I rent <u>an air mattress</u>?	에어 매트리스를 빌 수 있읍니까? <u>Eŏ maet'ŭrisŭrŭl</u> pil su issŭmnikka?

a beach towel	비치 타월을	Pich'i t'aworŭl
a beach umbrella	비치 파라솔을	Pich'i p'arasorŭl
a boat	보트를	Pot'ŭrŭl
a motor boat	모터 보트를	Mot'ŏ pot'ŭrŭl
a sailboat	요트를	Yot'ŭrŭl
a swimming tube	튜브를	T'yubŭrŭl
water skis	수상 스키를	Susang sŭk'irŭl

How much is it per hour?
한 시간에 얼맙니까?
Han shigane ŏlmamnikka?

Do you want a deposit?
보증금 있읍니까?
Pojŭnggŭm issŭmnikka?

How much is the deposit?
보증금이 얼맙니까?
Pojŭnggŭmi ŏlmamnikka?

Is there a nice beach around here?
이 근처에 좋은 해변이 있읍니까?
I kŭnch'ŏe choŭn haebyŏni issŭmnikka?

Where is the closest beach?
가장 가까운 해변이 어딥니까?
Kajang kakkaun haebyŏni ŏdimnikka?

How can I get there?
거기에 어떻게 가는 것이 좋습니까? Kŏgie ŏttŏk'e kanŭn kŏshi chossŭmnikka?

Is there a <u>train</u> that goes there?
거기 가는 기차가 있읍니까? Kŏgi kanŭn <u>kich'aga</u> issŭmnikka?

bus
버스가 pŏsŭga

How long does it take to get there?
거기까지 얼마나 걸립니까? Kŏgikkaji ŏlmana kŏllimnikka?

Is there a hotel with a swimming pool?

수영장이 있는 호텔이 있읍니까? Suyŏngjang-i innŭn hot'eri i-ssŭmnikka?

Can hotel guests swim free of charge?

숙박객은 무료로 수영할 수 있읍니까? Sukpakkaegŭn muryoro suyŏnghal su issŭmnikka?

Is the hotel swimming pool for guests only?

호텔 수영장은 숙박객 전용입니까? Hot'el suyŏngjang-ŭn sukpak-kaek chŏnyong-imnikka?

How much is the charge?

요금은 얼맙니까? Yogŭmŭn ŏlmamnikka?

What hours is the swimming pool open?

수영장은 몇 시부터 몇 시까지 합니까? Suyŏngjang-ŭn myŏt shibut'ŏ myŏt shikkaji ham-nikka?

I like swimming.

저는 수영을 좋아합니다. Chŏnŭn suyŏng-ŭl choahamnida.

Do you like swimming?

수영 좋아하십니까? Suyŏng choahashimnikka?

Where do you go swimming?

수영하러 어디로 가십니까? Su-yŏngharŏ ŏdiro kashimnikka?

Could you tell me where I can swim?

어디서 수영할 수 있는지 가르쳐 주시겠읍니까? Ŏdisŏ suyŏng-hal su innŭnji karŭch'yŏ chu-shigessŭmnikka?

Is there a swimming pool nearby?

근처에 수영장이 있읍니까? Kŭn-ch'ŏe suyŏngjang-i issŭmni-kka?

Is it a public swimming pool?

거기 공공 수영장입니까? Kŏgi konggong suyŏngjang-imni-kka?

Korea has good beaches, but they're crowed —don't expect to enjoy the sun and sand in solitude. Pools are crowded too. Your hotel pool may be your best bet if you're a swimming enthusiast.

Golf

If I call today for a reservation, when can I play golf?	오늘 전화로 예약하면 언제 골프를 칠 수 있읍니까? Onŭl chŏnhwaro yeyak'amyŏn ŏnje kolp'ŭrŭl ch'il su issŭmnikka?
How much is the greens fee?	골프 코스 사용료가 얼맙니까? Kolp'ŭ k'osŭ sayongnyoga ŏlmamnikka?
Do I have to hire a caddy?	캐디를 써야 합니까? K'aedirŭl ssŏya hamnikka?
How much does the caddy cost per round?	캐디료는 라운드당 얼맙니까? K'aediryonŭn raundŭdang ŏlmamnikka?
Can I rent golf clubs?	골프채를 빌릴 수 있읍니까? Kolp'ŭch'aerul pil su issŭmnikka?
Is it a difficult course?	코스가 어렵습니까? K'osŭga ŏryŏpsŭmnikka?
What's par?	기준 타수가 얼맙니까? Kijun t'asuga ŏlmamnikka?
Can I use the clubhouse facilities?	클럽하우스 시설을 이용할 수 있읍니까? K'ŭllŏp'ausŭ shisŏrŭl iyonghal su issŭmnikka?

| Do you play golf? | 골프 치십니까? |
| | Kolp'ŭ ch'ishimnikka? |

| Where do you play golf? | 골프를 어디서 치십니까? Kolp'ŭrŭl ŏdisŏ ch'ishimnikka? |

| Could you tell me where I can play golf? | 골프를 어디서 칠 수 있는지 가르쳐 주시겠읍니까? Kolp'ŭrŭl ŏdisŏ ch'il su innŭnji karŭch'yŏ chushigessŭmnikka? |

| Is there a public golf course? | 공공 골프 코스가 있읍니까? Konggong k'olp'ŭ k'osŭga issŭmnikka? |

| Is there a hotel with a golf course? | 골프 코스가 있는 호텔이 있읍니까? Kolp'ŭ k'osŭga innŭn hot'eri issŭmnikka? |

Fishing

| Where can I rent fishing equipment? | 낚시 도구를 어디서 빌 수 있읍니까? Nakshi togurŭl ŏdisŏ pil su issŭmnikka? |

| a fishing boat | 낚시배를 Nakshibaerŭl |

| Where can I buy fishing gear? | 낚시 도구를 어디서 살 수 있읍니까? Nakshi togurŭl ŏdisŏ sal su issŭmnikka? |

| Where can I join a chartered fishing boat? | 낚시배를 어디서 탈 수 있읍니까? Nakshibaerŭl ŏdisŏ t'al su issŭmnikka? |

| What time does the fishing boat leave? | 낚시배가 언제 출발합니까? Nakshibaega ŏnje ch'ulbarhamnikka? |

Health & Fitness

Do I need to make a reservation?	예약을 해야 합니까? Yeyagŭl haeya hamnikka?
What's the charge?	요금이 얼맙니까? Yogŭmi ŏlmamnikka?
Do I need to take my own food and drinks?	음식을 가져가야 합니까? Ŭmshigŭl kajyŏgaya hamnikka?
Can I buy bait?	미끼를 살 수 있읍니까? Mikkirŭl sal su issŭmnikka?
What kind of bait is it?	그것은 무슨 미끼입니까? Kŭgŏsŭn musŭn mikkiimnikka?
Is there a fishing rights charge?	입어료가 있읍니까? Ibŏryoga issŭmnikka?
Do you like fishing?	낚시 좋아합니까? Nakshi choahamnikka?
Where do you go fishing?	낚시 어디로 가십니까? Nakshi ŏdiro kashimnikka?
Where is a nearby fishing spot?	가까운 낚시터가 어디에 있읍니까? Kakkaun nakshit'ŏga ŏdie issŭmnikka?
How can I get there?	거기에 어떻게 가는 것이 좋습니까? Kŏgie ŏttŏk'e kanŭn kŏshi chossŭmnikka?
How long does it take to get there?	거기까지 얼마나 걸립니까? Kŏgikkaji ŏlmana kŏlimnikka?
I like <u>river</u> fishing.	<u>강</u> 낚시를 좋아합니다. <u>Kang</u> nakshirŭl choahamnida.
sea	바다 Pada

surf	파도	P'ado
offshore	근해	Kŭnhae

What can you catch now?

요즘에는 어떤 걸 잡으십니까?
Yojŭmenŭn ŏttŏn kŏl chabŭshimnikka?

What kind of fishing equipment do you use?

어떤 낚시를 사용하십니까? Ŏttŏn nakshirŭl sayonghashimnikka?

CAMPING

Are there <u>toilets</u>?

<u>화장실이</u> 있읍니까?
<u>Hwajangshiri</u> issŭmnikka?

baths	욕실이	Yokshiri
tents	텐트가	T'ent'ŭga
cooking facilities	요리 설비가	Yori sŏlbiga

Can I rent <u>a sleeping bag</u>?

<u>슬리핑 백을</u> 빌 수 있읍니까?
<u>Sŭllip'ing paegŭl</u> pil su issŭmnikka?

a blanket	모포를	Mop'orŭl
cooking utensils	취사 용구를	Ch'wisa yonggurŭl
a lamp	램프를	Laemp'ŭrŭl
a tent	텐트를	T'ent'ŭrŭl

I intend staying <u>a day</u>.

<u>하루</u> 머물 예정입니다.
<u>Haru</u> mŏmul yejŏng-imnida.

two days	이틀	It'ŭl
three days	사흘	Sahŭl

How much is the charge per person per day?	요금이 하루 일인당 얼맙니까? Yogŭmi haru irindang ŏl-mamnikka?
Can I play <u>tennis</u> there?	거기서 테니스 할 수 있읍니까? Kŏgisŏ <u>t'enisŭ</u> hal su issŭm-nikka?

basketball	농구	nonggu
badminton	배드민턴	paedŭmint'ŏn
ping pong	탁구	t'akku
volleyball	배구	paegu

Can I go <u>fishing</u>?	낚시하러 갈 수 있읍니까? <u>Nak-shiharŏ</u> kal su issŭmnikka?

swimming	수영하러	Suyŏngharŏ
bicycling	자전거 타러	Chajŏn-gŏ t'arŏ

Where is the Tourist Information Center?	관광 안내소가 어디에 있읍니까? Kwan-gwang annaesoga ŏdie issŭmnikka?
Is there a camping site near here?	근처에 야영장이 있읍니까? Kŭnch'ŏe yayŏngjang-i issŭm-nikka?
I like camping at <u>a lake</u>.	<u>호수에서</u> 야영하는 걸 좋아합니다. <u>Hosuesŏ</u> yayŏnghanŭn kŏl choahamnida.

a mountain	산	San
the seashore	해변	Haebyŏn

Could you recommend a site?	어떤 야영장이 좋습니까? Ŏ-ttŏn yayŏngjang-i chossŭmni-kka?

Could you tell me how to get there?	거기에는 어떻게 가면 좋습니까? Kŏgienŭn ŏttŏk'e kamyŏn chossŭmnikka?
Where is it on the map?	거기가 지도에서 어딥니까? Kŏgiga chido-esŏ ŏdimnikka?
Do I need to make a reservation?	예약을 해야 합니까? Yeyagŭl haeya hamnikka?
Can I camp for the night?	하룻밤 야영할 수 있읍니까? Harutpam yayŏnghal su issŭmnikka?
Where can I spend the night?	어디에서 묵을 수 있읍니까? Ŏdiesŏ mugŭl su issŭmnikka?
Is there <u>drinking water</u>?	마실 물이 있읍니까? <u>Mashil muri</u> issŭmnikka?

running water	수도가	Sudoga
electricity	전기가	Chŏn-giga
a children's playground	어린이 놀이터가	Ŏrini norit'ŏga
a grocery	식료품점이	Shingnyop'umjŏmi

Is there a hiking trail nearby?	근처에 하이킹 코스가 있읍니까? Kŭnch'ŏe haik'ing k'osŭga issŭmnikka?
Is there a map for the hiking trail?	하이킹 코스 지도 있읍니까? Haik'ing k'osŭ chido issŭmnikka?
What a beautiful landscape!	경치 좋습니다! Kyŏngch'i chossŭmnida!
Look at the barn.	저 광 좀 보세요. Chŏ kwang chom poseyo.

Entertainment & Pastimes

AT NIGHT

Discotheques

Where is it?	그곳이 어디에 있읍니까? Kŭgoshi ŏdie issŭmnikka?
What time does it open?	몇 시에 엽니까? Myŏt shie yŏmnikka?
How late does it stay open?	몇 시까지 합니까? Myŏt shikkaji hamnikka?
Is there an admission charge?	입장료가 있읍니까? Ipchangnyoga issŭmnikka?
How much is the admission?	입장료가 얼맙니까? Ipchangnyoga ŏlmamnikka?
How much does a drink cost?	한 잔에 얼맙니까? Han chane ŏlmamnikka?
Is the music recorded?	레코드 음악입니까? Rek'odŭ ŭmagimnikka?
Do they have live music?	생음악이 있읍니까? Sang-ŭmagi issŭmnikka?
I feel like dancing in a disco.	디스코에서 춤추고 싶은데요. Tisŭk'o-esŏ ch'umch'ugo ship'ŭndeyo.
Is there a good disco nearby?	근처에 좋은 디스코가 있읍니까? Kŭnch'ŏe choŭn tisŭk'oga issŭmnikka?

Which discos are very popular now?	지금 어떤 디스코가 인기가 있읍니까? Chigŭm ŏttŏn tisŭk'oga inkiga issŭmnikka?
Could you recommend one?	어디가 좋습니까? Ŏdiga chossŭmnikka?
What's the name of it?	그곳이 어딥니까? Kŭgoshi ŏdimnikka?

Nightclubs and Cabarets

How much is the hostess fee?	<u>호스테스료가</u> 얼맙니까? <u>Hosŭt'esŭryoga</u> ŏlmamnikka?
cover charge	서비스료가 Sŏbisŭryoga
Is the hostess fee by the hour?	호스테스료는 시간제입니까? Hosŭt'esŭryonŭn shiganjeimnikka?
Are couples welcome?	커플도 입장됩니까? K'ŏp'ŭldo ipchangdoemnikka?
Do they have a floor show?	쇼가 있읍니까? Syoga issŭmnikka?
What kind of floor show do they have?	어떤 쇼가 있읍니까? Ŏttŏn syoga issŭmnikka?
What time does the floor show start?	쇼가 몇 시에 시작됩니까? Syoga myŏt shie shijaktoemnikka?
Do they have a good dance band?	댄스 밴드가 괜찮습니까? Taensŭ paendŭga kwaench'anssŭmnikka?

What kind of music does the band play?

밴드가 어떤 음악을 연주합니까?
Paendŭga ŏttŏn ŭmagŭl yŏnjuhamnikka?

Can I have dinner there too?

거기 저녁 식사도 됩니까?
Kŏgi chŏnyŏk shiksado toemnikka?

What kind of clothes do I need to wear?

어떤 옷을 입어야 합니까?
Ŏttŏn osŭl ibŏya hamnikka?

I'd like to visit a nightclub.

나이트클럽에 가고 싶은데요. Nait'ŭk'ŭllŏbe kago ship'ŭndeyo.

   cabaret

카바레에 K'abaree

Are the nightclubs and cabarets extremely expensive?

나이트클럽과 카바레가 굉장히 비쌉니까? Nait'ŭk'ŭllŏpkwa k'abarega koengjanghi pissamnikka?

For example, how much does it cost per person?

예를 들어 1인당 얼마나 됩니까?
Yerŭl tŭrŏ irindang ŏlmana toemnikka?

Do you know the best nightclub/ cabaret?

최고로 좋은 나이트클럽/카바레 아시는 데 있으세요? Ch'oegoro choŭn nait'ŭk'ŭllŏp/k'abare ashinŭn de issŭseyo?

   a cozy
   an inexpensive
   a nice
   a posh

아담한 Adamhan
싼 Ssan
좋은 Choŭn
멋진 Mŏtchin

Could you recommend a reasonable nightclub?

어떤 나이트클럽이 비싸지 않습니까? Ŏttŏn nait'uk'ŭllŏbi pissaji anssŭmnikka?

cabaret   카바레   k'abare

Do I need to make a reservation?

예약을 해야 합니까?
Yeyagǔl haeya hamnikka?

Do they have a cover charge?

서비스료 있읍니까?
Sǒbisǔryo issǔmnikka?

Bars

Is there a bar I can go to without worrying about the bill?

청구서 걱정 없이 갈 수 있는 바가 있읍니까?   Ch'ǒngguǒ kǒkchǒng ǒpshi kal su innǔn paga issǔmnikka?

Would you suggest which bar I should go to?

어느 바가 좋은지 가르쳐 주시겠읍니까?   Ǒnǔ paga choǔnji karǔch'yǒ chushigessǔmnikka?

Do you have a bar you go to often?

자주 가시는 바가 있읍니까?
Chaju kashinǔn paga issǔmnikka?

Do they have a minimum charge?

기본 요금이 있읍니까?
Kibon yogǔmi issǔmnikka?

Do I have to buy drinks for the hostesses?

호스테스에게 술을 사야 합니까?
Hosǔt'esǔege surǔl saya hamnikka?

Are strangers welcome there?

외국인도 들어갈 수 있읍니까?
Oegugindo tǔrǒgal su issǔmnikka?

How much will it be for <u>a bottle of beer</u> there?

거긴 맥주 한 병에 얼맙니까?
Kǒgin maekchu han pyǒng-e ǒlmamnikka?

    a shot of whiskey

위스키 한 잔에   wisǔk'i han chane

Do you think 5,000 won per person is enough?

1인당 5,000원이면 됩니까?
Irindang och'ŏn wonimyŏn toemnikka?

| 15,000 won | 15,000 원 | man och'ŏn won |
| 20,000 won | 20,000 원 | iman won |

I'd like to go to a bar.

바에 가고 싶습니다.
Pa-e kago shipsŭmnida.

Is there an inexpensive bar nearby?

이 근처에 비싸지 않은 바가 있읍니까? I kunch'ŏe pissaji anŭn paga issŭmnikka?

| a quiet | 조용한 | choyonghan |
| a pleasant | 쾌적한 | k'waejŏk'an |

Do you know of a bar with nice atmosphere?

분위기 좋은 바 알고 계신 데 있읍니까? Punwigi choŭn pa algo kyeshin te issŭmnikka?

with no hostesses	호스테스가 없는	Hosŭt'esŭga ŏmnŭn
with a nice reputation	평판이 좋은	P'yŏngp'ani choŭn
with clearly listed prices	정가제인	Chŏngkajein

Where is a bar that's popular among young people?

젊은이들 사이에 인기가 있는 바가 어디에 있읍니까? Chŏlmŭnidŭl saie inkiga innŭn paga ŏdie issŭmnikka?

| women | 여성들 | Yŏsŏngdŭl |
| office workers | 셀러리맨들 | Sellŏrimaendŭl |

Beer Halls

Do they have imported beer?

수입 맥주 있읍니까?
Suip maekchu issŭmnikka?

| American | 미국산 | Miguksan |
| German | 독일산 | Togilsan |

Do they serve food?

식사가 됩니까?
Shiksaga toemnikka?

Can I have a light meal?

간단한 식사 됩니까? Kandan-
han shiksa toemnikka?

Do they serve dinner?

저녁 식사가 됩니까?
Chŏnyŏk shiksaga toemnikka?

What kind of food do they have?

어떤 음식이 있읍니까?
Ŏttŏn ŭmshigi issŭmnikka?

Do they have entertainment?

쇼가 있읍니까?
Syoga issŭmnikka?

What kind of entertainment do they have?

어떤 쇼가 있읍니까?
Ŏttŏn syoga issŭmnikka?

What time do they open?

거기는 몇 시에 문을 엽니까?
Kŏginŭn myŏt shie munŭl
yŏmnikka?

close

닫습니까 tassŭmnikka

Do they open at lunchtime?

점심 시간에 문을 엽니까?
Chŏmshim shigane munŭl
yŏmnikka?

Do they serve only beer?

거기서는 맥주만 팝니까? Kŏgisŏ-
nŭn maekchuman p'amnikka?

Do they serve other drinks besides beer?

맥주 외에 다른 음료도 팝니까?
Maekchu oe-e tarŭn ŭmnyodo
p'amnikka?

Is there <u>ale</u>?   에일 있읍니까?
                           <u>Eil</u> issŭmnikka?

draft beer   생맥주   Saengmaekchu
light beer   라이트 비어   Lait'ŭ piŏ

Korean cities offer the usual variety of after-hours diversion, with one important difference: the costs can be astronomical. To avoid unpleasant surprises when your check arrives, you should know beforehand what kind of place it is. While some bars, clubs, cabarets, and discos are reasonable and affordable for most foreign visitors, many are not. A few drinks, a dish of peanuts or rice crackers, and some conversation with a hostess could add up to the won equivalent of hundreds of dollars.

Before you set out for an evening on the town—or for a drink or two anywhere other than your hotel bar—ask a Korean friend or acquaintance, or check with your hotel staff or a Tourist Information Center, to get information on the kind of place you're looking for. *Do not choose a bar, nightclub, or cabaret on you own.* And remember that appearances can be misleading. A modest-looking place could turn out to be extremely expensive. *Ask First!*

This section contains phrases useful for various kinds of nightlife. For ordering once inside, refer to the *Eating and Drinking Out* section, which gives complete listings for beverages and snacks.

CINEMA/THEATER

Is it a Korean film?	한국 영화닙니까? Han-guk yŏnghwamnikka?
an American	미국 Miguk
Do they show it in the original language?	원어로 상영합니까? Wonŏro sangyŏnghamnikka?
Is it dubbed in Korean?	한국어로 더빙한 겁니까? Han-gugŏro tŏbinghan kŏmnikka?
Does it have English subtitles?	영어 자막이 있읍니까? Yŏng-ŏ chamagi issŭmnikka?
Is it a first-run film?	개봉 영화닙니까? Kaebong yŏnghwamnikka?
Is the film black and white, or color?	영화가 흑백입니까 칼라입니까? Yŏnghwaga hŭkpaegimnikka k'allaimnikka?
What kind of story is it?	어떤 이야기입니까? Ŏttŏn iyagiimnikka?
Are the performers Americans or Koreans?	출연자들이 미국인입니까 한국인입니까? Ch'uryŏnjadŭri Miguginimnikka Han-guginimnikka?
Do they speak English or Korean?	출연자들이 영어로 말합니까 한국어로 말합니까? Ch'uryŏnja-dŭri Yŏng-ŏro marhamnikka Han-gugŏro marhamnikka?
Let's go to the movies.	우리 영화 보러 갑시다. Uri yŏnghwa porŏ kapshida.

I'd like to go see a <u>film</u>.	<u>영화가</u> 보고 싶은데요? <u>Yŏnghwaga</u> pogo ship'ŭndeyo.
play	연극이 Yŏn-gŭgi
Are there any good films in town?	시내에 뭐 볼 만한 영화 있읍니까? Shinaee mwo pol manhan yŏnghwa issŭmnikka?
Could you recommend one?	어떤 것이 좋습니까? Ŏttŏn kŏshi chossŭmnikka?
Where's the <u>movie theater</u>?	그 <u>영화관이</u> 어디에 있읍니까? Kŭ <u>yŏnghwagwani</u> ŏdie issŭmnikka?
theater	극장이 kŭkchang-i
What's the title of the <u>film</u>?	영화 제목이 뭡니까? <u>Yŏng-hwa</u> chemogi mwomnikka?
play	연극 Yŏn-gŭk
Who's the <u>director</u> of the film?	영화 감독이 누굽니까? <u>Yong-hwa kamdogi</u> nugumnikka?
director of the play	연출가가 Yonch'ulgaga
Who's playing the lead?	누가 주연입니까? Nuga chuyŏnimnikka?
Is it a <u>comedy</u>?	<u>희극입니까</u>? <u>Hŭigŭgimnikka?</u>
historical drama	사극 Sagŭk
musical	뮤지칼 Myujik'ar
mystery	미스테리 Misŭt'eri
romance	애정물 Aejŏngmur
science fiction film	공상 과학 영화 Kongsang kwahak yŏnghwa

thriller/horror movie	공포 영화	Kongp'o yŏnghwa
tragedy	비극	Pigŭk
Western	서부극	Sŏbugŭk
war film	전쟁 영화	Chŏnjaeng yŏnghwa

Is there a cloak-room?	휴대품 보관소 있읍니까? Hyudae-p'um pokwanso issŭmnikka?
Is there a program in English?	영어로 된 프로그램 있읍니까? Yŏng-ŏro toen p'ŭrogŭraem issŭmnikka?
Please show me to my seat.	이 자리가 어디에 있읍니까? I chariga ŏdie issŭmnikka?
Is there a Broadway show being performed now?	브로드웨이형 쇼 있읍니까? Pŭrodŭweihyŏng syo issŭmnikka?
What time does the first show begin?	첫 공연이 몇 시에 시작됩니까? Ch'ŏt kongyŏni myŏt shie shijaktoemnikka?
What time does the show end?	공연이 몇 시에 끝납니까? Kongyŏni myŏt shie kkŭnnamnikka?
What time does the performance begin?	공연이 몇 시에 시작됩니까? Kongyŏni myŏt shie shijaktoemnikka?
end	끝납니까 kkŭnnamnikka
How long will it run?	얼마나 오랫 동안 상연될까요? Ŏlmana oraet tong-an sang-yŏndoelkkayo?

Is there a matinee?	마티네가 있읍니까? Mat'inega issŭmnikka?
Where can I buy a ticket?	표를 어디서 삽니까? P'yorŭl ŏdisŏ samnikka?
Where's the box office?	매표소가 어디에 있읍니까? Maep'yosoga ŏdie issŭmnikka?
Do you have any tickets left for <u>tonight</u>?	<u>오늘 밤</u> 표 있읍니까? <u>Onŭl pam</u> p'yo issŭmnikka?
the next show	다음 회 Taŭm hoe
I'd like to buy <u>a ticket</u> for tonight.	오늘 밤 표 1매 부탁합니다. Onŭl pam <u>p'yo han mae</u> put'ak'amnida.
two tickets four tickets	표 2매 p'yo tu mae 표 4매 p'yo ne mae
I'd like to buy a ticket for <u>tomorrow night</u>.	<u>내일 밤</u> 표 1매 부탁합니다. <u>Naeil pam</u> p'yo han mae put'ak'amnida.
Friday Saturday Sunday Monday Tuesday Wednesday Thursday	금요일 Kŭmyoil 토요일 T'oyoil 일요일 Iryoil 월요일 Woryoil 화요일 Hwayoil 수요일 Suyoil 목요일 Mogyoil
Do you have seats in the <u>orchestra</u>?	<u>무대에 가까운</u> 좌석 있읍니까? <u>Mudaee kakkaun</u> chwasŏk issŭmnikka?
balcony mezzanine	2층 Ich'ŭng 2층 앞쪽 Ich'ŭng aptchok

Do you have better seats than that?	그것보다 더 좋은 좌석 있읍니까? Kŭgŏtpoda tŏ choŭn chwasŏk issŭmnikka?
Do you have seats a little more <u>for</u>ward?	더 앞쪽 좌석 있읍니까? Tŏ <u>ap-tchok</u> chwasŏk issŭmnikka?
to the rear	뒤쪽 twitchok

Foreign-made films are shown with their original sound tracks and Korean titles. Korean films, of course, have Korean sound tracks, but you might enjoy them just the same: For theater fans, there are good stage productions in Seoul and other Korean cities.

MUSIC-RELATED PERFORMANCES

Who is the <u>composer</u>?	작곡가가 누굽니까? Chakkokkaga nugumnikka?
lead dancer	주연 무용수가 Chuyŏn muyongsuga
lead singer	주연 가수가 Chuyŏn kasuga
violinist	바이올린 주자가 Paiollin chujaga
What time does tonight's performance start?	오늘 밤 연주는 몇 시에 시작합니까? Onŭl pam yŏnjunŭn myŏt shie shijak'amnikka?
Are tonight's tickets <u>sold out</u>?	오늘 밤 표 매진됐읍니까? Onŭl pam p'yo maejindwaessŭmnikka?

still available	아직 있읍니까	ajik issŭmnikka

Should I get tickets in advance?
표를 예매해야 합니까? P'yorŭl yemaehaeya hamnikka?

What are the least expensive seats?
제일 싼 좌석이 어떤 겁니까? Cheil ssan chwasŏgi ŏttŏn kŏmnikka?

I'd like to get good seats.
좋은 좌석으로 좀 부탁합니다. Choŭn chwasŏgŭro chom put'ak'amnida.

How much are the front-row seats?
전열 좌석이 얼맙니까? Chŏnnyŏl chwasŏgi ŏlmamnikka?

I'll take any seats available.
아무 좌석이나 좋습니다. Amu chwasŏgina chossŭmnida.

Could you show me where our seats are on the chart?
좌석표에 저희 좌석이 어디에 있읍니까? Chwasŏkp'yo-e chŏhŭi chwasŏgi ŏdie issŭmnikka?

Can I <u>see</u> well from there?
거기에서 잘 <u>보입니까</u>? Kŏgiesŏ chal <u>poimnikka</u>?

  hear
들립니까 tŭllimnikka

Is there an intermission?
중간에 휴식 시간이 있읍니까? Chunggane hyushik shigani issŭmnikka?

Is it nearby?
거기가 가깝습니까? Kŏgiga kakkapsŭmnikka?

Is a ballet being performed now?
지금 발레가 공연 중에 있읍니까? Chigŭm pallega kongyŏn chung-e issŭmnikka?

Is a concert being performed now?	지금 음악회가 열리고 있읍니까? **Chigŭm ŭmak'oega yŏlligo issŭmnikka?**
Which <u>ballet company</u> is performing?	어떤 <u>발레단이</u> 공연 중입니까? **Ŏttŏn <u>palledani</u> kongyŏn chung-imnikka?**
opera company	가극단이 kagŭktani
Which <u>orchestra</u> is playing?	어떤 <u>관현악단이</u> 연주하고 있읍니까? **Ŏttŏn <u>kwanhyŏnaktani</u> yŏnjuhago issŭmnikka?**
symphony orchestra	교향악단이 kyohyang-aktani
band	악단이 aktani
group	그룹이 kŭrubi
Is that a Korean <u>ballet company</u>?	한국의 <u>발레단</u>입니까? **Han-gugŭi <u>palledan</u>imnikka?**
opera company	가극단 kagŭktan
orchestra	관현악단 kwanhyŏnaktan
Is that a foreign <u>ballet company</u>?	외국 <u>발레단</u>입니까? **Oeguk <u>palledan</u>imnikka?**
opera company	가극단 kagŭktan
orchestra	관현악단 kwanhyŏnaktan
Which country do they come from?	어느 나라에서 왔읍니까? **Ŏnŭ nara-esŏ wassŭmnikka?**
What are they performing?	무엇을 공연하고 있읍니까? **Muŏsŭl kongyŏnhago issŭmnikka?**

Who's conduct-ing?

누가 지휘하고 있읍니까?
Nuga chihwihago issŭmnikka?

dancing	춤을 추고	ch'umŭl ch'ugo
playing	연주하고	yŏnjuhago
singing	노래하고	noraehago

I'd like to attend a ballet.

발레를 보고 싶은데요.
Pallerŭl pogo ship'ŭndeyo.

a concert	음악회에 가고	Ŭmak'oee kago
an opera	오페라를 보고	Op'erarŭl pogo

Do I need to dress formally?

정장을 해야 합니까? Chŏng-jang-ŭl haeya hamnikka?

What shall I wear?

어떤 옷을 입을까요?
Ŏttŏn osŭl ibŭlkkayo?

I prefer chamber music.

실내악을 더 좋아합니다.
Shillaeagŭl dŏ choahamnida.

classical music	고전 음악을	Kojŏn ŭmagŭl
concertos	협주곡을	Hyŏpchugogŭl
country music	컨트리 뮤직을	K'ŏnt'ŭri myujigŭl
folk songs	포크 송을	P'ok'ŭ song-ŭl
jazz	재즈를	Chejŭrŭl
modern music	현대 음악을	Hyŏndae ŭmagŭl
popular songs	팝송을	P'apsong-ŭl
rock'n'roll	로큰롤을	Rok'ŭnrorŭl
symphonies	심포니를	Shimp'onirŭl
classical ballet	고전 발레를	Kojŏn pallerŭl
modern ballet	현대 발레를	Hyŏndae pallerŭl

Where's the con-cert hall?

음악당이 어디에 있읍니까?
Ŭmaktang-i ŏdie issŭmnikka?

PASTIMES

Paduk and *Changgi*

Could you teach me how to play *paduk*.

바둑 좀 가르쳐 주시겠읍니까?
<u>Paduk</u> chom karŭchy'ŏ chushigessŭmnikka?

    how to play *changgi*

장기   Changgi

Is it difficult to learn *paduk*?

바둑 배우기가 어렵습니까? Paduk paeugiga ŏryŏpsŭmnikka?

Do you have a <u>*paduk* board and stones?</u>

바둑판과 바둑알 있읍니까?
<u>Padukp'an-gwa padugal</u> issumnikka?

    changgi board and pieces

장기판과 장기말   Changgip'an-gwa   changgimal

How do you decide the winner and loser?

승부는 어떻게 결정합니까?
Sŭngbunŭn ŏttŏk'e kyŏlchŏnghamnikka?

How do you capture your opponent's <u>stones</u>?

상대편 <u>돌을</u> 어떻게 땁니까?
Sangdaep'yŏn <u>torŭl</u> ŏttŏk'e ttamnikka?

    pieces

말을   marŭl

Do you play <u>*paduk*</u>?

바둑 두십니까?
<u>Paduk</u> tushimnikka?

    changggi

장기   Changgi

I don't know how to play *paduk*.

바둑 둘 줄 모릅니다.
Paduk tul chul morŭmnida.

I don't know how to play *changgi*.	장기 둘 줄 모릅니다. Changgi tul chul morŭmnida.
know	압니다 amnida
Could you play *paduk* with me?	바둑 한번 둘까요? Paduk hanbŏn tulkkayo?
changgi	장기 Changgi

These are two of Korea's oldest traditional board games. *Changgi* is similar to chess. *Paduk* is a territorial game, played with flat, round black and white stones. It's been in Korea for about 1300 years, and originally came from China. You probably won't master the fine points of *paduk* and *changgi* in a short time, but you can learn the basics, and then continue to play back home.

Reference Section

COUNTING YEARS

one year	1 년	il nyŏn
two years	2 년	i nyŏn
three years	3 년	sam nyŏn
four years	4 년	sa nyŏn
five years	5 년	o nyŏn
six years	6 년	yung nyŏn
seven years	7 년	ch'il nyŏn
eight years	8 년	p'al nyŏn

THE FOUR SEASONS

spring	봄	pom
summer	여름	yŏrum
fall	가을	kaŭl
winter	겨울	kyŏul

MONTHS OF THE YEAR

January	1월	irwol
February	2월	iwol

March	3월	samwol
April	4월	sawol
May	5월	owol
June	6월	yuwol
July	7월	ch'irwol
August	8월	p'arwol
September	9월	kuwol
October	10월	shiwol
November	11월	shibirwol
December	12월	shibiwol

DAYS OF THE MONTH

1st	1일	iril
2nd	2일	iil
3rd	3일	samil
4th	4일	sail
5th	5일	oil
6th	6일	yugil
7th	7일	ch'iril
8th	8일	p'aril
9th	9일	kuil

10th	10일	shibil
11th	11일	shibiril
12th	12일	shibiil
13th	13일	shipsamil
14th	14일	shipsail
15th	15일	shiboil
16th	16일	shimnyugil
17th	17일	shipch'iril
18th	18일	shipp'aril
19th	19일	shipkuil
20th	20일	ishibil
21st	21일	ishibiril
22nd	22일	ishibiil
23rd	23일	ishipsamil
24th	24일	ishipsail
25th	25일	ishiboil
26th	26일	ishimnyugil
27th	27일	ishipch'iril
28th	28일	ishipp'aril
29th	29일	ishipkuil
30th	30일	samshibil
31st	31일	samshibiril

COUNTING WEEKS

one week	1 주	il chu
two weeks	2 주	i chu
three weeks	3 주	sam chu
four weeks	4 주	sa chu
five weeks	5 주	o chu
six weeks	6 주	yuk chu
seven weeks	7 주	ch'il chu
eight weeks	8 주	p'al chu
nine weeks	9 주	ku chu
ten weeks	10 주	ship chu

DAYS OF THE WEEK

Sunday	일요일	iryoil
Monday	월요일	woryoil
Tuesday	화요일	hwayoil
Wednesday	수요일	suyoil
Thursday	목요일	mogyoil
Friday	금요일	kŭmyoil
Saturday	토요일	t'oyoil

COUNTING DAYS

one day	1 일	ir il
two days	2 일	i il
three days	3 일	sam il
four days	4 일	sa il
five days	5 일	o il
six days	6 일	yuk il
seven days	7 일	ch'ir il
eight dsys	8 일	p'ar il
nine days	9 일	ku il
ten days	10 일	ship il
eleven days	11 일	ship ir il

TIME PHRASES

today	오늘	onŭl
yesterday	어제	ŏje
the day before yesterday	그제	kŭje
tomorrow	내일	naeil
the day after to-morrow	모레	more

this week	금주	kŭmju
last week	지난주	chinanju
next week	다음주	taŭmchu
for one week	1주간	il chugan
for two weeks	2주간	i chugan
in one week	1주에	il chue
in two weeks	2주에	i chue
for two days	이틀간	it'ŭlgan
in one day	하루에	harue
in two days	이틀에	it'ŭre
three days ago	3일 전	sam il chŏn
four months ago	4개월 전	sa kaewol chŏn
five years ago	5년 전	o nyŏn chŏn
this year	금년	kŭmnyŏn
last year	작년	changnyŏn
next year	내년	naenyŏn
this morning	오늘 아침	onŭl ach'im
this afternoon	오늘 오후	onŭl ohu
tonight	오늘 밤	onŭl pam
tomorrow night	내일 밤	naeil pam
for six years	6년간	yung nyŏn-gan

for seven months	7개월간	ch'il kaewolgan
in the morning	아침에	ach'ime
in the afternoon	오후에	ohue
in the early evening	초저녁에	ch'ojŏnyŏge
in the evening	저녁에	chŏnyŏge
in summer	여름에	yŏrŭme
in winter	겨울에	kyŏure
by Tuesday	화요일까지는	hwayoilkkajinŭn
by June	6월까지는	yuwolkkajinŭn
by morning	아침까지는	ach'imkkajinŭn
What's today's date?	오늘 며칠입니까? Onŭl myŏch'irimnikka?	
It's ___.	오늘은 ___입니다. Onŭrŭn ___imnida.	
What day is today?	오늘 무슨 요일입니까? Onŭl musŭn yoirimnikka?	
It's ___.	오늘은 ___입니다. Onŭrŭn ___imnida.	

THE TIME

A.M.	오전	Ojŏn
P.M.	오후	ohu
noon	정오	chŏng-o

midnight	자정	chajŏng
o'clock	시	shi

First, a list of hours, then a list of minutes, then we'll put them together!

Hours

1 o'clock	1시	hanshi
2 o'clock	2시	tushi
3 o'clock	3시	seshi
4 o'clock	4시	neshi
5 o'clock	5시	tasŏssi
6 o'clock	6시	yŏsossi
7 o'clock	7시	ilgopshi
8 o'clock	8시	yŏdŏlshi
9 o'clock	9시	ahopshi
10 o'clock	10시	yŏlshi
11 o'clock	11시	yŏrhanshi
12 o'clock	12시	yŏltushi

Minutes

1 minute	1분	ilbun
2 minutes	2분	ibun
3 minutes	3분	sambun

4 minutes	4분	sabun
5 minutes	5분	obun
6 minutes	6분	yukpun
7 minutes	7분	ch'ilbun
8 minutes	8분	p'albun
9 minutes	9분	kubun
10 minutes	10분	shippun
11 minutes	11분	shibilbun
12 minutes	12분	shibibun
13 minutes	13분	shipsambun
14 minutes	14분	shipsabun
15 minutes	15분	shibobun
16 minutes	16분	shimnyukpun
17 minutes	17분	shipch'ilbun
18 minutes	18분	shipp'albun
19 minutes	19분	shipkubun
20 minutes	20분	ishippun
21 minutes	21분	ishibilbun
22 minutes	22분	ishibibun
23 minutes	23분	ishipsambun
24 minutes	24분	ishipsabun

Reference Section

25 minutes	25분	ishibobun
26 minutes	26분	ishimnyukpun
27 minutes	27분	ishipch'ilbun
28 minutes	28분	ishipp'albun
29 minutes	29분	ishipkubun
30 minutes	30분	samshippun
31 minutes	31분	samshibilbun
32 minutes	32분	samshibibun
33 minutes	33분	samshipsambun
34 minutes	34분	samshipsabun
35 minutes	35분	samshibobun
36 minutes	36분	samshimnyukpun
37 minutes	37분	samshipch'ilbun
38 minutes	38분	samshipp'albun
39 minutes	39분	samshipkubun
40 minutes	40분	sashippun
41 minutes	41분	sashibilbun
42 minutes	42분	sashibibun
43 minutes	43분	sashipsambun
44 minutes	44분	sashipsabun
45 minutes	45분	sashibobun

46 minutes	46분	sashimnyukpun
47 minutes	47분	sashipch'ilbun
48 minutes	48분	sashipp'albun
49 minutes	49분	sashipkubun
50 minutes	50분	oshippun
51 minutes	51분	oshibilbun
52 minutes	52분	oshibibun
53 minutes	53분	oshipsambun
54 minutes	54분	oshipsabun
55 minutes	55분	oshibobun
56 minutes	56분	oshimnyukpun
57 minutes	57분	oshipch'ilbun
58 minutes	58분	oshipp'albun
59 minutes	59분	oshipkubun

a quarter after ten   yŏlshi shibobun
a quarter to ten   yŏlshi shibobun chŏn

[Note: start using "chŏn," which means "to" or "before," at 15minutes before the hour.]

half past ten   yŏlshi pan

[Note: "pan" means "half."]

What time is it?   지금 몇 시입니까?
                    Chigŭm myŏt shiimnikka?

It's <u>5 : 00</u> o'clock. <u>5</u>시입니다. <u>Tasŏsshiimnida.</u>

5 : 05	5시 5분 Tasŏsshi obun
5 : 10	5시 10분 Tasŏsshi shippun
5 : 15	5시 15분 Tasŏsshi shibobun
5 : 20	5시 20분 Tasŏsshi ishippun
5 : 25	5시 25분 Tasŏsshi ishibobun
5 : 30	5시 30분 Tasŏsshi samshippun
5 : 35	5시 35분 Tasŏsshi samshibobun
5 : 40	5시 40분 Tasŏsshi sashippun
5 : 45[a quarter to six]	5시 45분[6시 15분 전] Tasŏsshi sashibobun[Yŏsŏsshi shibobun chŏn]
5 : 50[ten to six]	6시 10분 전 Yŏsŏsshi shippun chŏn
5 : 55[five to six]	6시 5분 전 Yŏsŏsshi obun chŏn
5 : 57[three to six]	6시 3분 전 Yŏsŏsshi sambun chŏn

For time schedules, as in railway and airline timetables, numbers 1 to 59 are used for minutes, not "a quarter to," or "ten to" the hour.

My train leaves at 1 : 48 P.M.   제 기차는 오후 1시 48분에 출발합니다.   Che kich'anŭn ohu hanshi sashipp'albune ch'ulbarhamnida.

| My plane arrives at 10 : 53 A.M. | 제 비행기는 오전 10시 53분에 도착합니다. Che pihaengginŭn ojŏn yŏlshi oshipsambune toch'ak'amnida. |

Transportation timetables are based on the 24-hour clock. Airline and train schedules are expressed in terms of a point within a 24-hour sequence.

PUBLIC HOLIDAYS

January 1 New Year's Day	설날	Sŏllal
March 1 Independence Movement Day	삼일절	Samilchŏl
April 5 Arbor Day	식목일	Shingmogil
8th of 4th lunar month Buddha's Birthday	석탄일	Sokt'anil
May 5 Children's Day	어린이 날	Ŏrini nal
June 6 Memorial Day	현충일	Hyŏnch'ung-il
July 17 Constitution Day	제헌절	Chehŏnjŏl
August 15 Liberation Day	광복절	Kwangbokchŏl

| 15th of 8th lunar month | | |
| Korean Thanks-giving Day | 추석 | Ch'usŏk |

| October 1 | | |
| Armed Forces Day | 국군의 날 | Kakkunŭi nal |

| October 3 | | |
| National Found-ation Day | 개천절 | Kaech'ŏnjŏl |

| October 9 | | |
| Han-gŭl Day | 한글날 | Han-gŭllal |

| December 25 Christmas | 성탄절 | Sŏngt'anjŏl |

COUNTRIES

Argentina	아르헨티나	Arŭhent'ina
Australia	오스트레일리아	Osŭt'ŭreillia
Austria	오스트리아	Osŭt'ŭria
Belgium	벨기에	Pelgie
Brazil	브라질	Pŭrajil
Canada	캐나다	K'aenada
Chile	칠레	Ch'ille
China	중국	Chungguk

Czechoslovakia	체코	Ch'ek'o
Denmark	덴마크	Tenmak'ŭ
Ecuador	에쿠아도르	Ek'uadorŭ
Egypt	이집트	Ijipt'ŭ
England	영국	Yŏngguk
Finland	핀란드	P'illandŭ
France	프랑스	P'ŭrangsŭ
Greece	그리스	Kŭrisŭ
Holland	네덜란드	Nedŏllandŭ
India	인디아	India
Indonesia	인도네시아	Indoneshia
Iran	이란	Iran
Ireland	아일랜드	Aillaendŭ
Israel	이스라엘	Isŭra-el
Italy	이태리	It'aeri
Jordan	요르단	Yorŭdan
Korea	한국	Han-guk
Kuwait	쿠웨이트	K'uweit'ŭ
Lebanon	레바논	Lebanon
Malaysia	말레이지아	Malleijia
Mexico	멕시코	Mekshik'o

New Zealand	뉴질랜드	Nyujillaendŭ
Norway	노르웨이	Norŭwei
Pakistan	파키스탄	P'ak'ist'an
Peru	페루	P'eru
Philippines	필리핀	P'illip'in
Poland	폴란드	P'ollandŭ
Portugal	포르투갈	P'orŭt'ugal
Saudi Arabia	사우디아라비아	Saudiarabia
Singapore	싱가포르	Shinggap'orŭ
South Africa	남아프리카	Namap'ŭrik'a
Soviet Union	소련	Soryŏn
Spain	스페인	Sŭp'ein
Sweden	스웨덴	Sŭweden
Switzerland	스위스	Sŭwisŭ
Thailand	태국	T'aeguk
Turkey	터키	T'ŏk'i
United States	미국	Miguk
Uruguay	우루과이	Urugwai
Venezuela	베네즈웰라	Penejŭwella
West Germany	서독	Sŏdok
Yugoslavia	유고슬라비아	Yugosŭllabia

NATIONALITIES

To express nationality, add *in* to the Korean expressions or the countries listed above. For example, to say "American," look up the country United States, which is Miguk, and add *in*. Thus American is Migugin. *In* literally means "person."

COUNTING TIMES

once	1 번	han pŏn
twice	2 번	tu pŏn
three times	3 번	se pŏn
four times	4 번	ne pŏn
five times	5 번	tasŏt pŏn
the first time	첫번째	ch'ŏtpŏntchae
the second time	두번째	tubŏntchae
the third time	세번째	sebŏntchae
the fourth time	네번째	nebŏntchae
the fifth time	다섯번째	tasŏtpŏntchae
the sixth time	여섯번째	yŏsŏtpŏntchae
the seventh time	일곱번째	ilgoppŏntchae
the eighth time	여덟번째	yŏdŏlpŏntchae
the ninth time	아홉번째	ahoppŏntchae

COUNTING THINGS

1 (one)	2 (two)	3 (three)	4 (four)
people			
han myŏng 1 명	tu myŏng 2 명	se myŏng 3 명	ne myŏng 4 명
pencils			
han charu 1 자루	tu charu 2 자루	se charu 3 자루	ne charu 4 자루
thin, flat objects (paper, bills, cloth, dishes, tickets, and so forth)			
han chang 1 장	tu chang 2 장	se chang 3 장	ne chang 4 장
bound objects (books, magazines, notebooks, and so forth)			
han kwon 1 권	tu kwon 2 권	se kwon 3 권	ne kwon 4 권
vehicles, machines			
han tae 1 대	tu tae 2 대	se tae 3 대	ne tae 4 대
things to wear (jackets, sweaters, shirts, coats, and so forth)			
han pŏl 1 벌	tu pŏl 2 벌	se pŏl 3 벌	ne pŏl 4 벌

pairs of things to wear on feet or legs (socks, shoes, slippers, and so forth)

han k'yŏlle	tu k'yŏlle	se k'yŏlle	ne k'yŏlle
1 켤레	2 켤레	3 켤레	4 켤레

pairs of people

han ssang	tu ssang	se ssang	ne ssang
1 쌍	2 쌍	3 쌍	4 쌍

boxes, cases, and so forth

han sangja	tu sangja	se sangja	ne sangja
1 상자	2 상자	3 상자	4 상자

floors of buildings

il ch'ŭng	i ch'ŭng	sam ch'ŭng	sa ch'ŭng
1 층	2 층	3 층	4 층

animals, insects, fish

han mari	tu mari	se mari	ne mari
1 마리	2 마리	3 마리	4 마리

houses

han ch'ae	tu ch'ae	se ch'ae	ne ch'ae
1 채	2 채	3 채	4 채

horses

han p'il	tu p'il	se p'il	ne p'il
1 필	2 필	3 필	4 필

bunches (grapes, bananas, and so forth)

han song-i	tu song-i	se song-i	ne song-i
1 송이	2 송이	3 송이	4 송이

slices			
han chogak 1조각	tu chogak 2조각	se chogak 3조각	ne chogak 4조각
portions, servings			
ir inbun 1인분	i inbun 2인분	sam inbun 3인분	sa inbun 4인분
small objects not in the categories listed above			
han kae 1개	tu kae 2개	se kae 3개	ne kae 4개

A Korean Grammar Guide

A few notes on grammatical details are provided for those who wish to grasp and understand the structure of the Korean language.

ARTICLE

The Korean language does not have articles like *a* or *the* in English. Also singular and plural forms are not as clear as in English. Thus, 개 *kae(dog)* may mean *a dog or dogs.*

TABLE OF PRONOUNS

En-glish	Korean	En-glish	Korean
I	nanŭn, naega	he	kŭnŭn, kŭga
we	urinŭn, uriga	his	kŭŭi
my	naŭi	him	kŭrŭl, kŭege
our	uriŭi	she	kŭ yŏjaga, kŭ yŏjanŭn
me	na-ege, narŭl	her	kŭ yŏjaŭi
us	uriege, urirŭl	her	kŭ yŏjarŭl, kŭ yŏja-ege
you	tangshinŭn, tangshini	they	kŭdŭrŭn, kŭdŭri
your	tangshinŭi	their	kŭdŭrŭi
you	tangshinege, tangshinŭl	them	kŭdŭrege, kŭdŭrŭl

ADJECTIVES

The position of adjectives in the Korean language is before the noun. Korean adjectives, like English ones, modifies the noun by being placed in front of the noun: *hŭin changmi* 흰 장미 *white rose*.

I have a white rose. Nanŭn hŭin changmirŭl kajigo issŭmnida.

A function of adjectives as in English is to describe the subject: *hŭimnida* 흽니다 *is white*, *yeppŭmnida* 예쁩니다 *is pretty*. Notice that these Korean words do not mean *white* or *pretty* but *is white* or *is pretty*.

This book is interesting. I ch'aegŭn chaemiissŭmnida.

NUMERALS

Arabic	Cardinal	Cardinal	Ordinal
0	yŏng		
1	il	hana	ch'ŏt(pŏn)tchae
2	i	tul	tultchae, tubŏntchae
3	sam	set	se(bŏn)tchae
4	sa	net	ne(bŏn)tchae
5	o	tasŏt	tasŏt(pŏn)tchae
6	yuk	yŏsŏt	yŏsŏt(pŏn)tchae
7	ch'il	ilgop	ilgop(pŏn)tchae
8	p'al	yŏdŏl	yŏdŏl(pŏn)tchae
9	ku	ahop	ahop(pŏn)tchae
10	ship	yŏl	yŏl(pŏn)tchae
11	ship il	yŏl hana	yŏl han(bŏn)tchae

12	ship i	yŏl tul	yŏl tu(bŏn)tchae
13	ship sam	yŏl set	yŏl se(bŏn)tchae
20	iship	sŭmul	sŭmu(bŏn)tchae
21	iship il	sŭmul hana	sŭmul han(bŏn)tchae
22	iship i	sŭmul tul	sŭmul tu(bŏn)tchae
30	samship	sŏrŭn	sŏrŭn(bŏn)tchae
40	saship	mahŭn	mahŭn(bŏn)tchae
50	oship	shwin	shwin(bŏn)tchae
60	yukship	yesun	yesun(bŏn)tchae
70	ch'ilship	irhŭn	irhŭn(bŏn)tchae
80	p'alship	yŏdŭn	yŏdŭn(bŏn)tchae
90	kuship	ahŭn	ahŭn(bŏn)tchae
100	paek	paek	paek(pŏn)tchae

For the numbers over hundred there is an only way of counting.

200	ibaek	2, 000	ich'ŏn
300	sambaek	3, 000	samch'ŏn
400	sabaek	4, 000	sach'ŏn
500	obaek	5, 000	och'ŏn
600	yukpaek	6, 000	yukch'ŏn
700	ch'ilbaek	7, 000	ch'ilch'ŏn
800	p'albaek	8, 000	p'alch'ŏn
900	kubaek	9, 000	kuch'ŏn
1, 000	ch'ŏn	10, 000	man
20, 000	iman	50, 000	oman

VERBS

A characteristic of the Korean sentence is the fact that it ends with verbs. The verb in Korean indicates that either something happens or someone does something in a certain manner.

Position of Verb

Note that the Korean verb is placed at the end of the sentence as follows:

English structure: I read a book.

Korean structure: I *nŭn* a book *ŭl* read.

$$(Na) \quad (ch'aek) \quad (iksŭmnida)$$

Verb Stem and Suffix

The verb in Korean consists of one verb stem plus one or more suffixes. For instance, the verb *oda* 오다 (to come) takes the suffixes in the following manner:

Korean	Stem-Suffix	Stem-Suffix	Meaning
오다	오-	o-	to come
옵니다	오-ㅂ니다	o-mnida	come
옵시다	오-ㅂ시다	o-pshida	let's come
옵니까	오-ㅂ니까	o-mnikka?	do(you)come?

Conjugation

In Korean dictionaries, verbs are shown in present tense ending with *-da* -다.

kada 가다 I [you, we, they] go(or to go)

However, in ordinary conversation the above forms of present tense are rarely used. Instead, the suffixes such as *-mnida* -ㅂ니다(after vowel) or *-ŭmnida* -읍니다(after consonant) are very common.

The following charts show changes of verb according to its tense. Please note that there are certain patterns (or rules) one can make from the examples which can be applied in making other various verb forms.

(1) Present tense

After	Suffix	Example	Meaning
Vowel	-mnida	sada사다→samnida	to buy
Consonant	-ŭmnida	ch'amta참다→ch'am-ŭmnida	to endure

(2) Past tense

After		Suffix	Example	Meaning
Vowel	a	-ssŭmnida	sada사다→sassŭmnida	bought
	o	-assŭmnida	ssoda쏘다→ssoassŭmnida	shot
	e		peda베다→peŏssŭmnida	cut
	i	-ŏssŏmnida	kida기다→kiŏssŭmnida	crept
	u		chuda주다→chuŏssŭmnida	gave
	ha	-yŏssŭmnida exception	hada하다→hayŏssŭmnida	did
			oda오다→wassŭmnida	came
Consonant	a+c.	-assŭmnida	ch'amta참다→ch'amass-ŭmnida	en-dured
	o+c.		nokta녹다→nogassŏmnida	melted
	other vowel +consonant	-ŏssŭmnida	chŏpta접다→chŏbŏssŭm-nida	folded
			ipta입다→ibŏssŭmnida	wore
			mutta묻다→mudŏssŭmnida	buried

(3) Future tense

After	Suffix	Example	Meaning
Vowel	-gessŭmnida	sada사다→sagessŭmnida	I will buy
		hada하다→hagessŭmnida	I will do
Consonant	-k[g]es-sŭmnida	ipta입다→ipkessŭmnida	I will wear
		kalda갈다→kalgessŭm-nida	I will grind

A Korean Grammar Guide

OMISSION OF SUBJECT

Like other languages, it is not unusual in the Korean language to drop the subject of sentence particularly when meaning is obvious without mentioning the details.

Kamnida[*go*] may mean *I*[*you, he, she, they, we*] *am*[*is, are*]*going. Kamnikka?*[*go?*] may mean *Is* [*Are*] *he*[*she, you, they*] *going?*

Taegu[to Taegu]*kamnida* [go].	(*I'm*) *going to Taegu.*
Naeil[Tomorrow]*Taegu* [to Taegu] *kamnida*[go].	(*I'm*) *going to Taegu tomorrow.*

DECLARATIVE AND INTERROGATIVE

Unlike English, the Korean language has different suffixes for declarative and interrogative sentence respectively.

Sonyŏni kamnida.	The boy is going.
Sonyŏni kamnikka?	Is the boy going?

In the above example, the suffix *-da* is used for a declarative and *-kka* for a interrogative sentence.

Vocabulary

⋯❧ A ❧⋯

abalone 전복 *chŏnbok*
accident 사고 *sago*
acupressure 지압 *chiap*
acupressurist 지압사 *chiapsa*
acupuncture 침술 *ch'imsul*
acupuncturist 침술사 *ch'imsulsa*
ad 광고 *kwanggo*
adapter plug 어댑터 플러그 *ŏdaept'ŏ p'ŭllŏgŭ*
address 주소 *chuso*
adhesive tape 반창고 *panch'angko*
admission fee 입장료 *ipchangnyo*
aerogram 항공 봉함 엽서 *hanggong ponham yŏpsŏ*
Africa 아프리카 *Ap'ŭrik'a*
after ⋯ 후에 ⋯ *hue*
afternoon 오후 *ohu*
again 다시 *tashi*
age limit 연령 제한 *yŏllyŏng chehan*
air conditioner 냉방 장치 *naengbang changch'i*
airplane 비행기 *pihaenggi*
airport 공항 *konghang*

aisle 통로 *t'ongno*
alcohol 알콜 *alk'ol*
ale 에일 *eil*
allergy 알레르기 *allerŭgi*
almonds 아몬드 *amondŭ*
alone 혼자 *honja*
also 또한 *ttohan*
alter (clothing) 고치다 *koch'ida*
altogether 전부 *chŏnbu*
always 항상 *hangsang*
ambulance 구급차 *kugŭpch'a*
America 미국 *Miguk*
American (adj.) 미국의 *Migugŭi*
American 미국인 *Migugin*
American music 미국 음악 *Miguk ŭmak*
American products 미제 *Mije*
and (between nouns) 와 *wa*, 과 *kwa*
and (between sentences) 그리고 *kŭrigo*
ankle 발목 *palmok*
another 또 하나의 *tto hanaŭi*
antacid 제산제 *chesanje*
antibiotics 항생제 *hang-*

saengje

antiques 골동품 *koltong-p'um*

antiseptic 소독약 *sodong-nyak*

aperitif 아페리티프 *ap'e-rit'ip'ŭ*

appendicitis 맹장염 *maengjangnyŏm*

appetizers 전채 *chŏnch'ae*

apple 사과 *sagwa*

appointment 약속 *yaksok*

April 4월 *sawol*

aquamarine 남옥 *namok*

aquarium 수족관 *sujok-kwan*

Arabic (lang.) 아랍어 *Ar-abŏ*

architect 건축가 *kŏn-ch'ukka*

architecture 건축 *kŏnch'uk*

area 지역 *chiyŏk*

arm 팔 *p'al*

around (approximate time) 경에 *kyŏng-e*

arrive 도착하다 *toch'ak'a-da*

art 미술 *misul*

art gallery 화랑 *hwarang*

artist 예술가 *yesulga*

go ashore 상륙하다 *sang-nyuk'ada*

ashtray 재떨이 *chaettŏri*

aspirin 아스피린 *asŭp'irin*

aspirin-free pain-killer 아스피린 성분이 없는 진통제 *asŭp'irin sŏngbuni ŏmnŭn chint'ongje*

assistant 조수 *chosu*

assorted food 모듬 요리 *modŭm yori*

at …에 …*e*

atmosphere 분위기 *pun-wigi*

attaché case 서류 가방 *sŏryu kabang*

attractions 인기거리 *inki-kŏri*

main attractions 주요 인기거리 *chuyo inkikŏri*

auburn 적갈색 *chŏkkalsaek*

August 8월 *p'arwol*

aunt 숙모 *sungmo*

Australia 오스트레일리아 *Osŭt'ŭreillia*

author 저자 *chŏja*

auto mechanic 자동차 정비공 *chadongch'a chŏng-bigong*

auto repair shop 정비 공장 *chŏngbi kongjang*

automatic transmission 자동 변속 *chadong pyŏn-sok*

autumn leaves 단풍 *tan-p'ung*

awful-tasting 맛이 없는 *mashi ŏmnŭn*

⊶ B ⊷

baby 아기 *agi*
baby-sitter 애 보는 사람 *ae ponŭn saram*
back (location) 뒤에 *twie*
back (body) 등 *tŭng*
bacon 베이컨 *peik'ŏn*
bad 안 좋은 *an choŭn*
badminton 배드민턴 *paedŭmint'ŏn*
baggage 수하물 *suhamul*
baked 군 *kun*
bakery 빵집 *ppangchip*
balcony (theater) 2층석 *ich'ŭngsŏk*
ballet 발레 *palle*
ballet theater 발레 극장 *palle kŭkchang*
ballpoint pen 볼펜 *polp'en*
bamboo 대나무 *taenamu*
bamboo basket 대바구니 *taebaguni*
bamboo craft shop 죽세공점 *chuksegongjŏm*
banana 바나나 *panana*
band 악단 *aktan*
bandages 붕대 *pungdae*
bandaids 1회용 반창고 *irhoeyong panch'anggo*
bangs 단발머리 *tanbalmŏri*
bank 은행 *ŭnhaeng*
bar 바 *pa*
barbershop 이발소 *ibalso*

barn 광 *kwang*
baseball 야구 *yagu*
basket 바구니 *paguni*
basketball 농구 *nonggu*
bath 욕실 *yokshil*
bathing suit 수영복 *suyŏngbok*
bathtub 욕조 *yokcho*
bathroom 화장실 *hwajangshil*
batter-fried food 튀김 *t'wigim*
battery 전지 *chŏnji*
battery (car) 배터리 *paet'ŏri*
bay 만 *man*
beach 해안 *haean*
beach umbrella 비치 파라솔 *pich'i p'arasol*
bean curd 두부 *tubu*
beard 턱수염 *t'ŏksuyŏm*
beautiful, pretty 예쁜 *yeppŭn*
beauty parlor 미용실 *miyongshil*
bed 침대 *ch'imdae*
beef 쇠고기 *soegogi*
beer 맥주 *maekchu*
before 전에 *chŏne*
bellhop 보이 *poi*
belt 벨트 *pelt'ŭ*
better 더 좋은 *tŏ choŭn*
bicycle, bike 자전거 *chajŏn-gŏ*

bicycling 사이클링 *saik'ŭlling*

bicycling course 사이클링 코스 *saik'ŭlling k'osŭ*

big 큰 *k'ŭn*

bills(currency) 지폐 *chip'ye*

bird 새 *sae*

birthdate 생년월일 *saengnyŏnworil*

biscuits 비스켓 *pisŭk'et*

black 검은 *kŏmŭn*

black and white 흑백 *hŭkpaek*

blanket 담요 *tamnyo*

blender 믹서 *miksŏ*

blond 금발 *kŭmbal*

blood 피 *p'i*

blood pressure 혈압 *hyŏrap*

blouse 블라우스 *pŭllausŭ*

blow dry 드라이 *tŭrai*

blown glass 불어 만든 글래스 *purŏ mandŭn kŭllaesŭ*

blue 청색 *ch'ŏngsaek*

boat 보트 *pot'ŭ*

bobby pins 머리핀 *mŏrip'in*

body 몸 *mom*

body lotion 바디 로션 *padi losyŏn*

boiled 익힌 *ik'in*

bone 뼈 *ppyŏ*

book 책 *ch'aek*

bookstore 서점 *sŏjŏm*

boots 부츠 *puch'ŭ*

bottle 병 *pyŏng*

bourbon 버번 *pŏbŏn*

bow 인사 *insa*

bow (v.) 인사하다 *insahada*

bowl 사발 *sabal*

boxed 상자에 넣은 *sangja-e nŏŭn*

box office 매표소 *maep'yoso*

bra, brassiere 브라자 *pŭraja*

bracelet 팔찌 *p'altchi*

brakes 브레이크 *pŭreik'ŭ*

brake fluid 브레이크 오일 *pŭreik'ŭ oil*

Brazil 브라질 *Pŭrajil*

Brazilian 브라질의 *Pŭrajirŭi*

bread 빵 *ppang*

break down 고장나다 *kojangnada*

breakfast 조반 *choban*

bridge 다리 *tari*

bright 밝은 *palgŭn*

British 영국의 *Yŏnggugŭi*

Britisher 영국인 *Yŏnggugin*

Broadway hits 브로드웨이 히트 작품 *Pŭrodŭwei hit'ŭ chakp'um*

broccoli 브라컬리 *pŭrak'ŏlli*

broiled 불에 구운 *pure*

kuun

broken 부러진 *purŏjin*

broken, out of order 고장난 *kojangnan*

brown 갈색 *kalsaek*

bruise 타박상 *t'abaksang*

brunette 브루넷의 *pŭrunesŭi*

brushes 솔 *sol*

Buddhist temples 절 *chŏl*

buffet car 부페 차 *pup'e ch'a*

building 빌딩 *pilding*

built 지은 *chiŭn*

burn 화상 *hwasang*

bus 버스 *pŏsŭ*

bus stop 버스 정거장 *pŏsŭ chŏnggŏjang*

business 사업/비즈니스 *saŏp/pijŭnisŭ*

business district 비즈니스가 *pijinisŭga*

business trip 출장 *ch'ulchang*

but 그러나 *kŭrŏna*

butcher 정육점 *chŏngyukchŏm*

butter 버터 *pŏt'ŏ*

button 단추 *tanch'u*

buy 사다 *sada*

by (means of) …(으)로 … *(ŭ)ro*

by the aisle 통로측 *t'ongnoch'ŭk*

by the hour 시간당 *shigandang*

by the way 그런데 *kŭrŏnde*

by the window 창측 *ch'angch'ŭk*

—◁ **C** ▷—

cabaret 카바레 *k'abare*

cabbage 배추 *paech'u*

cable car 케이블 카 *k'eibŭl k'a*

caddy 캐디 *k'aedi*

cake 케이크 *k'eik'ŭ*

calendar 캘린더 *k'aellindŏ*

call 전화 걸다 *chŏnhwa kŏlda*

camera 카메라 *k'amera*

camera shop 카메라점 *k'amerajŏm*

camping 캠핑 *k'aemp'ing*

camping site 캠핑장 *k'aemp'ingjang*

can 캔 *k'aen*

Canada 캐나다 *K'aenada*

Canadian 캐나다인 *K'aenadain*

candy 캔디 *k'aendi*

candy store 과자점 *kwajajŏm*

capital 수도 *sudo*

car 차 *ch'a*

car rental agency 렌트카사

rent'ŭk'asa

carburetor 기화기 *kihwagi*

card (business, personal) 명함 *myŏngham*

cardigan 카디건 *k'adigŏn*

cards(playing) 카드 *k'adŭ*

carp 잉어 *ing-ŏ*

carrots 당근 *tanggŭn*

carry-on 기내 소지품 *kinae sojip'um*

cartridges 카트리지 *k'at'ŭriji*

carved objects 조각품 *chogakp'um*

cassette 카세트 *k'aset'ŭ*

cassette recorder 카세트 녹음기 *k'aset'ŭ nogŭmgi*

castle 성 *sŏng*

catalog 카탈로그 *k'at'allogŭ*

cavity 충치 *ch'ungch'i*

celery 셀러리 *sellŏri*

center 중앙 *chung-ang*

ceramics 도자기 *tojagi*

ceramics store 도자기점 *tojagijŏm*

cereal 곡물식 *kongmulshik*

chain 체인 *ch'ein*

chamber music 실내악 *shillaeak*

change (money) 거스름돈 *kŏsŭrŭmton*

change 바꾸다 *pakkuda*

change 갈아타다 *karat'ada*

channel (TV) 채널 *ch'aenŏl*

chauffeur 운전 기사 *unjŏn kisa*

cheap 싼 *ssan*

check, bill 계산서 *kyesansŏ*

check (personal) 수표 *sup'yo*

checks (pattern) 체크 무늬 *ch'ek'ŭ munŭi*

check (baggage) 맡기다 *matkida*

check (examine) 검사하다 *kŏmsahada*

check in 체크인하다 *chek'ŭinhada*

cheek 뺨 *ppyam*

cheese 치즈 *ch'ijŭ*

cherries 버찌 *bŏtchi*

cherry blossoms 벚꽃 *pŏtkkot*

chest 가슴 *kasŭm*

chestnuts 밤 *pam*

chicken 통닭 *t'ongdak*

chicken soup 치킨 수프 *ch'ik'in sup'ŭ*

child 애 *ae*

chill 오한 *ohan*

china 도자기 *tojagi*

China 중국 *Chungguk*

Chinese (lang.) 중국어 *Chunggugŏ*

Chinese tile game 마작 *majak*

chocolate 초콜렛 *ch'o-*

k'ollet

chopsticks 젓가락 *chot-karak*

chrysanthemum 국화 *kuk'wa*

church 교회 *kyohoe*

citizenship 시민권 *shiminkwon*

civilian 민간인 *min-ganin*

civilization 문명 *munmyŏng*

classical music 고전 음악 *kojŏn ŭmak*

clay 진흙 *chinhŭk*

clench 꽉 쥐다 *kkwak chwida*

clergyman 목사 *moksa*

clever 영리한 *yŏngnihan*

climax 절정 *chŏlchŏng*

clown 익살꾼 *iksalkkun*

coast 해안 *haean*

coeducation 공학 *konghak*

cocoa 코코아 *k'ok'oa*

coffee shop 다방 *tabang*

collapse 무너지다 *munŏjida*

collection 수집 *sujip*

come 오다 *oda*

comedian 희극 배우 *hŭigŭk paeu*

comedy 희극 *hŭigŭk*

commencement 졸업식 *chorŏpshik*

companion 친구 *ch'in-gu*

company 회사 *hoesa*

competition 경쟁 *kyŏng-jaeng*

complain 불평하다 *pulp'yŏnghada*

comprehend 이해하다 *i-haehada*

compromise 타협 *t'ahyŏp*

conceal 감추다 *kamch'uda*

concentrate 집중하다 *chipchunghada*

concert 음악회 *ŭmak'oe*

concert hall 음악당 *ŭmaktang*

concerto 협주곡 *hyŏpchugok*

constipation 변비 *pyŏnbi*

construction 건설 *kŏnsŏl*

consulate 영사관 *yŏngsagwan*

cotton 면 *myŏn*

cough 기침 *kich'im*

counter 카운터 *k'aunt'ŏ*

country (nation) 나라 *nara*

countryside 시골 *shigol*

cover charge 서비스료 *sŏbisŭryo*

cozy 안락한 *allak'an*

crackers 크래커 *k'ŭraek'ŏ*

crafts 공예 *kongye*

craftsman 공예가 *kongyega*

cramps (stomach) 복통 *pokt'ong*

cream 크림 *k'ŭrim*

cream rinse 크림 린스 *k'ŭrim rinsŭ*

credit card 크레디트 카드 *k'ŭredit'ŭ k'adŭ*

cruise 항해 *hanghae*

customs 관세 *kwanse*

—◆◄ **D** ►◆—

damage 손해 *sonhae*

dandelion 민들레 *mindŭlle*

daughter 딸 *ttal*

day 일 *il*

dealer 장사꾼 *changsakkun*

decent 점잖은 *chŏmjanŭn*

declaration 선언 *sŏnŏn*

decoration 장식 *changshik*

dedicate 바치다 *pach'ida*

defense 방어하다 *pang-ŏ-hada*

defendant 피고 *p'igo*

deficient 부족한 *pujok'an*

delegate 대표 *taep'yo*

delicious 맛있는 *madinnŭn*

delivery 배달 *paedal*

demonstration 시범 *shibŏm*

dentist 치과 의사 *ch'ikwa ŭisa*

denture 틀니 *t'ŭlni*

depart 출발하다 *ch'ulbarhada*

departure 출발 *ch'ulbal*

description 묘사 *myosa*

dessert 후식 *hushik*

destruction 파괴 *p'agoe*

devotion 헌신 *hŏnshin*

dialogue 대화 *taehwa*

diamond 다이아몬드 *taiamondŭ*

dictionary 사전 *sajŏn*

diesel 디젤 *tijel*

diet 다이어트 *taiŏt'ŭ*

diplomat 외교관 *woegyo-gwan*

disappointment 실망 *shilmang*

disapproval 불찬성 *pulch'ansŏng*

disco 디스코 *tisŭk'o*

discontent 불만 *pulman*

discount 할인 *harin*

discouragement 낙심 *nakshim*

disgraceful 수치스러운 *such'isŭrŏun*

dishonesty 부정직 *pujŏngjik*

dislocated 탈구된 *talgudoen*

disorder 무질서 *mujilsŏ*

distress 고민 *komin*

distribution 분배 *punbae*

doctor 의사 *ŭisa*

dominate 지배하다 *chibaehada*

doughnuts 도나스 *tonasŭ*

doze 졸다 *cholda*

dress 드레스 *tŭresŭ*
drink 마시다 *mashida*
dry 건조한 *kŏnjohan*
dry cleaner 세탁소 *set'akso*
dry cleaning service 드라
이 서비스 *tŭrai sŏbisŭ*
duck 오리 *ori*
during … 중에 … *chung-
-e*

—◁• E •▷—

ear 귀 *kwi*
earnings 수입 *suip*
earthquake 지진 *chijin*
Easter 부활제 *puhwalche*
ebb 썰물 *ssŏlmul*
eclipse 일식 *ilshik*
economics 경제학 *kyŏng-
jehak*
ecstasy 황홀 *hwanghol*
editor 편집자 *p'yŏnjipcha*
efficiency 능률 *nŭngnyul*
egg 달걀 *talgyal*
eggplant 가지 *kaji*
electricity 전기 *chŏn-gi*
elementary school 국민 학
교 *kungmin hakkyo*
embassy 대사관 *taesagwan*
embroider 수놓다 *sunot'a*
emergency 긴급 *kin-gŭp*
emigrate 이민하다 *imin-
hada*
emperor 황제 *hwangje*

employee 종업원 *chong-ŏb-
won*
enchant 황홀하게 하다
hwanghorhage hada
encyclopaedia 백과 사전
paekkwa sajŏn
endless 끝없는 *kkŭdŏmnŭn*
endurance 참을성 *ch'a-
mŭlsŏng*
enemy 적 *chŏk*
energy 힘 *him*
engagement 약혼 *yak'on*
engrave 조각하다 *choga-
k'ada*
enjoyment 향락 *hyangnak*
enlarge 확대하다 *hwak-
taehada*
enmity 증오 *chŭng-o*
enroll 등록하다 *tŭngno-
k'ada*
enterprise 기업 *kiŏp*
entertainment 오락 *orak*
enthusiastic 열광적인
yŏlgwangjŏgin
entrance 입구 *ipku*
enumerate 헤아리다 *hea-
rida*
environment 환경 *hwan-
gyŏng*
epidemic 유행병 *yuhaeng-
pyŏng*
equality 평등 *p'yŏngdŭng*
essay 수필 *sup'il*
establishment 설립 *sŏllip*

European products 구라파 제 *Kurap'aje*

evidence 증거 *chŭnggŏ*

excitement 흥분 *hŭngbun*

excursion 소풍 *sop'ung*

exhibition 전람회 *chŏllamhoe*

existence 존재 *chonjae*

expedition 원정 *wonjŏng*

experiment 실험 *shirhŏm*

exploration 탐험 *t'amhŏm*

exterior 외부 *woebu*

extraordinary 특별한 *t'ŭkpyŏrhan*

extreme 극단의 *kuktanŭi*

eyesight 시력 *shiryŏk*

—◆❘ **F** ❘◆—

fable 동화 *tonghwa*

factory 공장 *kongjang*

failure 실패 *shilp'ae*

faith 믿음 *midŭm*

faithfulness 충실 *ch'ungshil*

famine 기근 *kigŭn*

fancy 공상 *kongsang*

farmhouse 농가 *nongga*

fasting 단식 *tanshik*

fate 운명 *unmyŏng*

fatigue 피곤 *p'igon*

fertilizer 비료 *piryo*

fiction 소설 *sosŏl*

finance 재정 *chaejŏng*

fisherman 어부 *ŏbu*

flattery 아첨 *ach'ŏm*

flock 떼 *tte*

flood 홍수 *hongsu*

flourish 무성하다 *musŏnghada*

foot 발 *pal*

football 축구 *ch'ukku*

foreigner 외국인 *woegugin*

fork 포크 *p'ok'ŭ*

formal clothing 정장 *chŏngjang*

formation 구성 *kusŏng*

founder 창립자 *ch'angnipcha*

fragrance 향기 *hyanggi*

free 빈 *pin*

freedom 자유 *chayu*

friend 친구 *ch'in-gu*

friendship 우정 *ujŏng*

frontier 국경 *kukkyŏng*

full moon 보름달 *porŭmtal*

function 기능 *kinŭng*

furious 격분한 *kyŏkpunhan*

futile 무익한 *muik'an*

—◆❘ **G** ❘◆—

gaiety 명랑 *myongnang*

gallant 훌륭한 *hullyunghan*

garage 차고 *ch'ago*

garbage 쓰레기 *ssŭregi*

garden 정원 *chŏngwon*
garlic 마늘 *maŭl*
garment 옷 *ot*
gender 성 *sŏng*
genealogy 족보 *chokpo*
generation 세대 *sedae*
generous 관대한 *kwandae-han*
gold plated 금도금 *kŭm-dogŭm*
gigantic 거대한 *kŏdaehan*
glisten 반짝거리다 *pan-tchakkŏrida*
gloomy 어두운 *ŏduun*
glory 영광 *yŏnggwang*
goodness 착함 *ch'ak'am*
gospel 복음 *pogŭm*
government 정부 *chŏngbu*
governor 도지사 *tojisa*
graceful 인자한 *injahan*
graduation 졸업 *chorŏp*
grammar 문법 *munpŏp*
grammar book 문법 책 *munpŏp ch'aek*
gratitude 감사 *kamsa*
gray 회색 *hoesaek*
greedy 욕심 많은 *yok-shim manŭn*
grocery store 식료품점 *shingnyop'umjŏm*
grumble 불평하다 *pul-p'yŏnghada*
guardian 보호자 *pohoja*
gym 체육관 *ch'eyukkwan*

⤙ H ⤚

hair 머리 *mŏri*
hammer 망치 *mangch'i*
handbag 손가방 *sonkabang*
handkerchief 손수건 *son-sugŏn*
happiness 행복 *haengbok*
harmony 조화 *chohwa*
harsh 거친 *kŏch'in*
harvest 추수 *ch'usu*
haughty 거만한 *kŏmanhan*
headache 두통 *tut'ong*
headline 제목 *chemok*
headquarters 본부 *ponbu*
healthy 건강한 *kŏn-gang-han*
heavy 무거운 *mugŏun*
hedge 울타리 *ult'ari*
helmet 철모 *ch'ŏlmo*
helpful 도움이 되는 *to-umi toenŭn*
heredity 유전 *yujŏn*
hero 영웅 *yŏng-ung*
heroine 여장부 *yŏjangbu*
highland 고지 *koji*
historian 역사가 *yŏksaga*
hobby 취미 *ch'wimi*
homesickness 향수 *hyangsu*
honeymoon 신혼 여행 *shinhon yŏhaeng*
horizon 지평선 *chi-p'yŏngsŏn*

horserace 경마 *kyŏngma*
hospitality 환대 *hwandae*
hot spring 온천 *onch'ŏn*
housekeeper 가정부 *ka-jŏngbu*
humble 겸손한 *kyŏmsonhan*
humid 습한 *sŭp'an*

———◆❙ I ❙◆———

I 나 *na*
idleness 게으름 *keŭrŭm*
ignorance 무지 *muji*
illiteracy 무식 *mushik*
illness 병 *pyŏng*
illumination 조명 *cho-myŏng*
imagination 상상 *sangsang*
imitation 모방 *mobang*
impatient 참을 수 없는 *ch'amŭl su ŏmnŭn*
imported 수입한 *suip'an*
improvement 개선 *kaesŏn*
I'm sorry 미안합니다 *Mi-anhamnida*
in 안에 *ane*
in advance 미리 *miri*
incense 향 *hyang*
Indian 인도의 *Indoŭi*
indigestion 소화 불량 *so-hwa pullyang*
industrious 부지런한 *puji-rŏnhan*
industry 산업 *sanŏp*

infantry 보병 *pobyŏng*
influence 영향 *yŏnghyang*
information 정보 *chŏng-bo*
inhabitant 주민 *chumin*
injustice 부정 *pujŏng*
inn 여관 *yŏgwan*
insignia 휘장 *hwijang*
inspection 검열 *kŏmnyŏl*
insurance 보험 *pohŏm*
international 국제적인 *kukchejŏgin*
interpreter 통역자 *t'ong-yŏkcha*
invention 발명 *palmyŏng*
investigation 조사 *chosa*
iron 다리미 *tarimi*
island 섬 *sŏm*
itinerary 여행 계획 *yŏ-haeng kyehoek*

———◆❙ J ❙◆———

jacket 상의 *sang-ŭi*
jade 비취 *pich'wi*
janitor 수위 *suwi*
jaw 턱 *t'ŏk*
jaunty 경쾌한 *kyŏng-kwaehan*
jealousy 질투 *chilt'u*
joke 농담 *nongdam*
judge 판사 *p'ansa*
justification 정당화 *chŏngdanghwa*

⚜ K ⚜

kettle 주전자 *chujŏnja*
kindergarten 유치원 *yu-ch'iwon*
kite 연 *yŏn*
knee 무릎 *murŭp*
knitting 뜨개질 *ttŭgaejil*
knowledge 지식 *chishik*

⚜ L ⚜

lacquerwear 칠기 *ch'ilgi*
ladies' room 여자 화장실 *yŏja hwajangshil*
lake 호수 *hosu*
lament 슬퍼하다 *sŭlp'ŏhada*
lass 소녀 *sonyŏ*
lavatory 화장실 *hwajangshil*
lawyer 변호사 *pyŏnhosa*
lecture 강의 *kang-ŭi*
legation 공사관 *kongsagwan*
leisure 여가 *yŏga*
lenient 너그러운 *nŏgŭrŏun*
lens 렌즈 *lenjŭ*
letter 편지 *p'yŏnji*
lettuce 상치 *sangch'i*
librarian 사서 *sasŏ*
library 도서관 *tosŏgwan*
license 면허 *myŏnhŏ*
lightning 번개 *pŏn-gae*

livelihood 생계 *saenggye*
locomotive 기관차 *kigwanch'a*
lonesome 쓸쓸한 *ssŭlssŭrhan*
longevity 장수 *changsu*
luminous 빛나는 *pinnanŭn*
lusty 기운 좋은 *kiun choŭn*
luxury 사치 *sach'i*

⚜ M ⚜

machine 기계 *kig'ye*
magistrate 치안관 *ch'ian-gwan*
magnificent 장엄한 *chang-ŏmhan*
magnify 확대하다 *hwaktaehada*
maiden 처녀 *ch'ŏnyŏ*
majority 다수 *tasu*
malady 질병 *chilbyŏng*
man 남자 *namja*
management 관리 *kwalli*
manager 관리인 *kwalliin*
mansion 저택 *chŏt'aek*
manufacturer 제조업자 *chejŏŏpch'a*
manuscript 원고 *won-go*
maple 단풍 *tanp'ŭng*
marriage 결혼 *kyŏrhon*
marry 결혼하다 *kyŏrhonhada*
marvellous 놀라운 *nollaun*

mask 탈 *t'al*
masseur 안마사 *anmasa*
match 성냥 *sŏngnyang*
maybe 아마 *ama*
mayor 시장 *shijang*
medicine 약 *yak*
memornadum 메모 *memo*
merchant 상인 *sang-in*
meteorology 기상학 *ki-sanghak*
militia 민병 *minbyŏng*
millionaire 백만 장자 *paengman changja*
minimum 최소의 *ch'oesoŭi*
minority 소수 *sosu*
miracle 기적 *kijŏk*
misfortune 불행 *purhaeng*
missionary 선교사 *sŏn-gyosa*
modesty 겸손 *kyŏmson*
moment 순간 *sun-gan*
monotonous 단조로운 *tanjoroun*
monument 기념비 *ki-nyŏmbi*
morality 도덕 *todŏk*
mother country 모국 *moguk*
movie 영화 *yŏnghwa*
mud 흙 *hŭk*
museum 박물관 *pangmul-gwan*
mystery 신비 *shinbi*
myth 신화 *shinhwa*

N

nail file 손톱 줄 *sont'op chul*
nail polish 매니큐어액 *maenik'yuŏaek*
nail polish remover 아세톤 *aset'on*
name 이름 *irŭm*
nationality 국적 *kukchŏk*
nature 자연 *jayŏn*
necessity 필수품 *p'ilsu-p'um*
negligence 태만 *t'aeman*
negotiation 교섭 *kyosŏp*
neighbor 이웃 사람 *iut-saram*
NewYear 새해 *saehae*
nobleman 귀족 *kwijok*
nominate 지명하다 *chi-myŏnghada*
nourish 기르다 *kirŭda*
novelist 소설가 *sosŏlga*
nullify 무효로 하다 *mu-hyoro hada*
nursery 육아실 *yugashil*
nutrition 영양 *yŏngyang*
nylon 나일론 *naillon*

O

oak 참나무 *ch'amnamu*
oath 맹세 *maengse*
oatmeal 오트밀 *ot'ŭmil*

obvious 명백한 *myŏngbaek'an*

occupation 직업 *chigŏp*

ocean 바다 *pada*

October 10월 *shiwol*

opinion 의견 *ŭigyŏn*

opponent 반대자 *pandaeja*

opportunity 기회 *kihoe*

optimism 낙천주의 *nakch'ŏnjuŭi*

orchestra 관현악단 *kwanhyŏnaktan*

ornament 장식 *changshik*

other 다른 *tarŭn*

outline 윤곽 *yun-gwak*

owner 소유자 *soyuja*

—◁ P ▷—

Pacific Ocean 태평양 *t'aepyŏngnyang*

painter 화가 *hwaga*

palace 궁전 *kungjŏn*

parachute 낙하산 *nak'asan*

park (n.) 공원 *kongwon*

park 주차하다 *chuch'ahada*

parliament 의회 *ŭihoe*

passion 정열 *chŏngnyŏl*

pastor 목사 *moksa*

pasture 목장 *mokchang*

path 길 *kil*

patience 인내 *innae*

pavement 포장 *p'ojang*

payment 지불 *chibul*

peach 복숭아 *poksung-a*

peasant 농부 *nongbu*

pedestrian 보행자 *pohaengja*

pencil 연필 *yŏnp'il*

pepper 후추 *huch'u*

performance 공연 *kongyŏn*

performer 출연자 *ch'uryŏnja*

perfume 향수 *hyangsu*

permanent wave 파마 *p'ama*

per person 일인당 *irindang*

persimmon 감 *kam*

person 사람 *saram*

pharmacy 약국 *yakkuk*

Philippines 필리핀 *P'illip'in*

photograph 사진 *sajin*

photography shop 사진관 *sajin-gwan*

picture postcard 그림 엽서 *kŭrim yŏpsŏ*

pie 파이 *p'ai*

pier 부두 *pudu*

pillow 베개 *pegae*

pin 핀 *p'in*

pineapple 파인애플 *p'ain-aep'ŭl*

ping pong 탁구 *t'akku*

pink 분홍 *punhong*

pipe 파이프 *p'aip'ŭ*

plant 식물 *shingmul*

plastic 플라스틱 *p'ŭllasŭt'ik*

plate 접시 *chŏpshi*

platinum 백금 *paekkŭm*

play 연극 *yŏn-gŭk*

playground 운동장 *undongjang*

pleasant 쾌적한 *k'waejŏk'an*

Pleased to meet you. 만나 뵈어 반갑습니다. *Manna poeŏ pan-gapsŭmnida.*

pliers 뻰찌 *ppentchi*

plum 건포도 *kŏnp'odo*

points of interest 명소 *myŏngso*

police 경찰 *kyŏngch'al*

police officer 경관 *kyŏng-gwan*

polish 닦다 *takta*

pond 연못 *yŏnmot*

popcorn 팝콘 *p'apk'on*

popular songs 팝송 *p'apsong*

pork 돼지 고기 *twoeji kogi*

potato 감자 *kamja*

purse 핸드백 *haendŭbaek*

—◦◦ Q ◦◦—

question 질문 *chilmun*

quick 빠른 *pparŭn*

quiet 조용한 *choyonghan*

—◦◦ R ◦◦—

rabbit 토끼 *t'okki*

railroad 철도 *ch'ŏlto*

rainbow 무지개 *mujigae*

rainy season 장마철 *changmach'ŏl*

rare 드문 *tŭmun*

rate 요금 *yogŭm*

razor 면도기 *myŏndogi*

realization 실현 *shirhyŏn*

rebellion 반역 *panyŏk*

receipt 영수증 *yŏngsujŭng*

recollection 회상 *hoesang*

recommend 추천하다 *ch'uch'ŏnhada*

reconfirm 재확인하다 *chaehwaginhada*

recovery 회복 *hoebok*

recreation 오락 *orak*

referee 심판관 *shimp'an-gwan*

reformation 개혁 *kaehyŏk*

refrigerator 냉장고 *naengjanggo*

refugee 피난민 *p'inanmin*

registration 등록 *tŭngnok*

reinforce 보강하다 *poganghada*

religion 종교 *chonggyo*

renaissance 문예 부흥 *munye puhung*

rent 빌다 *pilda*

replacement 교대 *kyodae*

reputation 명성 *myong-sŏng*

reservation 예약 *yeyak*

resignation 사직 *sajik*

responsibility 책임 *ch'aegim*

restaurant 레스토랑 *resŭt'orang*

restroom 화장실 *hwajangshil*

resurrection 부활 *puhwal*

retirement 은퇴 *ŭnt'oe*

romantic 낭만적인 *nangmanjŏgin*

route 길 *kil*

ruler 자 *cha*

rumor 소문 *somun*

rural 시골의 *shigorŭi*

rye 호밀 *homil*

⤛ S ⤜

safe (adj.) 안전한 *anjŏnhan*

safe (n.) 금고 *kŭmgo*

safety 안전 *anjŏn*

safety pin 핀 *p'in*

sailboat 보트 *pot'ŭ*

sailor 선원 *sŏnwon*

saint 성인 *sŏng-in*

salary 봉급 *ponggŭp*

sanitation 위생 *wisaeng*

satire 풍자 *p'ungja*

satisfaction 만족 *manjok*

Saturday 토요일 *t'oyoil*

Scandinavian 스칸디나비아의 *Sŭk'andinabiaŭi*

scarf 스카프 *suk'ap'ŭ*

schedule 시간표 *shiganp'yo*

scheme 계획 *kyehoek*

scientist 과학자 *kwahakcha*

scotch 스카치 *sŭk'ach'i*

scripture 성경 *sŏnggyŏng*

seagull 갈매기 *kalmaegi*

secret 비밀 *pimil*

security 안전 *anjŏn*

semester 학기 *hakki*

senator 상원 의원 *sangwon ŭiwon*

send 보내다 *ponaeda*

September 9월 *kuwol*

serpent 뱀 *paem*

servant 하인 *hain*

sex 성 *sŏng*

shameful 수치스러운 *such'isŭrŏun*

sheep 양 *yang*

shelter 피난처 *p'inanch'ŏ*

ship 배 *pae*

shooting 사격 *sagyŏk*

shower 소낙비 *sonakpi*

shrine 사당 *sadang*

sickness 병 *pyŏng*

sightseeing 관광 *kwangwang*

signboard 간판 *kanp'an*

sing 노래하다 *noraehada*

singer 가수 *kasu*

skyscraper 마천루 *ma-ch'ŏllu*

sleep 자다 *chada*

sleeping car 침대차 *ch'imdaech'a*

sleeping pill 수면제 *sumyŏnje*

sleepy 졸리는 *chollinŭn*

solemn 엄숙한 *ŏmsuk'an*

solitude 고독 *kodok*

sorcerer 마술사 *masulsa*

souvenir 기념품 *kinyŏmp'um*

space 공간 *konggan*

speaker 연사 *yŏnsa*

specimen 견본 *kyŏnbon*

spectator 구경꾼 *kugyŏngkkun*

speech 연설 *yŏnsŏl*

spider 거미 *kŏmi*

spiritual 정신적인 *chŏngshinjŏgin*

spokesman 대변인 *taebyŏnin*

sponsor 후원인 *huwonin*

sportsman 운동 선수 *undong sŏnsu*

stability 안정 *anjŏng*

stay 묵다 *mukta*

station 역 *yŏk*

stationery shop 문방구점 *munbanggujŏm*

steamship 기선 *kisŏn*

stockings 스타킹 *sŭt'ak'ing*

stomach 위 *wi*

stone 돌 *tol*

storm 폭풍 *p'òkp'ung*

streetcar 전차 *chŏnch'a*

strong 튼튼한 *t'ŭnt'ŭnhan*

student 학생 *haksaeng*

submission 복종 *pokchong*

subscription 구독 *kudok*

success 성공 *sŏnggong*

summer 여름 *yŏrŭm*

Sunday 일요일 *iryoil*

sunflower 해바라기 *haebaragi*

superstition 미신 *mishin*

supporter 지지자 *chijija*

suppository 좌약 *chwayak*

surgeon 외과 의사 *oekwa ŭisa*

survey 조사하다 *chosahada*

sweet 단 *tan*

Swiss 스위스의 *Sŭwisŭŭi*

swollen 부은 *puŭn*

symphony 교향악 *kyohyang-ak*

system 체계 *ch'egye*

───◆❧ T ❧◆───

table 테이블 *t'eibŭl*

tavern 술집 *sulchip*

tearoom 다방 *tabang*

telegram 전보 *chŏnbo*

temperature 온도 *ondo*

temple 절 *chŏl*

tent 텐트 *t'ent'ŭ*

terrace 테라스 *t'erasŭ*

Thai 태국의 *T'aegugŭi*

Thai (n.) 태국인 *T'aegugin*

thank you 감사합니다 *kamsahamnida*

that 저 *chŏ*

that 저것 *chŏgŏt*

thatch 초가 지붕 *ch'oga chibung*

theft 도난 *tonan*

theme 주제 *chuje*

there 저기 *chŏgi*

thermometer 온도계 *ondogye*

themostat 온도 조절기 *ondo chojŏlgi*

they 그들 *kŭdŭl*

thick 두꺼운 *tukkŏun*

thigh 사타구니 *sat'aguni*

thin 가는 *kanŭn*

think 생각하다 *saengga-k'ada*

thirsty 목마른 *mong-marŭn*

this (pron.) 이것 *igŏt*

this (adj.) 이 *i*

thriller 공포물 *kongp'omul*

throat 목구멍 *mokkumŏng*

thumb 엄지 *ŏmji*

Thursday 목요일 *Mogyoil*

ticket 표 *p'yo*

ticket machine 표 판매기 *p'yo p'anmaegi*

ticket window 표 파는 창구 *p'yo p'anŭn ch'anggu*

tie 타이 *t'ai*

tight 끼는 *kkinŭn*

tighten 죄다 *choeda*

time 시간 *shigan*

timetable 시간표 *shigan-p'yo*

tire 타이어 *t'aiŏ*

tired 피곤한 *p'igonhan*

tissues 화장지 *hwajangji*

title 제목 *chemok*

to …에 …*e*

toast (n.) 토스트 *t'osŭt'ŭ*

toast 건배하다 *kŏnbaehada*

toaster 토스터 *t'osŭt'ŏ*

tobacco 담배 *tambae*

today 오늘 *onŭl*

toe 발가락 *palkarak*

together 함께 *hamkke*

toilet 화장실 *hwajangshil*

tomato 토마토 *t'omat'o*

tomorrow 내일 *naeil*

tongue 혀 *hyŏ*

tonight 오늘 밤 *onŭl pam*

tonsils 편도선 *p'yŏndosŏn*

toothache 치통 *ch'it'ong*

toothbrush 칫솔 *ch'issol*

toothpick 이쑤시개 *issu-shigae*

topaz 황옥 *hwang-ok*

tour 관광 *kwan-gwang*

tour guide 관광 안내원 *kwan-gwang annaewon*

tourist 관광객 *kwan-gwanggaek*

tourist information center 여행 안내소 *yŏhaeng annaeso*

towels 수건 *sugŏn*

town 소도시 *sodoshi*

tow truck 견인차 *kyŏninch'a*

toy store 완구점 *wangujŏm*

traditional 전통적인 *chŏnt'ongjŏgin*

train 기차 *kich'a*

track 홈 *hom*

tragedy 비극 *pigŭk*

tranquilizers 안정제 *anjŏngje*

translate 번역하다 *pŏnyŏk'ada*

translation 번역 *pŏnyŏk*

transportation 교통편 *kyot'ongp'yŏn*

travel agency 여행사 *yŏhaengsa*

travelers check 여행자 수표 *yŏhaengja sup'yo*

tree 나무 *namu*

trip 여행 *yŏhaeng*

trout 송어 *song-ŏ*

try on 입어 보다 *ibŏ poda*

Tuesday 화요일 *hwayoil*

tuna 참치 *ch'amch'i*

turn 돌다 *tolda*

turquoise 터키옥 *t'ŏk'iok*

tweezers 족집게 *chokchipke*

type 종류 *chongnyu*

typewriter 타자기 *t'ajagi*

typing paper 타자 용지 *t'aja yongji*

typhoon 태풍 *t'aep'ung*

typical 전형적인 *chŏnhyŏngjŏgin*

--- U ---

ugly 추한 *ch'uhan*

uncle 숙부 *sukpu*

umbrella 우산 *usan*

understand 이해하다 *ihaehada*

underwear 내의 *naeŭi*

United States 미국 *Miguk*

university 대학 *taehak*

up 위로 *wiro*

urgent 긴급한 *kin-gŭp'an*

use 사용하다 *sayonghada*

--- V ---

vacation 휴가 *hyuga*

valley 계곡 *kyegok*

veal 송아지 고기 *song-aji kogi*

vegetables 채소 *ch'aeso*

venetian blind 차양 *ch'ayang*

video equipment shop 비디오 가게 *pidio kage*

Vietnamese 월남인 *Wollamin*

view 경치 *kyŏngch'i*

village 마을 *maŭl*

vinegar 식초 *shikch'o*

vinyl 비닐 *pinil*

vitamin 비타민 *pit'amin*

vodka 보드카 *podŭk'a*

volcano 화산 *hwasan*

voltage 전압 *chŏnap*

—◄ W ►—

wait 기다리다 *kidarida*

waiting room 대합실 *taehapshil*

walk 걷다 *kŏtta*

wallet 지갑 *chigap*

walnut 호두 *hodu*

want 원하다 *wonhada*

warm 따뜻한 *ttattŭt'an*

warmup suit 트레이닝 *t'ŭreining*

wash 씻다 *ssitta*

watch 시계 *shigye*

watch repair shop 시계 수리점 *shigye surijŏm*

water 물 *mul*

waterfall 폭포 *p'okp'o*

watermelon 수박 *subak*

water skis 수상 스키 *susang sŭk'i*

waves 파도 *p'ado*

we 우리 *uri*

weak 약한 *yak'an*

wear 입다 *ipta*

weather 날씨 *nalssi*

weather forecast 일기 예보 *ilgi yebo*

Wednesday 수요일 *suyoil*

week 주 *chu*

weekend 주말 *chumal*

welcome 환영하다 *hwanyŏnghada*

welldone 잘 익은 *chal igŭn*

west 서쪽 *sŏtchok*

western (film) 서부극 *sŏbugŭk*

Western-style 서양식 *sŏyangshik*

what 무엇 *muŏt*

what time 몇 시 *myŏt shi*

when 언제 *ŏnje*

where 어디서 *ŏdisŏ*

which 어느 *ŏnŭ*

wiskey 위스키 *wisŭk'i*

white 흰 *hŭin*

who 누구 *nugu*

why 왜 *wae*

wide 넓은 *nŏlbŭn*

wife 아내 *anae*

wind 바람 *param*

window 창 *ch'ang*

windshield 앞 유리 *ap*

yuri

windshield wiper 와이퍼 *waip'ŏ*

wine 술 *sul*

winter 겨울 *kyŏul*

wipe 닦다 *takta*

with pleasure 기꺼이 *ki-kkŏi*

woman 여자 *yŏja*

women's clothing 부인복 *puinbok*

wonderful 좋은 *choŭn*

wood 나무 *namu*

wooden 나무의 *namuŭi*

woodblock prints 목판화 *makp'anhwa*

woodblock print shop 판화점 *p'anhwajŏm*

wool 울 *ul*

wrapping paper 포장지 *p'ojangji*

wrist 팔목 *p'almok*

wristwatch 팔목 시계

p'almok shigye

write 쓰다 *ssŭda*

writer 작가 *chakka*

wrong 틀린 *t'ŭllin*

⋙ XYZ ⋘

X-ray 엑스레이 *eksŭrei*

yellow 노란 *noran*

yes 예 *ye*

Yes, it is. 예, 그렇습니다. *Ye, kŭrŏssŭmnida.*

you 당신 *tangshin*

young 젊은 *chŏlmŭn*

young people 젊은이 *chŏlmŭni*

younger brother 남동생 *namdongsaeng*

younger sister 여동생 *yŏdongsaeng*

your 당신의 *tangshinŭi*

zipper 지퍼 *chip'ŏ*

zoo 동물원 *tongmurwon*